UNDERSTANDING JAMAICA KINCAID
S ANNIE JOHN   A STUDENT CASEB
OOK TO ISSUES, SOURCES, AND HI
STORICAL D

MISTRON, DEBORAH E. 1950-

Understanding Jamaica Kincaid's
Annie John

Recent titles in
The Greenwood Press "Literature in Context" Series

Understanding *Of Mice and Men, The Red Pony,* and *The Pearl*: A
Student Casebook to Issues, Sources, and Historical Documents
Claudia Durst Johnson

Understanding Anne Frank's *The Diary of a Young Girl*: A Student
Casebook to Issues, Sources, and Historical Documents
Hedda Rosner Kopf

Understanding *Pride and Prejudice*: A Student Casebook to Issues,
Sources, and Historical Documents
Debra Teachman

Understanding *The Red Badge of Courage*: A Student Casebook to
Issues, Sources, and Historical Documents
Claudia Durst Johnson

Understanding Richard Wright's *Black Boy*: A Student Casebook to
Issues, Sources, and Historical Documents
Robert Felgar

Understanding *I Know Why the Caged Bird Sings*: A Student Casebook
to Issues, Sources, and Historical Documents
Joanne Megna-Wallace

Understanding *The Crucible*: A Student Casebook to Issues, Sources,
and Historical Documents
Claudia Durst Johnson and Vernon E. Johnson

Understanding *A Tale of Two Cities*: A Student Casebook to Issues,
Sources, and Historical Documents
George Newlin

Understanding Shakespeare's *Julius Caesar*: A Student Casebook to
Issues, Sources, and Historical Documents
Thomas Derrick

Understanding *A Raisin in the Sun*: A Student Casebook to Issues,
Sources, and Historical Documents
Lynn Domina

Understanding *The Great Gatsby*: A Student Casebook to Issues,
Sources, and Historical Documents
Dalton Gross and MaryJean Gross

Understanding *Hamlet*: A Student Casebook to Issues, Sources, and
Historical Documents
Richard Corum

UNDERSTANDING
Jamaica Kincaid's
Annie John

A STUDENT CASEBOOK TO ISSUES, SOURCES, AND HISTORICAL DOCUMENTS

Deborah Mistron

The Greenwood Press
"Literature in Context" Series
Claudia Durst Johnson, Series Editor

GREENWOOD PRESS
Westport, Connecticut • London

Library of Congress Cataloging-in-Publication Data

Mistron, Deborah E., 1950–
    Understanding Jamaica Kincaid's Annie John : a student casebook to issues, sources, and historical documents / Deborah Mistron.
      p. cm.—(The Greenwood Press "Literature in context" series, ISSN 1074–598X)
    Includes bibliographical references and index.
    ISBN 0–313–30254–5 (alk. paper)
    1. Kincaid, Jamaica. Annie John—Sources. 2. Mothers and daughters—Antigua—History—Sources. 3. Literature and society—Antigua—Sources. 4. Teenage girls—Antigua—History—Sources. 5. Women and literature—Antigua—Sources. 6. Antigua—History—Sources. I. Title. II. Series.
PR9275.A583K563436   1999
813—dc21   98–12158

British Library Cataloguing in Publication Data is available.

Library of Congress Catalog Card Number: 98–12158
ISBN: 0–313–30254–5
ISSN: 1074–598X

First published in 1999

Greenwood Press, 88 Post Road West, Westport, CT 06881
An imprint of Greenwood Publishing Group, Inc.

Printed in the United States of America

The paper used in this book complies with the Permanent Paper Standard issued by the National Information Standards Organization (Z39.48–1984).

10 9 8 7 6 5 4 3 2 1

Contents

Introduction

Since its publication in 1985, *Annie John* has become one of the most widely read novels in high schools in the United States. It was named one of the best books of 1985 by *Library Journal* and was cited in several lists of the most popular books in secondary school English classes. In 1993, the *School Library Journal* recommended *Annie John* on its list for English classes in middle school and high school of the best books written by women authors.

What is the appeal, in the United States of the 1990s, of a novel about a young girl growing up on the small Caribbean island of Antigua in the 1960s? In part, it may be its universal elements—its sensitive portrayal of a young girl's adolescence, including her painful alienation from her mother, her friendships, her education, the formation of her ideas, and her final separation from her family and from her country when she leaves to make her own way in the world.

But another part of this novel's appeal may be its unique setting. While students can identify with Annie's problems, perhaps quite similar to their own, they may also be intrigued by certain elements of difference. Annie grows up in a different country, with its own history, culture, customs, and foods; Antigua has its own educational, health, and religious systems. In Antigua, the overwhelming majority of inhabitants are of African descent, so the girl who is different in the school is the blond one, Ruth, who is from England. Although it is an independent country now, at the time the novel takes place, Antigua was still a colony of Great Britain and educated its citizens according to British values, often conflicting with Antigua's own perspectives. Like most of the Caribbean islands, Antigua has a long history of emigration from the home country in search of work elsewhere. Annie leaves Antigua at the end of the novel, just as her mother before her emigrated from Dominica to Antigua.

This combination of universality and uniqueness gives the novel a strong appeal. Students may gain insight into their own lives and, at the same time, enter into a multicultural experience. Students can see that forces such as familial relationships shape all of us, while the historical and cultural forces within each country shape its inhabitants. In this way, students can walk in the shoes of a girl their own age who lives in a different time and culture and see both the similarities and the differences between their experiences.

All of these elements give rise to certain questions in readers' minds. What is the significance of the history of slavery in Antigua, which Annie mentions? Why does she dislike Columbus? If they are Methodist, why is the Anglican church bell always ringing? And why does Annie's mother consult an Obeah woman? What is Obeah, anyway? Why does Annie's father have other women and children in his past life? Why are Annie's mother's hair and skin different from Annie's? What is Mrs. John's ethnicity? What is unique about her island of origin, Dominica? What is Annie's social position in Antigua? Is her way of life typical? Why do so many people leave their islands?

During the course of this study of *Annie John*, many of these questions will be answered, and many more will be posed for the reader to think through. Perhaps the first important issue to contemplate is the debate concerning how fiction should be studied. Should a novel like *Annie John* be studied as a self-contained unit, using, for analysis, only information found within the novel itself? Or would a student's understanding of the novel be enhanced by going beyond the story to look at the author, the history and culture of the time and setting, and the history of certain social issues brought up by the novel?

The approach taken by this book can best be described as interdisciplinary. In this study, we begin with a literary analysis that refers mainly to the forms and themes of the novel, adding biographical information about the author when relevant. In the subsequent chapters, documents from a variety of disciplines, such as history, sociology, culture, legal studies, anthropology, and other literature (such as memoirs, letters), not just literary criticism, aid in the study of the novel.* This book makes the assumption that these sources can provide useful information and issues to enhance our analysis and understanding of a literary text.

The documents in this collection raise broad questions about the novel:

- How can the forms and themes of *Annie John* be evaluated independently of other documents?
- How does knowledge of the author's life, particularly in an autobiographical novel such as *Annie John*, enhance our understanding of the novel?
- How does understanding the history of the island of Antigua, particularly its slave past, deepen our appreciation of the novel's themes?
- How does knowledge of Caribbean history, and of the many opinions surrounding Columbus's life, enhance our understanding of Annie's rebellious attitude in school?
- How does knowledge of spiritual practices, such as Obeah, increase our understanding of events in the novel?
- How does information about issues such as family life, education, and emigration in the Caribbean deepen our understanding of the novel?

A variety of different records are excerpted here as source material for study of *Annie John*:

- Newspaper articles
- Interviews
- Editorials
- Position papers from national organizations
- Magazine articles

*Spelling has been modernized in documents written before 1900 to facilitate reading.

- Historical, sociological, and legal studies
- Photographs
- Memoirs
- Letters

In addition to the documents, each section of the text contains an introductory discussion, study questions, topics for written or oral exploration, and a list of suggested readings.

1

Literary Analysis of *Annie John*: Coming of Age in Antigua

THEMES

The popularity of *Annie John* can be attributed to its strong, universal themes. One central theme is the sense of loss and betrayal that accompanies losing the love of a once-adoring mother. Early in the novel, Annie describes her relationship with her mother as a kind of paradise in which she followed her mother around all day, was included in all her activities, and was showered with love and kisses. As Annie enters puberty, however, her mother begins to distance herself from her daughter, becoming critical and harsh, sending her out to learn feminine skills such as sewing, and refusing to go through the trunk that contains artifacts from Annie's childhood. At first, Annie attempts to replace this love with intense friendships with other girls and tries to excel at school to win her mother's approval. Then she rebels against her mother's treatment by taking up with the Red Girl and playing the forbidden game of marbles. When Annie looks at herself in a shop window, feeling lonely, ugly, and forlorn, and is mocked by some boys, her mother is in the shop, watching her. Instead of seeing Annie for the lonely girl she is, her mother sees a girl trying to be a flirt. This argument over sexuality drives the final wedge between mother and daughter, causing Annie to suffer a breakdown. After going through a kind of rebirth under the care of her grandmother, Annie decides that she will have to leave her mother and the island in order to sustain her new, independent identity.

This theme, of growing up and separating from the mother during adolescence, has a universal appeal. The issues that *Annie John* treats, of adolescent relationships with parents, friends, and schoolteachers, of physical maturation and sexuality, of growing independence and maturity, are processes that most adolescents experience, in one way or another. In this novel, Annie must deal with the psychological loss of the loving mother and then struggle to form and maintain an identity separate from her mother in order to survive. This book shows one way in which this eternal, universal struggle can evolve.

Colonialism is a second important theme that runs throughout the novel. The authority of the mother is often associated with the British colonial authority. Both attempt to control Annie's behavior, to maintain Annie as a dependent subject, to dictate what she should think and feel. Annie's "crime" of defacing a photo of Columbus demonstrates her rebellion against both—against her Anglophile mother, who wants Annie to have a proper, middle-class upbringing in which British values are revered, and against the school system, which teaches the descendants of slaves to revere the man who brought the slave system to the New World, that is, to blindly and unquestioningly adhere to British values.

Both of these authorities threaten the girl's growing independence and individual identity. They refuse to see Annie as she is and resist any of her attempts to forge her own identity. Mrs. John appears to see Annie as an extension of herself and rejects her when she shows signs of a separate identity. The colonial authorities refuse to see Antiguans as people with their own history, culture, and identity and inculcate British values instead. When the values taught at school seem to conflict with reality, and in fact, seem to erase the local reality, children may suffer a damaging loss of identity and self-esteem. Annie's struggle against this threat contributes to her final decision to leave, not just her mother but her island home as well.

ELEMENTS OF FICTION

The novel is successful because the elements that make up the narrative support its themes. These elements consist of (1) point of view (or voice) and language, (2) tone, (3) time and place of setting, (4) characters, (5) plot structure, and (6) imagery and symbols.

In terms of the first element, the author has adopted a first-person *point of view*. Annie's mature voice narrates vivid, poetic descriptions of key episodes in her early life, with little dialogue or background explanation of time or place. The story is told from her point of view, describing events and feelings as she perceived them at the time. The reader is immediately situated within the consciousness of the young girl, but the *language* is the complex, eloquent, and evocative one of the adult writer.

The second element of the novel's structure, closely related to voice, is *tone*, which can range from comic to serious. The tone of this novel, in keeping with the child's point of view, is simple yet also very evocative and vivid. It is honest and direct but also quite suggestive. The novel seems to hint at psychological depths and mysteries that cannot be articulated, that circle around the descriptions of events and thoughts. The effect is somewhat dreamlike, as though actions are being filtered through her consciousness long after the events took place.

Another important element in this novel is the *setting*. The setting of *Annie John* is never explicitly stated within the novel; at first the reader seems to inhabit a psychological universe on an island somewhere. But it soon becomes clear, through references and allusions, that it takes place on a small Caribbean island belonging to the British Empire, some time in the twentieth century, before independence and the growth of the tourist industry. Because the novel is clearly autobiographical, a reader with knowledge of Jamaica Kincaid's life is able to discern that the setting is Antigua in the 1960s. But the setting, and the central themes depicted within it, would also be valid for other islands in the British West Indies.

Within the general setting of a town in the British West Indies are several arenas in which the action occurs: the Johns' family home, Annie's school, the cemetery, the downtown shopping area, the docks, and outdoor paths and fields that serve as play areas for children. Most of these arenas encompass particular institutions within the community: the family, the neighborhood, the educational system, the commercial areas. But the play areas seem to be an arena of temporary freedom for the children, before they must enter into the responsibilities of adulthood. Many of Annie's initial acts of defiance against her mother and teachers take place in this arena, before moving into the public, institutional arenas.

The fourth element is the *characters*. Most of the characters are Antiguans, except for Annie's mother and grandmother, who are from Dominica, and the headmistress and a girl in school, who are from England. Significantly, the narrator does not explicitly explain that everyone is of African descent—a given in that environment; race is not remarked upon except in the case of the two white characters. A reader with knowledge of Jamaica Kincaid's background, or perhaps of the history of Dominica, can guess that Annie's mother, with her long, wavy hair, whiter hands, and thinner lips, is part Carib Indian. Jamaica Kincaid's own mother is part Carib, from Dominica, and that island has a Carib Indian reservation, where most of the remnants of the Carib nation, many intermarried with Dominicans of African descent, live today. This oblique reference to the native Caribs, who were annihilated within a century after the arrival of Columbus, can add richness to the reader's perception of the theme of Columbus and colonialism.

All of the other characters represent local Antiguan residents—the father, who is a carpenter; the fishermen who deliver fish; the seamstress who tries to teach Annie to sew; the local Obeah woman; the neighbors; the girls and teachers at Annie's school; the local boys. All contribute to Annie's development and to her growing sense of oddness, of alienation. She is brighter than most of the girls in her school and has different, and often rebellious, attitudes and ideas. After her breakdown and "rebirth," Annie acts quite eccentrically in front of the other girls and alienates herself further, before leaving the island.

Another element that supports the main ideas of the novel is *plot structure*. The story of Annie John's adolescence covers about six years, from the age of ten in the first chapter to the end of her schooling at about the age of sixteen. The story is told episodically, focusing on important events and skipping other time periods. The novel is arranged in a rough chronological order, with occasional references to earlier or later incidents within a chapter. The action is divided into eight chapters, or episodes. "Figures in the Distance" tells of Annie's preoccupation with funerals and of her association of her mother with death. This association prefigures Annie's later fear that her identity could be obliterated by her mother, that she would never know whether her mother's shadow was standing between her and the world. "The Circling Hand" recounts Annie's idyllic life with her parents, which includes going through her trunk, and her mother and father's past. It also tells of the first acts of distancing between mother and daughter, after Annie's twelfth birthday. Mrs. John decides they will no longer dress alike, refuses to go through the trunk with Annie, and sends her out to learn feminine skills instead of allowing Annie to follow her around the house. Annie also witnesses her mother and father making love, which increases Annie's sense of alienation from them. By the end of the episode, she has found a new friend to love—Gwen. The third chapter, "Gwen," relates the stories of their friendship, Annie's first menstruation, and her essay about her separation from her mother at the beach, in which she includes an idealized, wish-fulfilling (but untrue) conclusion of unity between mother and daughter. At the end, Annie declares that she no longer loves her mother. In the next episode, "The Red Girl," Annie deliberately befriends a girl of a lower class of whom her mother would never approve and takes up the forbidden game of marbles. When her mother tries to trick her into revealing where she has hidden her marbles, Annie feels betrayed. The fifth chapter, "Columbus in Chains," focuses on Annie's education, particularly history, and on her punishment for defacing the picture of Columbus. Her mother betrays Annie again, by pretending that the hated breadfruit is really rice. In the sixth chapter, "Somewhere, Belgium," Annie is fifteen, extremely unhappy, and fantasizes about leaving the island for Europe, as did the author of her favorite novel, *Jane Eyre*, by Charlotte Brontë. She has an awkward encounter with local boys and recounts her earlier friendship with one, Mineu. The final break between mother and daughter occurs, and Annie asks her father to make her a trunk of her own. In the seventh episode, "The Long Rain," Annie suffers a breakdown and is nursed back to mental health by her maternal grandmother, Ma Chess. In the final episode, "A Walk to the Jetty," Annie leaves Antigua. Despite breaks in time, the sequence of episodes shows a progressive separation between mother and daughter throughout adolescence, culminating in the final argument, a breakdown accompanied by a rebirth, and the decision to leave.

The last of the elements of fiction discussed here is *imagery and symbolism*. The poetic, evocative language of the novel produces many important images that reinforce its central themes. One significant image is of Annie being remothered by her grandmother, with Annie curled up inside the curve of her grandmother's body like a "little comma." This fetuslike image suggests a pause before Annie's symbolic "rebirth" as an independent young woman. Several of the chapter titles suggest important symbols within the work. "The Circling Hand" represents the beginning of her feelings of alienation from her mother, particularly after her description, in the first chapter, of her mother's hands in relation to death and funerals. "Columbus in Chains" represents Annie's attitude toward colonialism. "Somewhere, Belgium" symbolizes her longing to live independently elsewhere, as well as her love of fiction.

One of the most important symbols in the novel is the trunk. The first trunk, which belonged to her mother and now contains Annie's baby things, represents Annie's emotional dependence on her mother; when she asks her father to build her a new one of her own, she is asserting her independence and indicating her intention to leave.

Perhaps most significant of all in analyzing *Annie John* is looking at it as a coming-of-age novel, which is considered an important genre (type) of fiction. In this case, the coming-of-age experience of the fictional character closely parallels that of the author. In several interviews (see the Suggested Readings), Jamaica Kincaid has stated that her novels are intensely autobiographical and that many of the events are emotionally true. It would be useful at this point, therefore, to outline the salient events in Jamaica Kincaid's life, because they closely parallel, particularly in time and place, those of Annie John's fictional life.

Jamaica Kincaid was born on May 25, 1949, with the name Elaine Potter Richardson, in St. John's Antigua. Her mother, a Richardson, was from a family of landed peasants in Dominica. Her maternal grandmother was a Carib Indian and a believer in Obeah; her paternal grandfather was a Methodist policeman. Kincaid's mother moved to Antigua at the age of sixteen and met Jamaica's father, Roderick Potter, a taxi driver who is now an employee of the Mill Reef Club in Antigua. Her mother never married Kincaid's father. She later married David Drew, Kincaid's stepfather, a carpenter and cabinetmaker. Kincaid attended a Moravian school, the Antiguan Girls School, and Princess Margaret School and was, for a time, also apprenticed to a seamstress. In 1958, Kincaid's first brother,

Joseph Drew, was born, followed closely by Dalma Drew in 1959 and Devon Drew in 1961. According to Kincaid, the arrival of the three brothers in close succession, and the illness of her older stepfather, caused great economic hardship and her ultimate removal from school to help care for them. In 1965, Kincaid left Antigua to become an au pair in Scarsdale, New York. Later, she worked as a receptionist, file clerk, and secretary in New York City. She obtained her high school diploma and studied photography at the New School for Social Research and later attended Franconia College in New Hampshire. She published her first article in 1973; became a freelance writer for *Ms., Ingenue*, and the *Village Voice*; and changed her name to Jamaica Kincaid. In 1976, she became a staff writer for *New Yorker* magazine and began a long friendship with editor William Shawn. She married his son Allen, a composer, in 1979. In 1983, she won the Morton Dauwen Zabel Award of the American Academy and Institute of Arts and Letters for *At the Bottom of the River*, a collection of short stories. She published *Annie John* and gave birth to a daughter, Annie, in 1985. In 1988, she published a long essay about Antigua, called *A Small Place*, and gave birth to a son, Harold. She published *Lucy*, a story about an au pair working in New York, in 1990, then began publishing a series of articles on gardening in the *New Yorker* in 1992. In 1994, she published *Autobiography of My Mother*, based on her mother's life story, and in 1997, she published *My Brother*, a book-length memoir about her youngest brother, Devon Drew, who remained in Antigua and died of AIDS (acquired immunodeficiency syndrome) several years ago. Jamaica Kincaid now lives in Bennington, Vermont, where her husband is a professor at Bennington College, and she continues to write, garden, and care for her two children.

The reader can immediately see the similarities of time and place between the author's early life and *Annie John*. Annie's life closely parallels Jamaica Kincaid's, but without the three brothers, the economic hardship, and the removal from school. The main focus is on the emotional relationship between mother and daughter. Most important, Kincaid's life and her novel include the break between mother and daughter, the attempts to forge her own identity, and the decision to leave her family and her island in order to maintain her hard-won sense of self. The formation of the author's identity included fashioning a new name for herself, Jamaica Kincaid, just as Annie, in the final chapter, insists on being called Annie John and is no longer called "Little Miss."

The story of a young person's growth to maturity—or "coming of age"—is a popular type, or genre, of fiction that originated in the nineteenth century with Johann Wolfgang von Goethe's *The Sorrows of Young Werther*. This genre is often called the novel of development, or, by its German name, *Bildungsroman*, meaning a novel (*Roman*) about growing up (*Bildungs*). According to literary critics, the *Bildungsroman* often includes the story of childhood and adolescence, with a conflict between generations. It often shows a young person growing up in a provincial society and moving into a larger, more cosmopolitan one. The genre also includes the story of the character's education, both academic and emotional, and the character's search for his or her own vocation/identity/values/working philosophy. This type of autobiographical novel is often a novelist's first one, with a strong focus on character; it is often narrated in the first person, with an episodic form and an open ending, allowing for future growth.

The reader can readily see that *Annie John* meets most of these criteria for the novel of development, although the search for a vocation and values is left for the future at the open-ended finish of the novel. The fact that the character is female can change the outcome somewhat: Female novels of development often entail rupture rather than integration—a rebellion, sometimes successful, sometimes not, against the repressive structures of a society with strong rules about a woman's place in it. With *Annie John*, one may also add the repressive strictures of a colonial society. Ultimately, it becomes clear to Annie that she will be unable to forge her own identity without leaving the familial, as well as the colonial, strictures behind.

Considerations of the elements of fiction, the author's biography, and the genre structures of the novel enhance the reader's understanding of a novel. In the following chapters, other historical and social considerations will be taken up in order to sharpen our understanding of the context of Jamaica Kincaid's most widely read novel.

STUDY QUESTIONS

1. Think about the first-person point of view in the novel. Is it consistent? Does it add to or detract from the narrative? Why or why not?

2. Outline the steps in the gradual breakdown of Annie's relationship with her mother. What issues or conflicts appear to undermine their relationship the most?

3. Describe Mrs. John's hopes and fears for Annie and her future. Do they conflict with Annie's? Do you think Mrs. John is an unsympathetic character? Why or why not?

4. Describe the relationships that Mr. and Mrs. John had with their parents or guardians, as far as we can tell from the novel. Do you think these past relationships had any influence on the manner in which they treat Annie?

5. To get a clearer picture of Annie's hometown, compare and contrast it with the place where you grew up.

6. Characterize Annie's friends. Do their friendships appear to be positive? Why or why not?

7. Do you think it was ultimately necessary for Annie to leave the island in order to forge her own identity? Why or why not?

8. Describe Annie's curriculum in school. What does she study? Compare and contrast it with your own studies.

TOPICS FOR WRITTEN OR ORAL EXPLORATION

1. Compare *Annie John* with another *Bildungsroman* (novel about growing up) that you have read. Do the main characters in each have similar problems? Is the narrative point of view similar? What similarities or differences do you notice between the two novels?

2. Compare and contrast Annie's relationship with her parents with your own relationship with your parent(s) or guardian(s). What similarities and/or differences do you notice?

3. Write a paper in which you describe the most important imagery used in the novel. Show how these images reinforce the major themes.

4. Discuss other works of literature that are mentioned in the novel. Make note of when and where these references occur. What role does each reference play in the major themes of the novel?

5. Describe the social codes and practices regarding male/female rela-

tionships that the novel reveals. What similarities and differences do you notice between that particular time and place and your own?

SUGGESTED READINGS

Other Books by Jamaica Kincaid

At the Bottom of the River. New York: Farrar, Straus and Giroux, 1983.
Autobiography of My Mother. New York: Farrar, Straus and Giroux, 1994.
Lucy. New York: Farrar, Straus and Giroux, 1990.
My Brother. New York: Farrar, Straus and Giroux, 1997.
A Small Place. New York: Farrar, Straus and Giroux, 1988.

Uncollected Fiction by Jamaica Kincaid

"Antigua Crossing." *Rolling Stone*, June 29, 1978, 48–50.
"Ovando." *Conjunctions* 14 (1989): 75–83.
"Song of Roland." *New Yorker*, April 12, 1993, 94–98.

Literary Criticism: Books and Articles

Dutton, Wendy. "Merge and Separate: Jamaica Kincaid's Fiction." *World Literature Today* 63 (Summer 1989): 396–411.

Ferguson, Moira. *Jamaica Kincaid: Where the Land Meets the Body*. Charlottesville: University Press of Virginia, 1994.

Murdoch, H. Adlai. "Severing the (M)other Connection: The Representation of Cultural Identity in Jamaica Kincaid's *Annie John*." *Callaloo* 13 (1990): 325–340.

Natov, Roni. "Mothers and Daughters: Jamaica Kincaid's Pre-Oedipal Narrative." *Children's Literature* 18 (1990): 1–16.

Simmons, Diane. *Jamaica Kincaid*. New York: Twayne, 1994.

———. "The Mother Mirror in Jamaica Kincaid's *Annie John* and Gertrude Stein's *The Good Anna*." In *The Anna Book: Searching for Anna in Literary History*, edited by Mickey Pearlman. Westport, Conn.: Greenwood, 1992. 99–104.

Tapping, Craig. "Children and History in the Caribbean Novel: George Lamming's *In the Castle of My Skin* and Jamaica Kincaid's *Annie John*." *Kunapipi* 9 (1989): 51–59.

Timothy, Helen Pyne. "Adolescent Rebellion and Gender Relations in *At the Bottom of the River* and *Annie John*." In *Caribbean Women Writers: Essays from the First International Conference*, edited by Selwyn Cudjoe. Wellesley, Mass.: Calaloux Publications, 1990. 233–242.

Interviews with Jamaica Kincaid

Bonetti, Kay. "An Interview with Jamaica Kincaid." *Missouri Review* 15, no. 2 (1992): 122–142.

Cudjoe, Selwyn R. "Jamaica Kincaid and the Modernist Project: An Interview." *Callaloo* 12 (Spring 1989): 396–411.

Ferguson, Moira. "A Lot of Memory: An Interview with Jamaica Kincaid." *Kenyon Review* 16 (Winter 1994): 163–188.

Perry, Donna, ed. "Jamaica Kincaid." In *Backtalk: Women Writers Speak Out: Interviews by Donna Perry*. New Brunswick, N.J.: Rutgers University Press, 1983. 127–141.

Vorda, Allan. "An Interview with Jamaica Kincaid." *Mississippi Review* 20 (1991): 7–26. Also in: Vorda, Allan, ed. *Face to Face: Interviews with Contemporary Novelists*. Houston, Tex.: Rice University Press, 1993. 78–105.

Information on the Bildungsroman

Abel, Elizabeth, Marianne Hirsch, and Elizabeth Langland, eds. *The Voyage In: Fictions of Female Development*. Hanover, N.H.: University Press of New England, 1983.

Buckley, Jerome Hamilton. *Season of Youth: The Bildungsroman from Dickens to Golding*. Cambridge, Mass.: Harvard University Press, 1974.

2

Historical Context: Slavery and Its Aftermath

Annie John takes place on the small Caribbean island of Antigua, a former British colony marked by 200 years of slavery. The slave past of Antigua is a backdrop to Annie John's environment and her thoughts. It forms a part of the climate in which she lives—the ancestry of her people—and shapes her ideas and attitudes. When asked about the name she chose for the main character of another novel, author Jamaica Kincaid replied, "She was going to have a name that would refer to the slave part of her history, so why not my own? I write about myself for the most part, and about things that have happened to me" (Bonetti, 125). This awareness of the slave past is also a part of Annie's story. Some knowledge of the history and environment of this island, especially of its slave system, is essential for a deeper understanding of the novel.

Antigua is located in the eastern Caribbean, at the southern end of the Leeward Islands, which extend out in an arc beyond Puerto Rico. Since 1981, it has been an independent nation called Antigua and Barbuda and is composed of three islands. Antigua, the largest, has an area of 108 square miles. It is low, mostly a plateau of flat limestone and sandstone, except for a few hills in the southwest. It has no mountains, forests, rivers, or streams and experiences frequent droughts in spite of an average annual rainfall of about forty inches. The climate is generally dry and sunny, with an average temperature of about eighty-one degrees Fahrenheit. The coastline has many bays and inlets, with beautiful beaches and excellent ports. On the northwest coast lies the capital, St. John's, which is the largest city and principal port. Another important port is English Harbor, in the southeast, the location of Nelson's dockyard, port of the famous Admiral Horatio Nelson of the British navy during the colonial period. Barbuda is a small island of 62 square miles situated 25 miles to the north, with only one small city, Codrington, and a game reserve. Redonda, the third island, is an uninhabited rock of about one-half a square mile.

The overwhelming majority of people on Antigua are of African heritage, descendants of African slaves who were brought over during colonial times to work on the island's sugar plantations. There are about 79,000 people living there today, mostly involved in tourism or agriculture ("Antigua and Barbuda," 454). The official language is English, and most people are Christian, predominantly Anglican (English Protestantism), with large numbers of Methodists and Moravians (Tolson, Niddrie, and Momsen, 762–763). These denominations sent missionaries to the islands during the colonial period. Annie, then, is a typical resident of this island in the 1950s and 1960s—English-speaking, black, Methodist, living in St. John's, attending British schools.

The island of Antigua was originally settled by Arawak and Carib Indians, the two principal groups of indigenous peoples in this area. The Arawaks of the Caribbean disappeared soon after the arrival of the Europeans, due to epidemics of communicable European diseases such as smallpox, measles, and influenza, for which they had no immunity, as well as war, displacement, enslavement, cruel treatment, and suicide. Most Caribs also died or were driven off their islands. Today, the few Carib Indians left in the Caribbean reside on the island of St. Vincent or on Dominica, which has a Carib reservation. Annie John's mother was born on Dominica and came to Antigua when she was sixteen. She is lighter skinned than Annie, with straighter hair, probably due to her Carib-African ancestry.

Christopher Columbus visited the island in 1493 and named it Antigua, after the Church of Santa Maria de la Antigua in Seville, Spain. English settlers from St. Kitts colonized it in 1632. At first they grew tobacco, but later in the seventeenth century, sugar, perhaps the most profitable crop of the Caribbean, became the predominant crop. The eighteenth century saw the rise of the large sugar plantation in Antigua. Because sugar was a labor- and capital-intensive crop, the English planters imported thousands of African slaves to perform the heavy, exhausting labor. Great Britain abolished the slave trade in 1808 and emancipated the slaves in its colonies in 1834. After that, the majority of Antiguans became wage earners on the same plantations. Antigua was still a crown colony and was administratively a part of the British colony of the Leeward Islands from 1871 until 1956. From 1958 to 1962 Antigua was a member of the West Indies Federation and then entered into a free association with Great Britain in 1967, shortly after Annie left the island for England. During this time, Antigua exercised its right of self-government in internal affairs. Antigua and Barbuda achieved full independence from Britain in 1981. Since independence, Antigua has had a parliamentary system with a prime minister. Political life has been dominated by Vere Bird, president of the Antigua Labour Party (ALP), which has won most of the elections since 1981 despite accusations of widespread graft, fraud, and mismanagement. The sugar industry declined in the twentieth century and finally disappeared in 1972, despite some efforts to revive it in the mid-1980s. Today most people are involved in trades (such as carpentry, like Annie's father), small-scale agriculture, and tourism, which has grown to be the most profitable industry in the last twenty years ("Antigua and Barbuda," 454; Rogozinski, 282–283).

The historical dates indicate that Antigua was still a British colony while Annie John was growing up there between 1949 and 1966. As a result, she received a classic British education, read English literature, had access to the services supplied by the British government—a public library and hospital—and was raised Methodist, a Protestant denomination.

Despite the strong British influence, Annie John has a keen awareness of Antigua's slave past and the fact that most of the inhabitants, including herself, are descendants of those slaves. She senses the hypocrisy of celebrating British events and figures (such as the Queen) and Christopher Columbus's discovery, as it resulted in slavery for her ancestors. In school, Annie thinks about the past as she looks at Ruth, an English girl whose father is a missionary, and imagines that she probably did not want to be in

the West Indies owing to her shame over what her ancestors had
done there and in Africa:

> Her ancestors had been the masters, while ours had been the slaves.
> She had such a lot to be ashamed of. . . . We could look everybody
> in the eye, for our ancestors had done nothing wrong except just
> sit somewhere, defenseless. Of course, sometimes, what with our
> teachers and our books, it was hard for us to tell on which side we
> really now belonged—with the masters or the slaves—for it was all
> history, it was all in the past, and everybody behaved differently
> now; all of us celebrated Queen Victoria's birthday, even though
> she had been dead a long time. But we, the descendants of the
> slaves, knew quite well what had really happened, and I was sure
> that if the tables had been turned we would have acted differently.
> (76)

It is interesting to note that instead of feeling any stigma attached to being a descendant of slaves, Annie John believes that
the descendants of the British are the ones who should feel
ashamed of the deeds of their ancestors. Just how terrible were
these deeds? Extremely so, especially on sugar islands such as Antigua, as historical documents and studies of slavery amply demonstrate.

Slavery has existed for well over 4,000 years of human history,
but the institution took an especially virulent form during the four
centuries (sixteenth to nineteenth) of slavery in the Americas. The
rapid demise of the indigenous people, coupled with the formation of highly profitable but labor-intensive plantations and estates
in the New World, created an enormous demand for slaves from
Africa. This demand created a transatlantic slave trade that went
from the coast of Africa (from the coasts of present-day Senegal,
Ivory Coast, Ghana, Benin, Nigeria, Cameroon, on south to Angola/
Namibia) to the Americas. African people were chained together
and tightly packed into the holds of slave ships for the voyage
(called "the Middle Passage") to the New World. The voyage took
anywhere from several weeks to months. The harsh conditions in
holds, particularly the lack of sanitation, created an average mortality rate of about 13 percent during the voyage—that is, thirteen
out of one hundred people died on the slave ships. This is an
extraordinarily high number, considering that most of the people

were young and able-bodied when they boarded. Conditions were so atrocious that it was said at the time that you could smell a slave ship on the high seas from over a mile away.

It has been estimated that over 10 million slaves were brought to the New World between 1510 and 1870, when the last slaves were brought to the Americas. Of these, the Caribbean islands received 3.5 to 4 million, or 40 percent of the total; the United States, 500,000, or 5 percent of the total; and Brazil, 3.5 to 4 million, or 40 percent of the total. The rest were scattered to other areas in the New World. Most slaves worked in agriculture. The most profitable crop was sugar, which was largely grown on the sugar estates of the Caribbean (Hellie, 21).

Slaves on the sugar estates suffered the harshest conditions of all the slaves in the New World and had the highest death rates. They were organized into highly regimented gangs and driven by overseers with whips to carry out the backbreaking labor required to plant, fertilize, tend, harvest, and process sugarcane. They worked from dawn til dusk, with two breaks for meals, or about ten to twelve hours per day, and sixteen to eighteen hours a day during the harvest, when the cane was cut by hand with a machete and taken to the mill to be processed. In order to plant the cane, large holes were dug by hand, because the planters refused to use plows. Sugarcane exhausts the soil quickly, so the crop was intensively fertilized with animal dung, which was very heavy and carried in baskets by hand. The planters seldom used beasts of burden, preferring human labor.

Because sugar was a labor-intensive crop that required immediate processing in expensive mills, planters needed to make large capital investments in slaves and machinery and were often in debt to banks and investors in Europe. Planters found that it was more economical to scrimp on food, clothing, housing, and medical care for their slaves, then replace them as needed, than to pay for any more than their bare subsistence. The slaves received a small food allotment for the week, which was high in carbohydrates but low in protein and fat. Their clothing allowance was so inadequate that they were often nearly naked, in rags. And their huts were small, flimsy, vermin infested, and leaky, with no bedding or furniture. Slaves were usually allowed a small plot of land to grow some of their own food to supplement their diet or to sell at Sunday market (their one day off, with three days off at Christmas). Physical punishment was frequent and harsh. The estate hospitals for sick slaves were actually pest houses. Due to the harsh living conditions, the constant hard labor, and especially malnutrition, the slaves were highly susceptible to disease, especially dysentery, tuberculosis, typhoid, and varieties of malaria and yellow fever that they had not been exposed to in Africa.

One measure of the condition of slaves is their mortality rate. Taking into account the number of new arrivals from Africa, scholars have looked at whether the net number of slaves in an area decreased or increased (due to procreation). A comparison of figures for the United States with the figures for the Caribbean confirms the harsh conditions on the islands. In 1825 in the United States, there were 2 million slaves, after having brought in a total of 375,000 to 500,000. This population was able to reproduce and grow. In the Caribbean, on the other hand, there were also 2 million slaves, but only after having imported 3.5 to 4 million. These slaves died frequently, died young, and were often unable to procreate. Even if they did manage to have children, three out of four died before the age of five (Rogozinski, 122–139).

Not all slaves worked in the fields. The more fortunate ones were employed as domestics or in skilled trades and often lived in urban areas. Conditions for these slaves were somewhat better, although they varied from owner to owner.

The Caribbean saw a high rate of runaways and slave rebellions. Some islands, such as Cuba and Jamaica, had large areas of undeveloped forest in the interiors where slaves could hide. These slaves were called maroons and often formed communities that lasted for decades. On small islands like Antigua, however, after a few years all of the land was cultivated, so it was more difficult to hide; the only other escape was by sea, for which one needed access to a boat. The Caribbean also had a high number of rebellions and conspiracies to rebel. The one successful slave rebellion in the Americas took place in St. Dominque (present-day Haiti); in 1789–1804, slaves drove the white French planters off the island and formed the first independent republic in the New World. Antigua had several conspiracies to rebel that were crushed before they broke out. The largest and most famous occurred in the early eighteenth century; excerpts from the official report on that conspiracy are reproduced in this chapter.

Since Antigua's land was filled with labor-intensive estates, the black population was large, with an extremely small white and free colored population (usually the offspring or descendants of white men and black or colored mistresses). At the end of the eighteenth century, the population of the British Leeward Islands (including Antigua, St. Kitts, Montserrat, and Nevis) was 83,000 slaves and 3,000 whites or free people of color. The ratio of slaves to free people was about 10:1 but often reached 50:1 in rural areas. The white planters were highly aware of the danger of rebellion—hence, the need for strict control of the slaves' behavior and for a strict social hierarchy based on race. People of color were not socially accepted until after several generations had passed and some "whitening" of the complexion had occurred; slaves, of course, were outcasts (Rogozinski, 122–139). So in these former slave societies like Antigua, almost the entire population is of African heritage, which means that racial relations are very different from those in the United States, where people of African descent are in the minority. Notice that in *Annie John* the narrator seldom mentions skin color unless the character is white; the assumption is that most people are black. In narratives in the United States, usually the opposite is true.

At the end of the eighteenth century, the sugar estates were in economic decline. Many British citizens, spurred on by the growing evangelism of religious denominations such as the Quakers and the Methodists, began to campaign for the end of slavery. The strategy was to end the slave trade first, then eventually to emancipate all the slaves in the British colonies. Economic concerns about slavery dovetailed with humanitarian concerns. After several decades of pamphlets, essays, speeches, petitions, and hearings in Parliament, the British government abolished the slave trade in 1808 and emancipated the slaves in its colonies in 1834 with a four-year apprenticeship, which was later repealed. The compensation paid to slave owners enabled them to pay off their debts and revitalized the sugar industry (Goveia, 260–261; Hellie, 293).

Antigua was the only island that enjoyed an immediate emancipation with no apprenticeship. The former slaves became (very low) wage earners on the estates and were free to come and go. The economic status quo, however, of rich white planters and poor black laborers, remained largely unchanged for many years, as did the social structure, which was stratified according to race, with whites at the top, coloreds or mulattoes in the middle, and blacks at the bottom of the hierarchy (Goveia, 260–262).

For this order to change, the economic structure of the island would need to change first. This process would take many years. At first, there was little land available for the newly freed black people to buy, even when they had saved money from their wages. Gradually, however, small villages sprang up, and some Antiguans were able to leave the sugar estates. Later, the sugar industry was mechanized, and many workers joined labor unions in order to improve working conditions. Black union workers and other black, educated Antiguans began to ascend into positions of power in Antigua in the twentieth century. Finally, the sugar industry vanished, and now most job opportunities are in the tourist industry.

The slave and sugar trades brought enormous wealth to England. Many English planters and their investors made huge fortunes from this trade, as did small merchants. The growth of the largest cities, especially the port of Liverpool, was a direct result of this trade. The suffering of the slaves made all this wealth possible for other people, in other places; the slaves received nothing but short, harsh lives. Today, Antigua is not a wealthy country. Most people are involved in tourism, small agriculture, or trades (such as Annie John's father, a carpenter) (Knight, 22).

In *A Small Place*, a long essay about Antigua published in 1988, after *Annie John*, Jamaica Kincaid describes Antigua's past of slavery and its present of tourism and corrupt government:

In Antigua, people speak of slavery as if it had been a pageant full of large ships sailing on blue water, the large ships filled up with human cargo—their ancestors; they got off, they were forced to work under conditions that were cruel and inhuman, they were beaten, they were murdered, they were sold, their children were taken from them and these separations lasted forever, there were many other bad things, and then suddenly the whole thing came to an end in something called emancipation. Then they speak of emancipation itself as if it just happened the other day . . . as if it, emancipation, were a contemporary occurrence, something everybody is familiar with. And perhaps there is something in that, for an institution that is often celebrated in Antigua is the Hotel Training School, a school that teaches Antiguans how to be good servants, how to be a good nobody, which is what a servant is. In Antigua, people cannot see a relationship between their obsession with slavery and emancipation and their celebration of the Hotel Training School (graduation ceremonies are broadcast on radio and television); people cannot see a relationship between their obsession with slavery and emancipation and the fact that they are governed by corrupt men, or that these corrupt men have given their country away to corrupt foreigners. (54–55)

In essence, Kincaid sees a new form of exploitation taking the place of the old slave system.

In *Annie John*, Antigua's slave past is an important element in Annie's environment. The slave system can be better understood by examining the documents that follow.

DESCRIPTIONS OF ANTIGUA DURING SLAVERY

John Luffman, an Englishman, lived in Antigua from 1786 to 1788 and wrote a series of forty letters describing the island and his experiences there. These letters were published with the title: *A Brief Account of the Island of Antigua, together with the customs and manners of its inhabitants, as well white as black: as also an accurate statement of the food, clothing, labor, and punishment, of slaves. In Letters to a Friend*, London, 1789. These letters have been reprinted several times, as they provide a clear and vivid portrait of Antigua at the time, particularly of slave conditions. The dates of the letters indicate that they were written at the height of the sugar/slave system in Antigua and at the time of intensive campaigns in England for the abolition of slavery. Luffman's descriptions and reactions to his observations reflect these historical conditions and lend credence to Annie's criticism of slavery in the novel.

FROM JOHN LUFFMAN, LETTERS FROM ANTIGUA (1789)

From Letter IX, December 6, 1786. The virtue of . . . [the white women] is said to be superior to the arts of seduction, infidelity to the marriage bed being very rarely known on their parts. I wish I could say as much for the men. Marriages are always solemnized in the houses, as are also baptisms (except those of negroes) and the churches are very thinly attended but on funerals or on particular public occasions.

This is the worst time of the year for thieving; the negroes will have some of the good things to keep Christmas with, and I have contributed thereto by my losses; a fine lamb and a young milch goat stole from me within the last twenty-four hours, and I am under no small apprehension for the fate of my poultry. The rogues rob generally at midnight, stark naked, their bodies greased, therefore if you get but slight hold of them, they slip through your hands and are off in an instant. . . .

From Letter XI, January 28, 1787. Here I must observe, that many of these gentlemen managers, [of the estates of absentee planters] as well as the overseers under them, contribute, in a great degree, to stock the plantation with mulatto and mestee slaves; it is impossible to say in what numbers they have such children, but the following fact is too often verified, "that, as soon as born, they are despised, not only by the very authors, under God, of their being, but by every white, destitute of humane and liberal principles," such is the regard paid to the hue of complexion in preference to the more permanent beauties of the mind.

From Letter XII, March 10, 1787. The tables of the opulent and also of many, who can very ill afford it, are covered with a profusion, known only in this part of the world; their attendants numerous, but it is not uncommon to see them waiting almost destitute of clothing, and the little they have mere rags. Even in the first houses, where an attendant slave may possibly have a shirt, jacket, and breeches, they are always without stockings, and generally wanting shoes. A few days since, being invited to a tea drinking party, where was collected from ten to a dozen ladies and gentlemen, a stout negro fellow waited, who had no other covering than an old pair of trousers. I believe I was the only person present who took the least notice of the indelicacy of such an appearance, and, indeed, it is my opinion, were the slaves to go quite naked, it would have no more effect on the feelings of the major part of the inhabitants of this country than what is produced by the sight of a dog, cat, or any other domesticated quadruped.

From Letter XIX, July 6, 1787. Being now about to commence my relation of the food, labor, and treatment of slaves within this island, it may not be uninteresting to you, to be previously acquainted with the mode of conveying these unfortunate people to our shores, and the method of disposing of them when brought hither; for the first part I can only say it comes from a person whose veracity is undoubted, for the last, my eyes have been witnesses to the act.

The slave trade, to the British dominions, is principally carried out by the merchants of Liverpool, Bristol does a little, and London less. Slaves are for the greatest part kidnapped, and many fall in the hands of the traders, from being prisoners of war to such of the country princes, whom the white men, or their black agents, have caused to commit hostilities on each other for the particular purpose of procuring the miserable captives as freight for their ships.

When a slave ship arrives on the coast, it is not generally a consideration with the captain or supercargo, what number of these people their vessel will take conveniently, but how many they can get, is the object; consequently even common humanity has no concern whatever in the employ, and it is customary to crowd as many of them into the ship as their efforts can procure. Between decks is their receptacle, the room allotted each man, is about six feet, by sixteen inches; women and children have a smaller, but proportionate allowance; very little regard is even paid to this rule of accommodation, although sufficiently small, and they are frequently so closely stowed together, as to be unable to lie down in any position but on one side. The captain and officers look with particular attention to their own security, for no sooner are the slaves on board, but the men are chained together in couples, the right hand and leg of one, to the left hand and leg of the other. When they are ordered up, which is generally when the watch is relieved, at eight o'clock in the morning, as each pair thus joined ascend from the hatches, a chain is passed through their irons, and made fast by ring bolts to the deck; and the precaution is absolutely necessary for the well doing of this nefarious commerce, lest if permitted the free use of their limbs, a spark of Heaven-born liberty should inspire them with revenge against their enslavers. In this situation (if the weather permits) they continue eight or ten hours, during which time they are fed, and the decks below cleansed, from such filth which is alone sufficient in one day to breed contagion. The women and children slaves are not shackled. . . .

The purchasers of slaves are as particular in examining them before they strike a bargain, as a butcher, at Smithfield market, when dealing for sheep. As soon as bought, they are walked to the respective plantations of their owner, where the hoe is frequently put into hands, hitherto unused to labor, and as soft as the finest lady's in Europe.

These cargoes average from thirty-seven to forty pounds sterling per head.

From Letter XXII, September 15, 1787. The clothing of a field slave consists of a blanket, which serves them not only to sleep upon (though some have beds of dried plantain leaves), but to fasten about their bodies in damp weather, also a piece of woolen cloth, called a babaw, which goes round the waist, a blue woolen jacket, and a party colored cap of the same material. Their drink, as per allowance, is water. . . . On every plantation is an hospital or sick-house, where the slaves, as soon as infected with disorder, or having received hurt (the latter of which frequently happens in crop time) are sent. These places, at least such as have come within my observation, are as bad as you can well suppose, being not only destitute of almost every convenience, but filthy in the extreme, and the attendants generally such negroes as are nearly superannuated or unfit for active employment.

From Letter XXIII, October 3, 1787. The negroes are turned out at sunrise, and employed in gangs from twenty to sixty, or upwards, under the inspection of white overseers, generally poor Scotch lads, who, by their assiduity and industry, frequently become masters of the plantation, to which they came out as indentured servants: subordinate to these overseers, are drivers, commonly called dog-drivers, who are mostly black or mulatto fellows, of the worst dispositions; these men are furnished with whips, which, while on duty, they are obliged, on pain of severe punishment, to have with them, and are authorized to flog wherever they see the least relaxation from labor; nor is it a consideration with them, whether it proceeds from idleness or inability, paying at the same time, little or no regard to age or sex.

From Letter XXIV, November 9, 1787. The punishments inflicted on slaves, in this island, are various and tormenting. . . . Many . . . cruelties . . . are practiced by the unfeeling, among which is the thumb-screw, a barbarous invention to fasten the thumbs together, which appears to cause excruciating pain. The iron necklace, is a ring, locked or rivetted about the neck; to these collars are frequently added what are here termed pot-hooks, additions, resembling the hooks or handles of a por-ridge pot, fixed perpendicularly, the bent or hooked parts turning out-wards, which prevents the wearers from laying down their heads with any degree of comfort. The boots are strong iron rings, full four inches in circumference, closed just above the ankles, to these some owners prefix a chain, which the miserable sufferers, if able to work, must man-age as well as they can, and it is not unfrequent to see in the streets of this town, at mid-day, negroes chained together by these necklaces as well as by the boots, when let out of their dungeon for a short time to breathe the fresh air, whose crime has been endeavoring to gain that liberty by running away, which they well knew could never be otherwise obtained from their owners. The spurs are rings of iron, similar to the boots, to which are added spikes from three to four inches long, placed horizontally. A chain fastened about the body with a padlock, is another mode of tormenting this oppressed race of beings. A boy who has not yet seen his fourteenth year, passes by my house several times in a day, and has done so for these six months past, with no other clothing; he also lays upon his chains, and although they are as much in point of weight as he ought reasonably to carry, yet he is obliged, through the day to fetch water from the country pond, at the distance of half a mile from the house of his mistress, who is an old widow-woman. To the chains thus put on, a fifty pounds weight is sometimes added, as an appendage; this is undoubtedly a prudent measure, and admirably well calculated to keep the slave at home, as it must of course prevent the object thus secured, from escaping the rigor of his destiny. The . . . severe floggings, and sundry other methods of torturing these unhappy people, as best suits the caprice or inventive cruelty of their owner or employers, are here inflicted. The public whipper is a white man, who executes his office by a negro deputy, and the price for every flogging is two bits.

However hurtful or disgusting the aforementioned punishments are to those who have minds fraught with humanity, every application to the magistrates to prevent the exercising such severities on these unfriended people, must be ineffectual while there is no existing law in the island code enabling them to take cognizance of the correction of slaves by their proprietors. I could therefore presume to advise those, to whom the power of making laws for the good government of the British empire, both at home and abroad, is delegated, to enact a law for establishing a committee of humanity, composed of men of liberal principles, and such, no doubt, can be found, not only in this island, but also in all those under the British government, who should have entire control in all cases between the master and the slave. To these men all complaints should be made, and by them and them only, should punishments be directed; an act of such a nature, would, I trust, not only be applauded by all good men, but bring on the authors of it, the blessings of Heaven, and the gratitude of a numerous body of unfortunate fellow creatures.

Slaves, for criminal offenses, have within these few years, been admitted to a trial by a jury of six white men, at which proceedings two justices preside as judges. They are seldom hanged, unless for murder, it being the interest of the owners of such as are convicted, to get them off, the country allowing the masters but half the appraised value of such as are executed; they are therefore in mitigation generally flogged under the gallows, and sometimes sent off the island to be sold.

From Letter XXV, December 8, 1787. Slaves are not permitted to marry consequently take one anothers words, and change their husbands and wives (as they term them) when, and as often as they please. Baptism is allowed by some owners, but the slave must pay the priest for executing his office and the price is a dollar. Negroes and colored people are not buried in the same church-yard as the white, even if free; the distinction, and the superiority which the European race claim over the African, are extended as far as they can possibly go: to the grave! but there they must cease, and the hereafter, when the reign of human pride is over, will be directed according to the fear we have had of God, and the love we have borne one another during our earthly state of trial.

From Letter XXVI, January 1, 1788. The general idea of Europeans, that blacks only are slaves, is very erroneous, for slavery extends to every descendant of negroes (slaves) by white men, such as mulattoes, mestees and quarteroons, and the two latter mentioned, are frequently as fair as Englishmen, at least such of them as have been habituated to a sea-faring life, or to tropical countries. I have seen persons sold here, having blue eyes and flaxen-hair, and complexions equal almost to any on your side the water, but such people fetch a lower price than blacks, unless they are tradesmen, because the purchasers cannot employ them in the drudgeries to which negroes are put to; the colored men, are therefore mostly brought up to trades or employed as house slaves, and the women of this description generally prostitutes. When taken into keeping by white men, they dress in a very ridiculous manner, assuming the name of their keeper for the time being, and laying it aside when turned off. There are persons in this island who let out their female slaves for the particular purpose of fornication, and that, as well as publicly cohabiting with them, is considered here merely as a venial error. Those women are much more subservient to the will of their enamoratos, from a dread of punishment than a white would be, or even the laws of the country suffer, for it is not uncommon for some men to beat, and otherwise severely correct their colored mistresses. This connexion strikes at the root of honorable engagements with the fair, prevents marriage, and is, thereby, detrimental to the increase of legitimate population.

From Letter XXVIII, February 7, 1788. What is it I hear from you? Not only that every appearance of war has subsided, but that the British legislature have serious thoughts of reforming the abuses in, if not totally abolishing the slave-trade to Africa, and slavery in the West Indies? . . . I think I hear you say, . . . "Let the banners of liberty, which are those of justice, and virtue also, be displayed in their fullest glory, in every clime under the British government." I join with you in the wish, and condemn the traffic to Africa, for human flesh and blood, as the most abominable, the most to be abhorred of any species of commerce ever carried on by our countrymen; it is a disgrace to those excellent laws we boast, and to the enlightened age we live in; it tends to the corruption of morals, and is totally repugnant to the immediate order of the Creator, delivered by the heavenly host, when the Saviour entered the world. *"Glory to God in the highest, and on earth peace, good will, towards men."* Nevertheless, if the African slave trade is abolished, and if slavery is still continued here, some wholesome laws for the better clothing and feeding of slaves will be absolutely necessary, for population will not increase under the disadvantages of hard labor, and indifferent food and raiment, and I have not a doubt, that if these people were well fed, and treated in such a manner as human beings ought to be treated, the stock of negroes already on this island, would be sufficient for all its purposes, without any further supplies from Africa. . . . Now if this business of abolition takes place and if there is not a very sharp look out kept, to prevent the smuggling of the produce of this island to the slave market, it will tend much to the hurt of the revenue and be a means of weakening our great national bulwark, the Navy. . . . It will also serve, without the before mentioned prevention, as a heavy tax upon the planter, without benefiting the mother country in the smallest degree, for what with the cost of the slaves, at the foreign-market, and the expenses attending thereon, they will stand him in double the price they are now purchased for. This is as it strikes me, but no doubt when such an event takes place, the wisdom and vigilance of a British Parliament, will provide every matter necessary to give the law its full effect.

From Letter XXX, March 14, 1788. Negroes are very fond of the discordant notes of the banjar, and the hollow sound of the toombah. The banjar is somewhat similar to the guitar, the bottom, or under part, is formed of one half of a large calabash, to which is prefixed a wooden neck, and it is strung with cat-gut and wire. This instrument is the invention of, and was brought here by the African negroes, who are most expert in the performances thereon, which are principally their own country tunes, indeed I do not remember ever to have heard any thing like European numbers from its touch. The toombah is similar to the tabor, and has gingles of tin or shells; to this music (if it deserves the name) I have seen a hundred or more dancing at a time, their gestures are extravagant, but not more so than the principal dancer at your Opera-house, and I believe were some of their steps and motions introduced into the public amusements at home, by French or Italian dancers, they would be well received; I do not mean, by the bye, to indicate that the movements of these sables are altogether graceful, but their agility and the surprising command of their limbs, is astonishing; this can be accounted for only by their being habituated to a warm climate, where elasticity is more general than in the colder latitudes: The principal dancing time is on Sunday afternoons, when the great market is over . . . , in fact Sunday is their day of trade, their day of relaxation, their day of pleasure, and may, in the strictest sense of the words, be called the negroes holiday.

From Letter XXXI, March 28, 1788. In my last I promised to give you an account of the Sunday market. . . . This market is held at the southern extremity of the town. [H]ere an assemblage of many hundred negroes and mulattoes expose for sale, poultry, pigs, kids, vegetables, fruit, and other things; they begin to assemble by daybreak and the market is generally crowded by ten o'clock; this is the proper time to purchase, for the week, such articles as are not perishable. The noise occasioned by the jabber of the negroes, and the squalling and cries of the children basking in the sun, exceeds any thing I ever heard in a London market: The smell is also intolerable, proceeding from the strong effluvia, naturally arising from the bodies of these people, and from the stinking salt-fish. . . . About three o'clock business is nearly over, when the hucksters shops are filled, and their doors crowded, and new rum grog is swilled in large quantities to the benefit of the retailers and destruction of the negroes; some, as I before wrote you, dance, others play at dice. . . . It is not uncommon for them, when intoxicated, to turn out to fight in Otto's pasture (adjoining the market). . . . They are punishable by law for fighting, but the law seldom interferes. The sight of a gun, or a white man, laying about him with a whip, will disperse them immediately; and a negro durst not return a blow, under the forfeiture of their right hand.

This rigid law was introduced, I learn, to prevent the insurrections of slaves; which, about fifty years ago, had nearly proved fatal to the white inhabitants of this island.

From Letter XXXIX, July 21, 1788. It must be a matter of surprise to Britons, that the people in power in the colony should so much neglect that best of institutions for public safety, and internal protection, the Militia, when the great disproportion of twelve blacks and colored persons to one white is considered as now existing, and when it is observed that eleven twelfths of the blacks are slaves . . . and when it is remarked that at this particular period the people of Britain seem almost determined on the abolition of the slave-trade to Africa, and may possibly extend their project to at least an amendment of the slave-laws in the West Indies, from a knowledge of which proceedings it is next to an impossibility to keep them ignorant, it is but reasonable to suppose, if they catch the idea that the people at home favor their cause, a confidence may be raised in them, hitherto unknown to the race, and the love of liberty, which I believe pervades the heart of man, whether black or white, as the first and ruling principle, might inspire them to make a grand effort to throw off the yoke, under which they at present groan, and recover their natural right, their liberty. Now in such a case, and in such a cause, suppose about twelve hundred men, almost as ignorant of military discipline as the negroes, opposed to forty thousand persons (for the women are as capable as the men of enduring fatigue, and would, no doubt, join in the cause) what would be the consequence, but a dreadful carnage, if not the total annihilation of the whites! This observation does not apply to Antigua only, but to the other isles under the British government, in the West Indies, where the same disproportion reigns, from which I believe not one can be excepted but Barbadoes. It therefore doth behove those in power, if only for the preservation of their own lives and properties, to keep up a strict military discipline, and endeavor also, by every possible encouragement, to increase the number of white inhabitants. To adopt measures effective of preservation from ill, is a duty imposed upon us by reason and common sense, and reason and common sense forbid that any set of men should turn a deaf ear to their dictates.

Reprinted in Vere Langford Oliver, *The History of the Island of Antigua, One of the Leeward Caribees in the West Indies, from the First Settlement in 1635 to the Present Time*, Vol. 1. London: Mitchell and Hughes, 1894, 128–138.

AUTOBIOGRAPHY OF A WEST INDIAN SLAVE WOMAN

The next document contains sections from the autobiography of an enslaved woman who lived in Antigua and other Caribbean islands. Her description of slave life emphasizes the absolute power that owners held over their slaves and how this power often led to unspeakable acts of cruelty against these human beings. Eventually, she is taken by her owners to England, where she leaves them in order to be free. The price of her freedom, however, is exile from her home in Antigua and separation from her husband. This document demonstrates the great strength and endurance of women in the West Indies, like the ancestors of Annie John.

FROM MARY PRINCE, *THE HISTORY OF MARY PRINCE, A WEST INDIAN SLAVE, NARRATED BY HERSELF* (1831)

[When Mary Prince is twelve years old, and her mistress dies, Mary is sold to another master and separated from her mother and sisters.] . . . Our mother, weeping as she went, called me away with the children Hannah and Dinah, and we took the road that led to Hamble Town, which we reached about four o'clock in the afternoon. We followed my mother to the marketplace, where she placed us in a row against a large house, with our backs to the wall and our arms folded against our breasts. I, as the eldest, stood first, Hannah next to me, then Dinah, and our mother stood beside, crying over us. My heart throbbed with grief and terror so violently, that I pressed my hands quite tightly across my breast, but I could not keep it still, and it continued to leap as though it would burst out of my body. But who cared for that? Did one of the many bystanders, who were looking at us so carelessly, think of the pain that wrung the hearts of the negro woman and her young ones? Not so! They were not all bad, I dare say, but slavery hardens white people's hearts towards the blacks; and many of them were not slow to make their remarks upon us aloud, without regard to our grief—though their light words fell like cayenne on the fresh wounds of our hearts. Oh, those white people have small hearts who can only feel for themselves. . . .

I then saw my sisters led forth, and sold to different owners; so that we had not the sad satisfaction of being partners in bondage. When the sale was over, my mother hugged and kissed us, and mourned over us, begging of us to keep up a good heart, and do our duty to our new masters. It was a sad parting; one went one way, one another, and our poor mammy went home with nothing. . . .

The next morning my mistress set about instructing me in my tasks. She taught me to do all sorts of household work; to wash and bake, pick cotton and wool, and wash floors, and cook. And she taught me (how can I ever forget it!) more things than these; she caused me to know the exact difference between the smart of the rope, the cart-whip, and the cow-skin, when applied to my naked body by her own cruel hand. And there was scarcely any punishment more dreadful than the blows I received on my face and head from her hard heavy fist. She was a fearful woman, and a savage mistress to her slaves.

There were two little slave boys in the house, on whom she vented her bad temper in a special manner. One of these children was a mulatto, called Cyrus, who had been bought while an infant in his mother's arms; the other, Jack, was an African from the coast of Guinea, whom a sailor had given or sold to my master. Seldom a day passed without these boys receiving the most severe treatment, and often for no fault at all. . . . They were never secure one moment from a blow, and their lives were passed in continual fear. . . . My pity for these poor boys was soon transferred to myself; for I was licked, and flogged, and pinched by her pitiless fingers in the neck and arms, exactly as they were. To strip me naked—to hang me up by the wrists and lay my flesh open with the cow-skin, was an ordinary punishment for even a slight offence. My mistress often robbed me too of the hours that belong to sleep. She used to sit up very late, frequently even until morning; and I had then to stand at a bench and wash during the greater part of the night, or pick wool and cotton; and often I have dropped down overcome by sleep and fatigue, till roused from a state of stupor by the whip, and forced to start up to my tasks. . . .

[Mary has several more masters, including Mr. D———.] . . . He had an ugly fashion of stripping himself quite naked, and ordering me then to wash him in a tub of water. This was worse to me than all the licks. Sometimes when he called me to wash him I would not come, my eyes were so full of shame. He would then come to beat me. . . .

During the time I worked there, I heard that Mr. John Wood was going to Antigua. I felt a great wish to go there, and I went to Mr. D———, and asked him to let me go in Mr. Wood's service. Mr. Wood did not then want to purchase me; it was my own fault that I came under him, I was so anxious to go. It was ordained to be, I suppose; God led me there. The truth is, I did not wish to be any longer the slave of my indecent master. . . .

My master and mistress went on one occasion into the country, to Date

Hill, for change of air, and carried me with them to take charge of the children, and to do the work of the house. While I was in the country, I saw how the field negroes are worked in Antigua. They are worked very hard and fed but scantily. They are called out to work before daybreak, and come home after dark; and then each has to heave his bundle of grass for the cattle in the pen. Then, on Sunday morning, each slave has to go out and gather a large bundle of grass; and, when they bring it home, they have all to sit at the manager's door and wait till he come out: often have they to wait there till past eleven o'clock, without any breakfast. After that, those that have yams or potatoes, or fire-wood to sell, hasten to market to buy a dog's worth [72nd part of a dollar] of salt fish, or pork, which is a great treat for them. Some of them buy a little pickle out of the shad barrels, which they call sauce, to season their yams and Indian corn. It is very wrong, I know, to work on Sunday or go to market; but will not God call the Buckra men [white men] to answer for this on the great day of judgment—since they will give the slaves no other day?

[Mary marries a free carpenter; then she is taken to England by the Wood family, without her husband. In England, legally, she is free, so she decides to leave their service.] And so I came out, and went and carried my trunk to the Moravians. I then returned back to Mash the shoe-black's house, and begged his wife to take me in. I had a little West Indian money in my trunk; and they got it changed for me. This helped to support me for a little while. The man's wife was very kind to me. I was very sick, and she boiled nourishing things up for me. She also sent for a doctor to see me, and he sent me medicine, which did me good, though I was ill for a long time with the rheumatic pains. I lived a good many months with these poor people, and they nursed me, and did all that lay in their power to serve me. The man was well acquainted with my situation, as he used to go to and fro to Mr. Wood's house to clean shoes and knives; and he and his wife were sorry for me.

About this time, a woman of the name of Hill told me of the Anti-Slavery Society, and went with me to their office, to inquire if they could do any thing to get me my freedom, and send me back to the West Indies. The gentlemen of the Society took me to a lawyer, who examined very strictly into my case; but told me that the laws of England could do nothing to make me free in Antigua. However they did all they could for me: they gave me a little money from time to time to keep me from want; and some of them went to Mr. Wood to try to persuade him to let me return a free woman to my husband; but though they offered him, as I have heard, a large sum for my freedom, he was sulky and obstinate, and would not consent to let me go free. . . .

At last I went into the service of Mr. and Mrs. Pringle, where I have been ever since, and am as comfortable as I can be while separated from my dear husband, and away from my own country and all old friends and connections. My dear mistress teaches me daily to read the word of God, and takes great pains to make me understand it. I enjoy the great privilege of being able to attend church three times on the Sunday: and I have met with many kind friends since I have been here, both clergymen and others. . . .

I still live in the hope that God will find a way to give me my liberty, and give me back to my husband. I endeavour to keep down my fretting, and to leave all to Him, for he knows what is good for me better than I know myself. Yet, I must confess, I find it a hard and heavy task to do so.

I am often much vexed, and I feel great sorrow when I hear some people in this country say, that the slaves do not need better usage, and do not want to be free. They believe the foreign people [West Indians], who deceive them, and say slaves are happy. I say, Not so. How can slaves be happy when they have the halter round their neck and the whip upon their back? and are disgraced and thought no more of than beasts?—and are separated from their mothers, and husbands, and children, and sisters, just as cattle are sold and separated? Is it happiness for a driver in the field to take down his wife or sister or child, and strip them, and whip them in such a disgraceful manner?—women that have had children exposed in the open field to shame! There is no modesty or decency shown by the owner to his slaves; men, women, and children are exposed alike. Since I have been here I have often wondered how English people can go out into the West Indies and act in such a beastly manner. But when they go, to the West Indies, they forget God and all feeling of shame, I think, since they can see and do such things. They tie up slaves like hogs—moor [tie] them up like cattle, and lick them, so as hogs, or cattle, or horses never were flogged;—and yet they come home and say, and make some good people believe, that slaves don't want to get out of slavery. But they put a cloak about the truth. It is not so. All slaves want to be free—to be free is very sweet. I will say the truth to English people who may read this history that my good friend, Miss S——, is now writing down for me. I have been a slave myself—I know what slaves feel—I can tell by myself what other slaves feel, and by what they have told me. The man that says slaves be quite happy in slavery—that they don't want to be free—that man is either ignorant or a lying person. I never heard a slave say so. I never heard a Buckra man say so, till I heard tell of it in England. Such people ought to be ashamed of themselves. They can't do without slaves, they say. What's the reason they can't do without slaves as well as in England? No slaves here—no whips—no stocks—no punishment, except for wicked people. They hire servants in

England; and if they don't like them, they send them away; they can't lick them. Let them work ever so hard in England, they are far better off than slaves. If they get a bad master, they give warning and go hire to another. They have their liberty. That's just what we want. We don't mind hard work, if we had proper treatment, and proper wages like English servants, and proper time given in the week to keep us from breaking the Sabbath. But they won't give it: they will have work—work—work, night and day, sick or well, till we are quite done up; and we must not speak up or look amiss, however much we be abused. And then when we are quite done up, who cares for us, more than for a lame horse? This is slavery. I tell it, to let English people know the truth; and I hope they will never leave off to pray God, and call loud to the great King of England, till all the poor blacks be given free, and slavery done up for evermore.

London: Westley and Davis, 1831, 4–23.

SLAVE RESISTANCE AND REBELLION

In *Annie John*, Annie's story is one of rebellion—against her mother, her teachers, and some aspects of Antigua's past and present, such as slavery, Christopher Columbus's heroic status, and British colonialism. This attitude has some important historical precedents in Antigua, and it is one that *Annie John*'s author shares. In an interview, when asked whether Lucifer's comment in *Paradise Lost* that it is "Better to reign in Hell than serve in Heav'n" could be applied to Antigua's colonial situation, Kincaid replied: "Yes. It is better to reign and to have self-possession in Hell than to be a servant in Heaven. . . . I always say, 'It's better to be dead than to live like this. It's better to risk dying than to live as a slave' " (Vorda, 18). Jamaica Kincaid's and Annie's historical ancestors were also rebellious, in their case, against their status as slaves. Their resistance to slavery took many forms. On an individual level, they could work slowly or inefficiently, behave insolently, sabotage the machinery, run away, or commit suicide. On a wider scale, slaves planned several revolts involving large groups of people. Perhaps the most widespread conspiracy to rebel occurred in 1736 when a slave of African origin joined with a Creole, or native-born slave, to lead a rebellion in which the whites were to be killed and the slaves were to take over the island. When the ball at which the revolt was to begin was postponed, the white elite had time to discover the plot. To their horror, the conspiracy appeared to be island wide and included the free colored people as well. There were numerous trials, with executions and banishments, before the conspiracy was crushed. John Luffman mentions this famous conspiracy in Letter XXXI to explain certain slave laws. The document that follows is an official report on the conspiracy, written by the men commissioned to investigate it and sent to the governor of the Caribbean islands immediately after a large number of the trials and executions had taken place. Although all the slaves who were tried were men, slave women were also active in resisting slavery and perhaps in the conspiracy of 1736 as well.

FROM *A GENUINE NARRATIVE OF THE INTENDED CONSPIRACY
OF THE NEGROES AT ANTIGUA, EXTRACTED FROM AN
AUTHENTIC COPY OF A REPORT MADE TO THE CHIEF
GOVERNOR OF THE CARABEE ISLANDS* (1737)

In obedience to an order of your Excellency and Council made the
ninth day of this instant December, we attend you with a report of our
proceedings, upon the weighty affair of the late conspiracy of our slaves,
instructed to us by your Excellency, with the consent of the Council and
Assembly. The substance of what appeared to us therein is; that the slaves
had formed and resolved to execute a plot, whereby all the white inhabitants of this island were to be murdered, and a new form of government
to be established by the slaves among themselves, and they entirely to
possess the island.

The slaves chiefly concerned in this conspiracy, were those born upon
the Gold Coast [Ghana] in Africa, whom we style Coromantees [also
called Akan]; and those born in one or other of the American sugar colonies, whom we call Creoles. At the head of the former was Court, alias
Tackey, Coromantee Negro man-slave, belonging to Thomas Kerby, Esq;
and at the head of the latter was Tomboy, a Creole born in Antigua, a
master carpenter, belonging to Mr. Thomas Hanson. The persons and
characters of these two chiefs were so well known to your Excellency,
and to this island in general, that little need be said of either, however
we shall beg so much of your time as just to mention that (as we are
told) Court was of a considerable family in his own country, but not as
was commonly thought of royal blood; and yet it was fully proved that
he had for many years covertly assumed among his countrymen here, the
title of King, and had been by them addressed and treated as such. He
appeared to us artful, and ambitious, very proud, and of few words; was
brought hither as a slave at about ten years of age, and was executed
about thirty five. His indulgences from his master were great, and uncommon, which gave him an opportunity of acquiring much more money
than slaves are usually masters of, which he perverted by engaging his
poorer countrymen in his evil designs. At the time of his execution, he
endeavored to put on a port and mien suitable to his affected dignity of
King. Tomboy was also very kindly used by his master, being admitted
for his own advantage to take Negro apprentices, and to make all the
profits he could of his own, and their labor, paying his master only a
monthly sum, far short of his usual earnings; so that he too was generally
master of much money, and did not fail applying it upon all occasions
to the promotion of his vile purposes among the Creoles; and being a

fellow of a robust strong body, and resolute temper, he had a great awe and influence over them, and had a genius formed for caballing.

To these two chiefs were joined other principals, viz. Hercules, belonging to Mr. John Christopher, Jack and Scipio, belonging to Mr. Philip Darby, Ned belonging to Col. Jacob Morgan, Fortune belonging to Mrs. Joanna Lodge, and Toney belonging to Col. Samuel Martin. These were all Creoles (except Fortune, of whom it's doubted whether he was a Creole or brought hither sucking at the breast) and had all, with their Chief, Tomboy, been lately baptized, and several of them could read and write. But the most active incendiaries under Tomboy, were, Freeman's Secundi, and Sir William Codrington's Jacko, both Creoles, of French parentage, and initiated into Christianity to the Romish Church. Of these chiefs and principals we can assuredly say, that they had heads to conceive, and hearts to perpetrate the most bloody and seditious machinations, even that unparalleled hellish plot formed by them against his Majesty's government of this island, and our lives and fortunes; and yet they could none of them justly complain of the hardships of slavery, their lives being as easy as those of our white tradesmen and overseers; and their manner of living much more plentiful than that of our common whites, who were looked upon by some of them for their poverty, with contempt: their employments were handicraft trades, overseers, and domestic servants. . . .

But we have by all the evidence, reason to believe Court was the first author, and have proof, that it was undoubtedly in agitation about November 1735, at which time Martin's Jemmy, by an artifice of Tomboy's making him drunk at Treblins, was brought in to take an oath, or engagement, as one of the conspirators for Court, who being sensible how impossible it was to effect his designs by Coromantees only, found himself under a necessity of engaging the Creoles, who are the most numerous, sensible, and able body of our slaves; and to that end after a long coldness between him and Tomboy, courted Tomboy's friendship, and obtained it, and found him every way ready for, and equal to his purposes.

The chief measures used by the two heads to corrupt our slaves, were, entertainments of dancing, gaming, and feasting, some of which were very expensive, always coloured with some innocent pretense, as of commemorating some deceased friend, by throwing water on his grave, or christening a house, or the like, according to the Negro customs, where they were debauched with liquor, their minds embittered against their masters, and against their condition of slavery, by strong invectives thrown out against both, and freedom and the possession of their master's estates were to be the rewards of their perfidy and treachery; and they never failed to bind their new proselytes to fidelity and secrecy, and to bring all assistance in their power, as they had done each other, by oaths taken after their country customs, mentioned hereafter more at large. A new government was to be established, when the white inhabitants were entirely extirpated; Court, amused and flattered by all with being king of the island; but the Creoles had resolved unknown to him, and his Coromantees, to settle a Commonwealth, and to make slaves of the Coromantees, and Negroes of all other nations, and to destroy Court, and all such who should refuse to submit to the terms the Creoles should please to prescribe or impose.

Towards the body of Coromantees, Court had hitherto acted with reserve and caution, but resolved upon one grand test, by which he might at once make proof of his numbers. This seems to be the masterpiece of the plot, and was to be done in open daylight, by a military dance and show, of which the whites, and even the slaves who were not Coromantees, not let into the secret, might be spectators, and yet ignorant of the meaning, the language and ceremonies used at it being all Coromantine. The evidence of witnesses, and confessions of many of the criminal Coromantees, make it appear to us, that it is the custom in Africa, when a Coromantee king has resolved upon a war with a neighboring state, to give public notice among his subjects, that the Ikem dance will be performed at a certain time, and place; and there the prince appears in royal habit, under an umbrella, or canopy of state. . . . Then the prince stepping into the area of the semi-circle, with his chief general, and taking a cutlass in his hand, moves with a whirling motion of his body round about, but dancing and leaping up at the same time . . . he takes an oath, (highly reverenced by the Coromantees) which is to the following purport: He swears to the general, that where he falls he will drop by his side rather than forsake or desert him in battle; and that he will behave as a brave prince ought, but in case he should fail in his oath, he agrees with, and desires his subjects present to take off his head, and makes them a grant of his houses, lands, and all his substance. This oath . . . [is] understood to be made to all the people, as well as to him, if he is answered by three huzzas from those present. By the custom of their country this signifies not only a declaration of their believing that he will observe his oath, but it is an actual and solemn engagement on their side to do as he does, and to join and go forth with him to the war, for the breach thereof, they are regarded as traitors. Brasso standing behind Court with a wooden cutlass cried Tackey, Tackey, Tackey, Coquo Tackey which signifies, King, King, King, great King, which words are used in the Coromantee country every morning at the King's door. . . .

This show and dance, the usurping traitor Court exhibited on Thursday the 3d. of October last, at about two of the clock in the afternoon, in Mrs. Dunbar Parke's pasture, near the town, in the presence of some whites, whose curiosity led them thither, and of a very great number of

Coromantee and Creole slaves; and he took the oath, and observed all the ceremony of it, only that there was no umbrella, which Emanual (a faithful slave of Mr. Gregory's guessing at Court's design) had refused to make: Court had a good sabre by his side with a red scabbard, and appeared as King, having on a particular cap proper to the kings of his country; this cap was made of green silk, embroidered with gold, with a deep border either of black fur, or black feathers, and three plumes of feathers in it; he had often worn it before, but without the feathers. . . . Tomboy was the greatest general, to whom the ceremony of the oath in the Coromantee language was addressed by Court, the by standing slaves huzzaed three times; the Coromantees knowing, but the Creoles not understanding the engagement they entered into by it: For to some who knew it, the thing appeared so audacious and terrible, that some of the Coromantees endeavoured by means of jumping among the dancers and spectators, and otherwise endeavouring to prevent its being performed, apprehending the meaning of it might be discovered; being sensible nothing could be intended by it less than a declaration of war, and that of necessity against the whites. . . . The nature of this part of the plot, being very uncommon, required a more particular description.

The method first proposed for executing the plot, was, that Tomboy should procure the making of the seats at a great ball, at which they knew all the people of distinction in the island would be present, by your Excellency's invitation; and which was appointed on the eleventh of October last, being the anniversary of his present Majesty's coronation: Then he was to contrive the laying a quantity of gun-powder in the house, and when the company was dancing, fire was to be set to three trains, upon the notice of firing a gun, and beating a drum, which were a notice also to the Negro musicians, and attendants (who were to be let into the secret) first to depart. When the blast was over, and all in the utmost confusion, three at least, if not four parties (intended to consist of three or four hundred men each) were to enter the town at different parts, and to put all the white people there, to the sword; seven strong guards to be placed on the out-parts of the town to prevent relief; St. John's Fort to be seized, with all the shipping in the harbour, and signals to be given to those in the country, to begin there the same tragical scene, and proceed onwards to the town, destroying all in their way, Monk's Hill (our chief fort and arsenal) was to be seized, and the arms distributed; the guard there destroyed, and all the avenues secured by strong guards of slaves. But the ball, upon notices sent by your Excellency's order, before the eleventh of October, was put off to the thirtieth, being his Majesty's birthday. This occasioned a meeting and a warm debate among the principal conspirators, whether or no they should execute their plot by immediately falling on with fire and sword or wait for the ball: All, except Court, were for an immediate execution, but his opinion happily prevailed, and it was deferred till the intended ball, before which the goodness of God wrought our deliverance from this execrable massacre. The suspicions of a plot were first owing to the uncommon licentious behaviour, and speech of some slaves in or about the town; unusual sounds of cockleshells, blown in the dead of night, without any apparent cause; the assembling of great numbers of slaves at unseasonable times; great feastings and caballings; at one of which, Court, was then reported to have been crowned, and honoured as King: And lists of officers, soldiers, provisions, and ammunition spoken of, and enquired after among them. . . . The discovery of the blowing up was entirely owing, being a secret, that Court and Tomboy had made known to few, if any of the conspirators, and discovered by Cuffee's over-hearing a private conversation held between those two, in a dark night, at Mr. Kerby's back door; the discovery was wonderful, but not more so than we think the concealment for so long a time, of a plot, whereon it afterwards appeared such numbers were concerned; the latter we remark, as an extraordinary proof of the fidelity of slaves to each other, and of the contrary to their masters.

Upon the evidence of those facts, the first twelve of the conspirators, mentioned in the annexed list, were executed; and this satisfaction was had by the imperfect confessions of Court and Tomboy, that the whole evidence against themselves, was confirmed, and the plot put past the possibility of being doubted, though neither of these confessed till after condemnation, the former making no confession, but at the place of execution, after having been tied about half an hour upon the wheel, and then untied at his own request, in order to confess: but the latter freely confessed before he came to the place of execution, and without any pain inflicted.

Now we thought the work was concluded, the witnesses being able to give us no further light; Court and Tomboy had assured us, the plot was stifled in its birth, and before the poison of it had been far spread, the truth of which though we doubted, we were not able to disprove; and for want of evidence, were put to a full stop: But though we were far from penetrating into the bottom of their secret villainies, God's all-seeing eye looked through them, and his merciful Providence laid them open to our view; for by voluntary information of Phillida (a sister of Tomboy's who was taken up upon suspicion of some virulent expressions, used upon her brother's account) who upon examination discovered (and her brother Jemmy, after being taken into custody confirmed,) that frequent Saturday night meetings of great numbers of the conspirators, had been for a great while held, at the house of Treblin, a Creole slave of Mr. Samuel Morgan's who was thereupon secured, and threw himself into our hands, without hope of mercy, making an ample discovery, and was the first who informed us of their oath, and gave an account of its having been taken by many over a grave at the Point, and at his own house. By these lights we saw that much remained to be discovered, and that our danger was as great as ever. This spurred us on to a vigorous pursuit of our inquiry, in which by the evidence of Treblin, Phillida, and Jemmy her brother, and of others afterwards admitted as evidence . . . there was convicted and condemned by us, and accordingly executed thirty five slaves more; and forty two other slaves, against whom the evidence was not so full, we humbly recommend to the consideration of the legislature for banishment. . . .

We conceive our narrative would be imperfect, without giving some account of this new scene, opened by the evidence of Treblin and the other witnesses, since the execution of the first twelve conspirators, which was in substance, "That the oath of secrecy and fidelity, had been taken both by Court and Tomboy, and almost by every one of the first twelve, and by every one that was since condemned and executed, or stands recommended for banishment." The manner of administering the oath, was by drinking a health in liquor, either rum, or some other kind, with grave-dirt, and sometimes cock's blood infused, and sometime the person swearing, laid his hand on a live cock: The words were various, but the general tenor, was to stand by, and be true to each other, and to kill the whites, man, woman, and child; and to assist in the execution of this, when called upon by the chief; and to suffer death, rather than discover; with damnation and confusion to those who should refuse; or having drank or sworn, should afterwards discover; sometimes too the person swearing chewed malageta pepper. This oath was administered in great numbers, before the execution of Court and Tomboy, and to many since, and had been administered at no less than seven places discovered to us. . . .

Upon the execution of the first twelve, it might have been reasonably thought, that at least a present stop might have been put to their prosecuting this bloody conspiracy, but the conspirators spirits seemed rather raised, than sunk by it; for at a little supper . . . the number of fifty at least, took the oath . . . but yet they thought proper, to appoint another meeting . . . where they were to resolve upon speedy measures of executing their execrable conspiracy: But this was happily prevented by the taking up Treblin, and soon after him Langford's Billy, and many other principals.

As it seems to us agreeable to the intent of the last order of your Excellency and Council, that we should report what our opinion is as to the safety of the island, we think it not improper to touch . . . upon what we think encouraged our slaves to attempt our ruin and destruction: And though we cannot be absolutely certain, on what particular inducements the plot was first set on foot, yet we may say with some certainty, that next to hopes of lawless liberty, the greatest was, the vast superiority in number of the blacks, to the white people. Neither can we presume to point out a certain remedy to the evil, but think it would lessen it much, if gentlemen resided on their own estates here, and that men of the best figure and fortune, would not so generally slight the Commissions of the Peace, and military commissions; and that slaves were disabled from being handicraft tradesmen, overseers, distillers, shop-keepers, hawkers, pedlars, or sailors; nor suffered to keep horses, nor to work out for themselves, and that more of our menial servants, and our wet and dry nurses, were to be whites: and that no fiddlers for gain except whites be suffered; and that generally, more encouragement should be given to whites by our laws and practice, and less to slaves; and our present wholesome laws, for government of our slaves vigorously executed. . . . With relation to the King's troops . . . the exact discipline shown by the officers, with the perfect obedience, and regularity of the soldiers, and the gallant appearance of the whole, did not only animate all our white inhabitants, but greatly intimidated the slaves. An additional number therefore of such forces . . . would make our safety far less precarious. How far we may be in danger still from this conspiracy, we cannot determine; since undoubtedly there are hundreds by us undiscovered, who have bound themselves by impious oaths to destroy us, man, woman, and child: From hence it may be collected, what must be the spirit and inclination of the slaves, and how weak and vain it would be in us, to say the country is in safety, or to advise your Excellency to put a stop to any further enquiry; since these are points of too great importance and delicacy to be determined by us. . . .

Antigua, December 20, 1736

A List of Slaves executed for the late conspiracy. December 15, 1736

1. Kirby's   Court
2. Hanson's   Tomboy
3. Christopher's   Hercules
4. Lodge's   Fortune

[etc., through number 47, with lists of two slaves fled from justice, four free Negroes in prison for the conspiracy, forty-three slaves proposed to be banished, and seven witnesses to be sent off.]

By the Commissioners, or Judges Appointed to try the Conspirators, Dublin, 1737.
    R. Reilly, 3–22.

WOMEN AND SLAVE RESISTANCE IN ANTIGUA

This document is a current scholarly article that discusses the role that women played in slave resistance in Antigua. It speculates on the part that women might have played in the conspiracy of 1736. Again, we see that Annie's attitude of resistance has many precedents in Antiguan history.

FROM DAVID BARRY GASPAR, "FROM 'THE SENSE OF THEIR SLAVERY': SLAVE WOMEN AND RESISTANCE IN ANTIGUA, 1632–1763" (1996)

Throughout the Americas slaves carved out more livable spaces for themselves by working to transform privileges allowed by the master class into customary rights. By the early decades of the eighteenth century, Caribbean slaves had earned the right to hold markets on Sundays, and these markets became a significant feature of slave life. When the legislature of the sugar island of Antigua abolished Sunday markets in March 1831 without allowing substitute time for marketing by law, the slaves vented their frustration in a number of ways that frightened most whites into believing that a general insurrection was in the making. At the very start of this outburst of collective protest, slave women were involved conspicuously. . . .

The prominent involvement of slave women in the dramatic confrontation at the Saint John's Market deserves special notice because it immediately draws attention to the resistance of slave women to slavery in the years before 1831. . . .

For the period 1722–1763, during which compensation claims were systematically recorded . . . at least twenty-one slave women were executed or killed, or about 6 percent of the total number of 381 slaves; eleven, or nearly 53 percent, of these women were executed for running away. . . .

Slave resistance in response to work load or to masters' work expectations took many forms besides flight. The Coromantee slaves who killed Major Samual Martin of Greencastle plantation in 1701 allegedly did so in response to his unreasonable demand to work around Christmas, when they looked forward instead to enjoying the customary work-free holiday season. There may have been several similar serious disturbances in subsequent years because in 1723 Antigua legislators felt it necessary to guarantee by law the right of slaves to Christmas holidays, stating that "great Disorders have happened, and Murders have been committed by Slaves because their Masters have not allowed them the same Number of Days for their Recreation at Christmas, as several of their Neighbours have done" (Antigua Act no. 176 of 1723, article 32). . . .

The typical style of resistance of Antigua slave women was unquestionably of the day-to-day variety that nibbled away most insidiously at the efficiency of the slave system. Among these forms might be included the inventive means women used to obstruct sexual exploitation by white males. Other forms of such resistance, more subtle certainly, are encapsulated in the term *insolence*, which whites frequently used. A whole range of behavior was crowded into this category of resistance, the intensity and meaning of which might vary: displays such as gestures, attitudes, posture, facial expression, gait, or verbal play. Whites commonly dealt with such behavior in ways which kept the offenders out of the standard documentary sources historians rely on. For such acts, suspected acts, or intentions to act that whites construed as particularly disrespectful or challenging to their authority and status, slave women were frequently whipped in an attempt to crush their spirit and humiliate them. Evidence about whipping is frequently indicative of some form of resistance. . . .

Although there are no claims for slave women who were connected with the major islandwide plot for a slave rebellion in 1736, other sources indicate that some women were indeed involved. The planned revolt was masterminded by Court alias Tackey, aged about forty-five, the Coromantee slave of Thomas Kerby, justice of the peace and speaker of the Antigua assembly. Court shared leadership with Tomboy, the Creole or Antigua-born slave of Thomas Hanson, a merchant and planter. The plot grew out of a series of related developments that sharpened the slaves' awareness of the possibilities for seizing power from whites. Its etiology can be traced back to the desire of the slaves to destroy slavery, their long involvement in resistance short of revolt, and population imbalance greatly in their favor, lax enforcement of slave controls, and the general character of slavery. . . .

Shaken by the revelation that free people of color had made common cause with rebellious slaves, the authorities took the extraordinary step of admitting slave evidence against some of them, but they did not seek to prosecute any slave women, although evidence indicated that women participated in the organization of the plot in some way. . . .

The evidence suggests that Philida [Tomboy's sister] and other slave women were often present at special gatherings when the rebel leaders recruited their men, in the roles of informed onlookers or guests, or assisting with arrangements and serving food and drink, which was an especially critical role in the ceremonial initiation into the inner circles of the plot.

Recruits were initiated at these gatherings or feasts through a ritual ceremony which included taking a solemn "Damnation Oath" to support the plot and not betray it. . . . The dirt used in the ritual concoctions came from the graves of deceased relatives or other slaves, and indeed, many induction ceremonies were performed at grave sites, as the rebels sought assistance and approval from the ancestral spirits. The slave women Obbah (Aba among the Akan) therefore played a more central role in the organization of the plot than most other slave women when she held a feast and brought some "Dirt from her Sisters Grave (for whom this feast was made) in a Callabash," which the slave Watty mixed with wine (Trial Record, Council Minutes, January 12, 1737, CO 9/10).

Besides Obbah, another slave woman played much more than a peripheral part in the plot in a way that suggests, like the initiation rites, the slaves' preservation of links to Africa and the possibilities of cultural resistance under slavery. This woman the slaves called simply Queen. At the trial of Quawcoo . . . slave witness Quamina testified that "Court used to be very Often at Pares Plantation to go to an Old Womans house called Queen and sent Butter, Bread, and other things to her to sell for him. . . . Court sent a Boy on a white horse to Old Queen to tell her they were going to put him to Death, and She might keep what things She had of his" (Trial Record, Council Minutes, February 14, 1737, CO 9/11; Trial Record, Council Minutes, January 12, 1737, CO 9/10).

What was the real connection between Court, the rebel leader, and Obbah and Old Queen? If the Gold Coast slaves of Antigua accepted Court as their Akan ruler, could it be that Queen or Obbah, like Abena the Akan "Queen of Kingston" in Jamaica during the slave conspiracy of 1760, was "cast in the role of a traditional Akan queen-mother?"

In Akan/Asante society on the Gold Coast, the queen-mother, ohemaa, or female ruler, who was often really the chief's sister, was constitutionally regarded as his "mother." . . . "The queen-mother's obligation to advise and guide the chief, including her right to criticize and rebuke him in public, was a constitutional duty" (Agnes Akosua, Aidoo, "Asante Queen Mothers in Government and Politics in the Nineteenth Century," in *The Black Woman Cross-Culturally*, pp. 65–77). . . .

In Antigua, while Queen and Obbah were both probably Akan or of Akan descent and both were influential in the Coromantee slave community, it was probably Queen who acted as Court's principal advisor and confidant. She rather than Obbah may have been cast in the role of queen-mother to Court, the Akan king who was formally crowned "King of the Coromantees" in a public ceremony with nearly 2,000 slaves present, only a few days before the conspiracy to revolt was revealed to the utter consternation of whites. This coronation . . . accompanied an Akan military "ikem" ceremony which prepared participants for the intended war against the whites. This ceremony was a common practice in Akan communities of the Gold Coast, where it accompanied declarations of war. Court, who was uprooted from the Gold Coast as a child and shipped to Antigua, came to appreciate the significance of such Akan rituals during his rise to prominence within the Akan community of the island. The old slave women Queen most likely educated Court, who was of noble birth, in the workings of Akan tradition, particularly in regard to building collective support among his countrymen and other slaves for the revolt.

In regard to her probable role as a kind of queen-mother, Queen's anglicized creole name is most suggestive. Did her name carry more political and cultural than personal significance among the Akan slaves? The association between Queen and Court, which Quawcoo described in connection with petty trading, could have been good cover for more vital political relations that ultimately helped to pull the slave plot together. In this regard, it would be interesting to know the sort of goods or possessions that Court, facing execution, asked her to keep for him.

That slave women did not appear on the lists of slaves who were executed or banished for their part in the plot can perhaps be explained partly by the lack of understanding or interest among whites about how the slave community worked or about the significance of African culture and social organization. Slave women were not put on trial, even Queen or Obbah, though some women were questioned. Operating from European male-oriented perspectives, the authorities searched out slave men as the most dangerous conspirators or political actors, blind to the political meaning of the supportive functions of women within the slave community. They saw the plot primarily as a direct challenge issued by men; it was a challenge to the manhood, authority, and hegemony of white males and masters. We know the trials were ended because of heavy costs; eighty-eight male slaves were executed and forty-nine were banished. Had Vallentine Morris been able to persuade his colleagues on the court to continue with the trials regardless of cost, it is likely that many more slaves within the subsidiary ranks of the plot's membership would have been punished, including women. Indeed, had the revolt actually occurred, Antigua whites would have had ample evidence of the important political roles of slave women.

The Antigua authorities also may have been disinclined to seek out and prosecute women suspects because the plot did not represent the kind of resistance in which women were commonly involved. Thus it is possible that the commonly nonconfrontational resistance of Antigua slave women created the wide political space for many of them to support the plot without attracting attention from the authorities. When the time came for large-scale collective resistance, slave women were prepared by a life of day-to-day resistance and by African cultural antecedents to meet the challenge. Antigua slave women must have resisted enslavement in countless ways that the historical sources have not recorded, including the manner in which they raised their children to cope with slavery. In this way, as primary transmitters of culture, slave women were principal shapers of the culture of resistance.

From David Barry Gaspar and Darlene Clark Hine, eds., *More Than Chattel: Black Women and Slavery in the Americas*. Bloomington: Indiana University Press, 1996, 218–238. (Only direct quotes have sources listed. For historical references, refer to original document.)

ABOLITION OF THE SLAVE TRADE, EMANCIPATION, AND THE AFTERMATH OF SLAVERY

At the height of the British debate about the abolition of the slave trade, many people expressed their opinion in print, especially those involved in the church, in antislavery societies, and in commerce. But perhaps the most interesting type of writing to appear during this period was the narrative form by former slaves, who told searing and poignant stories of their lives and advocated the end of slavery. One such autobiography was that of Mary Prince, segments of which are quoted in a previous document; another was that of Olaudah Equiano, an African-born former slave who was kidnapped as a child, brought to Barbados, and sold to seafaring masters. Eventually, he was able to buy his freedom and spent the rest of his life in England. During hearings regarding the abolition of the slave trade, Equiano spoke to Parliament about his experiences as a former slave. In the excerpt that follows, he outlines several reasons for advocating the abolition of the slave trade, which sharpens our view of the lives and feelings of the slaves mentioned by Annie John.

FROM OLAUDAH EQUIANO, *THE LIFE OF OLAUDAH EQUIANO, OR GUSTAVUS VASSA, THE AFRICAN* (1789)

To the Lords Spiritual and Temporal, and the Commons of the Parliament of Great Britain.

My Lords and Gentlemen,

Permit me, with the greatest deference and respect, to lay at your feet the following genuine narrative; the chief design of which is to excite in your august assemblies a sense of compassion for the miseries which the slave-trade has entailed on my unfortunate countrymen. By the horrors of that trade was I first torn away from all the tender connexions that were naturally dear to my heart; but these, through the mysterious ways of Providence, I ought to regard as infinitely more than compensated by the introduction I have thence obtained to the knowledge of the Christian religion, and of a nation which, by its liberal sentiments, its humanity, the glorious freedom of its government, and its proficiency in arts and sciences, has exalted the dignity of human nature.

I am sensible I ought to entreat your pardon for addressing to you a work so wholly devoid of literary merit; but, as the production of an unlettered African, who is actuated by the hope of becoming an instrument towards the relief of his suffering countrymen, I trust that *such a man*, pleading in *such a cause*, will be acquitted of boldness and presumption.

May the God of heaven inspire your hearts with peculiar benevolence on that important day when the question of Abolition is to be discussed, when thousands, in consequence of your determination, are to look for happiness or misery!

I am, my Lords and Gentlemen, Your most obedient, And devoted humble Servant, Olaudah Equiano, or Gustavas Vassa. March 24, 1789. . . .

[Equiano and his sister are kidnapped and separated; they meet again, for one night, and are then separated forever.] She and I held one another by the hands . . . all night; and thus for a while we forgot our misfortunes in the job of being together: but even this small comfort was soon to have an end; for scarcely had the fatal morning appeared, when she was again torn from me for ever! I was now more miserable, if possible, than before. The small relief which her presence gave me from pain was gone, and the wretchedness of my situation was redoubled by my anxiety after her fate, and my apprehensions lest her sufferings should be greater than mine, when I could not be with her to alleviate them. Yes, thou dear partner of my joys and sorrows! happy should I have ever esteemed myself to encounter every misery for you, and to procure your freedom by the sacrifice of my own. Though you were early forced from my arms, your image has been always rivetted in my heart, from which neither *time nor fortune* have been able to remove it; so that, while the thoughts of your sufferings have damped my prosperity, they have mingled with adversity and increased its bitterness. To that Heaven which protects the weak from the strong, I commit the care of your innocence and virtues, if they have not already received their full reward, and if your youth and delicacy have not long since fallen victims to the violence of the African trader, the pesitlential stench of a Guinea ship, the seasoning in the European colonies, or the lash and lust of a brutal and unrelenting overseer. . . .

We [slaves] were not many days in the merchant's custody before we were sold after their usual manner, which is this: On a signal given, (as the beat of a drum) the buyers rush at once into the yard where the slaves are confined, and make choice of that parcel they like best. The noise and clamour with which this is attended, and the eagerness visible in the countenances of the buyers, serve not a little to increase the apprehensions of the terrified Africans, who may well be supposed to consider them as the ministers of that destruction to which they think themselves devoted. In this manner, without scruple, are relations and friends separated, most of them never to see each other again. I remember in the vessel in which I was brought over, in the men's apartment, there were several brothers, who, in the sale, were sold in different lots; and it was very moving on this occasion to see and hear their cries at parting. O, ye nominal Christians! might not an African ask you, learned you this from your God, who says unto you, Do unto all men as you would men should do unto you? Is it not enough that we are torn from our country and friends to toil for your luxury and lust of gain? Must every tender feeling be likewise sacrificed to your avarice? Are the dearest friends and relations, now rendered more dear by their separation from their kindred, still to be parted from each other, and thus prevented from cheering the gloom of slavery with the small comfort of being together and mingling their sufferings and sorrows? Why are parents to lose their children, brothers their sisters, or husbands their wives? Surely this is a new refinement in cruelty, which, while it has no advantage to atone for it, thus aggravates distress, and adds fresh horrors even to the wretchedness of slavery. . . .

As the inhuman traffic of slavery is to be taken into the consideration of the British legislature, I doubt not, if a system of commerce was established in Africa, the demand for manufactures would most rapidly augment, as the native inhabitants will insensibly adopt the British fashions, manners, customs, &c. In proportion to the civilization, so will be the consumption of British manufactures. . . .

Population, the bowels and surface of Africa, abound in valuable and useful returns; the hidden treasures of centuries will be brought to light and into circulation. Industry, enterprise, and mining, will have their full scope, proportionably as they civilize. In a word, it lays open an endless field of commerce to the British manufacturers and merchant adventurer. The manufacturing interest and general interests are synonymous. The abolition of slavery would be in reality an universal good.

Tortures, murder, and every other imaginable barbarity and iniquity, are practiced upon the poor slaves with impunity. I hope the slave trade will be abolished. I pray it may be an event at hand. The great body of manufacturers, uniting in the cause, will considerably facilitate and expedite it; and as I have already stated, it is most substantially their interest and advantage, and as such the nation's at large, (except those persons concerned in the manufacturing neck-yokes, collars, chains, hand-cuffs, leg-bolts, drags, thumbscrews, iron muzzles, and coffins; cats, scourges, and other instruments of torture used in the slave trade). In a short time one sentiment alone will prevail, from motives of interest as well as justice and humanity. Europe contains one hundred and twenty millions of inhabitants. Query—How many millions doth Africa contain? Supposing the Africans, collectively and individually, to expend 5l. a head in raiment and furniture yearly when civilized, &c. an immensity beyond the reach of imagination!

This I conceive to be a theory founded upon facts, and therefore an infallible one. If the blacks were permitted to remain in their own country, they would double themselves every fifteen years. In proportion to such increase will be the demand for manufactures. Cotton and indigo grow spontaneously in most parts of Africa; a consideration this of no small consequence to the manufacturing towns of Great Britain. It opens a most immense, glorious, and happy prospect—the clothing, &c. of a continent ten thousand miles in circumference, and immensely rich in productions of every denomination in return for manufactures.

Reprint. Boston: Isaac Knapp, 1837.

AMERICAN ANTI-SLAVERY SOCIETY

It is important to note that abolition of the slave trade, by Great Britain, which occurred in 1808, was not synonymous with the abolition of slavery; the slaves who were already in the British Caribbean remained slaves until their emancipation in 1834. This event changed the lives of all who resided in Antigua, and the transformation taking place there was closely watched by pro- and antislavery forces in the United States, where slaves were not to be emancipated for another thirty years. Antislavery forces were particularly interested in events in Antigua, since the immediate emancipation of the slaves there, without an apprenticeship, had occurred peacefully, without great turmoil. Antigua's success was used to argue the case for emancipation in the United States. This document contains excerpts of a favorable report made by the American Anti-Slavery Society after a fact-finding trip to Antigua in 1837. It provides interesting descriptions and details of life in Antigua after emancipation and insights into white attitudes toward black people in Antigua.

FROM JAS. A. THOME AND J. HORACE KIMBALL, *THE ANTI-SLAVERY EXAMINER: EMANCIPATION IN THE WEST INDIES: A SIX MONTHS' TOUR OF ANTIGUA, BARBADOES, AND JAMAICA, IN THE YEAR 1837* (1838)

It is hardly possible that the success of British West India Emancipation should be more conclusively proved, than it has been by the absence among us of the exultation which awaited its failure. But it is remarkable that, even since the first of August, 1834, the evils of West India emancipation on the lips of the advocates of slavery, or, as the most of them nicely prefer to be termed, the opponents of abolition, have remained in the future tense. . . . Not the slightest reference to the rash act, whereby the thirty thousand slaves of Antigua were immediately "turned loose," now mingles with the croaking which strives to defend our republican slavery against argument and common sense.

The Executive Committee of the American Anti-Slavery Society, deemed it important that the silence which the pro-slavery press of the United States has seemed so desirous to maintain in regard to what is strangely enough termed the "great experiment of freedom," should be thoroughly broken up by a publication of facts and testimony collected on the spot. To this end, Rev. James A. Thome, and Joseph H. Kimball, Esq., were deputed to the West Indies to make the proper investigations. . . .

Among the points established in this work, beyond the power of dispute or cavil, are the following: . . .

That the act of IMMEDIATE EMANCIPATION in Antigua, was not attended with any disorder whatever.

That the emancipated slaves have readily, faithfully, and efficiently worked for wages from the first. . . .

That the prejudice of caste is fast disappearing in the emancipated islands. . . .

That the emancipated people are perceptibly rising the scale of civilization, morals, and religion. . . .

We were kindly received at Millar's [Estate] by Mr. Bourne, the manager. . . . On the way, he remarked that we had visited the island at a very unfavorable time for seeing the cultivation of it, as every thing was suffering greatly from drought. . . . As we approached the laborers, the manager pointed out one company of ten, who were at work with their hoes by the side of the road, while a larger one of thirty were in the middle of the field. They greeted us in the most friendly manner. The manager spoke kindly to them, encouraging them to be industrious. . . . When we came up to the large company, they paused a moment, and with a hearty salutation, which ran all along the line, bade us "good mornin'," and immediately resumed their labor. The men and women were intermingled; the latter kept pace with the former, wielding their hoes with energy and effect. The manager addressed them for a few moments, telling them who we were, and the object of their visit. He told them of the great number of slaves in America, and appealed to them to know whether they would not be sober, industrious, and diligent, so as to prove to American slaveholders the benefit of freeing all their slaves. At the close of each sentence, they all responded, "Yes, massa," or "God bless de massas," and at the conclusion, they answered the appeal, with much feeling, "Yes, massa; please God massa, we will all do so." When we turned to leave, they wished to know what we thought of their industry. We assured them that we were much pleased, for which they returned their "thankee, massa." They were working a *job*. The manager had given them a piece of ground "to hole," engaging to pay them sixteen dollars when they had finished it. He remarked that he had found it a good plan to give *jobs*. He obtained more work in this way than he did by giving the ordinary wages, which is about eleven cents per day. It looked very much like slavery to see the females working in the field; but the manager said they chose it generally *"for the sake of the wages."* Mr. B. returned with us to the house, leaving the gangs in the field, with only an aged negro in charge of the work, as *superintendent*. Such now is the name of the overseer. The very *terms, driver* and *overseer*, are banished from Antigua; and the *whip* is buried beneath the soil of freedom.

When we reached the house we were introduced to Mr. Watkins, a *colored* planter, whom Mr. B. had invited to breakfast with us. . . .

Fitch's Creek Estate . . . presents the appearance . . . of a *resurrection* from the grave. In addition to his improved sugar and boiling establishment, he has projected a plan for a new village, (as the collection of negro houses is called,) and has already selected the ground and begun to build. The houses are to be larger than those at present in use, they are to be built of stone instead of mud and sticks, and to be neatly roofed. Instead of being huddled together in a bye place, as has mostly been the case, they are to be built on an elevated site, and ranged at regular intervals around three sides of a large square, in the centre of which a building for a chapel and school house is to be erected. Each house is to have a garden. This and similar improvements are now in progress, with the view of addding to the comforts of the laborers, and attaching them to the estate. It has become the interest of the planter to make it for the *interest of the people* to remain on his estate. This *mutual interest* is the only sure basis of prosperity on the one hand and of industry on the other.

The whole company heartily joined in assuring us that a knowledge of the actual working of abolition in Antigua, would be altogether favorable to the cause of freedom, *and that the more thorough our knowledge of the facts in the case, the more perfect would be our confidence in the safety of* IMMEDIATE *emancipation*.

Mr. A. said that the spirit of enterprise, before dormant, had been roused since emancipation, and planters were now beginning to inquire as to the best modes of cultivation, and to propose measures of general improvement. One of these measures was the establishing of *free villages*, in which the laborers might dwell by paying a small rent. When the adjacent planters needed help they could here find a supply for the occasion. This plan would relieve the laborers from some of that dependence which they must feel so long as they live on the estate and in the house of the planters. Many advantages of such a system were specified. We allude to it here only as an illustration of that spirit of inquiry, which freedom has kindled in the minds of the planters. . . .

As to prejudice against the black and colored people, all thought it was rapidly decreasing—indeed, they could scarcely say there was now any such thing. To be sure, there was an aversion among the higher classes of the whites, and especially among *females*, to associating in parties with colored people; but it was not on account of their *color*, but chiefly because of their *illegitimacy*. This was to us a new source of prejudice: but subsequent information fully explained its bearings. The whites of the West Indies are themselves the authors of that *illegitimacy*, out of which their aversion springs. It is not to be wondered at that they should be unwilling to invite the colored people to their social parties, seeing they might not unfrequently be subjected to the embarrassment of introducing to their white wives a colored mistress or an *illegitimate* daughter. This also explains the special prejudice which the *ladies* of the higher classes feel toward those among whom are their guilty rivals in a husband's affections, and those whose every feature tells the story of a husband's unfaithfulness!

New York: American Anti-Slavery Society, 1838, 5–11.

MEMOIRS OF AN ANTIGUAN
WORKINGMAN

The next document is from an autobiography of an Antiguan work-ingman who was born a few decades after emancipation and lived until 1982. He describes the life of a typical black man in Antigua over a hundred-year period. His account of life on the sugar estates after emancipation differs from the previous document, emphasiz-ing the harshness of the conditions and the cruelty and indiffer-ence of the estate owners. Eventually, Samuel Smith was able to build a house in a village, work in a sugar factory, join a labor union, witness the end of the sugar estates and the beginning of the tourist industry, and see conditions gradually improve over the years for Antiguans. His account describes the kind of life that An-nie's immediate ancestors probably led and brings us up to the time period in which Annie lives in Antigua.

FROM KEITHLYN B. SMITH AND FERNANDO C. SMITH, *TO SHOOT HARD LABOUR: THE LIFE AND TIMES OF SAMUEL SMITH, AN ANTIGUAN WORKINGMAN, 1877–1982* (1986)

From what I know, the life was worse, and that always make me won-der just how was it that the slaves survive.

Whenever there was a fight or quarrel among nega-house people [black people living and working on the sugar estate for wages], it would be massa who would decide who was to get punish and how the punish-ment would be. Some of the times the massa would punish everybody mixed up in it, and rightfully or wrongfully, them all get punish when them ready [when the estate owners felt like it]. But to be driven off the estate was the worst that could happen to you. People would settle for almost anything else—be whipped, be locked up in estate cellar for a time. The least punishment was to get suspended without pay for some time.

Now some people didn't understand the kind of gang-up that took place by the bakkra [white people] against the nega-house people and they believe that to have to leave the estate was the least punishment. But things was not as easy as that. A nega-house man could not live on another estate if he offend even one planter. If one planter tell him to leave, the others would usually refuse to let him work and live on the plantation, and that poor fellow wouldn't have a place to turn to for a long, long time. Dog better than he when that happen. . . .

The bakkra was hateful to the womenkind. I hear that in the last century it was the general feeling among the bakkra that nega woman was unclean, inferior and taint everlastingly with dirt and filth. But it seem that this belief get even worse when the century end and the women was terribly subject to rape and other things of that kind from the massa and his sons. Many times some planter would rape a mother and her daughters. If the women get pregnant in the event, they dare not tell how it happen. If they somehow be brave enough to tell them family or friend and the news spread, then massa would come down hard on the women, they could even lose them life.

At Jonas Estate there was a nega woman by the name of Missy Byam. She get raped by Massa Ted Cole, one of the English planters on the estate. . . . Then he go and rape Kate [her daughter], just thirteen years old, and get her pregnant. When Cole hear that Kate get pregnant, he threaten her and tell her never to come back to Jonas Estate for he have fear the news would reach the ears of his wife. Now Kate, she was either brave or stupid; she tell her friends about what happen and one of them take the story back to Cole. His pride was severely hurt. He did not want that news to spread, even though such a thing was common on the estates. Massa Cole would definitely get the cold shoulder by his white wife—not for the rape, but for being with a nega gal.

Some time pass and Massa Cole send for Kate and sternly warn her. . . . Kate answer back, something that never happen before. Another woman would just accept what happen and be saddle with a fatherless child. Not Kate. Well Cole took very unkindly to the rudeness of a little nega gal. He immediately let loose his dogs on her. Kate try to escape the beasts and she fall into Works Pond. That pond was deep. . . . [Kate drowns while the master watches. The estate workers, fearful of punishment, must look on and do nothing.]

Now I ask you, could there be any harder times? For a fact, at one stage, I was feeling that life wasn't worth living. I don't know how I escape that place. I believe God love me for there was nobody who could tell Massa Cole nothing. Planters kill king and rule country [planters were all-powerful].

I remember how bad was the housing on the estates. When the people find it hard to move from the estates to the villages after slavery end, the houses get to be very over-crowded. At the same time, you couldn't complain over the conditions, for planter say you free to leave. "The freedom that you wait on so long was granted long time ago, the people that were so big and generous to grant that freedom [the English Parliament] must also provide other things. Why look at us to provide?" was what they would say.

The conditions of the houses rapidly run down after the Emancipation even though they were strongly built. . . . Most of the houses were leak. . . . Neither were there screens in the houses. Nothing to separate one family from the other. . . . Try and understand, there was very little repairs done to them houses. When the floor start to rotten, the people living there would pluck up the floor—the whole thing—to keep themselves from falling in the cellar. The drop to the cellar would be about three and half feet and many children would get hurt that way when the floor was not pluck up. When the floor get pluck up, the bottom of the cellar would be the floor of the house. The bottom was earth.

Now the earth was generally full of jiggers [mite larvae that become attached to the skin]. . . . Rats, mice, spiders, centipedes, scorpions and other creatures also lived in the houses. . . .

Not only was the houses bad, there was no sanitation to speak of. There was no soap, neither was there disinfectants of any kind. My mother use to wash our skin with light carbolic water to keep the lice and fleas off our bodies. . . .

In the meanwhile, the planters always regard the reaping of the crop as a very serious matter and it better be reap in quick time too. Both the workers at the mills and the ones in the fields had to shoot [perform] hard labour. Particular care was taken during the grinding operations to make sure that the mills was always in operation. Now despite the special efforts to keep them mills turning over without stopping, they would get choked sometimes, mainly from being fed too much sugar cane. Whenever that would happen, the wrath of the planter would come down quick on the worker that get the blame. . . .

Trouble come with the first crop. Casper Thomas was walking on the millbed when he slipped and his hand get into the working mills. The force of the mills pull him in. The other workers move fast to stop the mills, but nothing could save Casper.

Young Massa Arthur heard the mills stop turning while he was away at lunch. He immediately rush to the mills. On reaching there he saw Casper lying on the ground with the workers all around him. Massa Arthur shout in great anger, "Who the hell told you all to stop my mill!" Nobody had the courage to answer. Them rush back to their jobs and the chief engineer start up the mills again. Work continue as though nothing happen. They left the body right there.

Massa Arthur make it clear in his fury that he was not about to lose money for the time the mills was down. After a while he send two workers to take the body away and tell Casper's parents. The estate give the family a coffin and that was that for Casper. At the end of the week, Massa

Arthur take out what he claim was a half a day's pay from everybody that work the day Casper die. And what he call "half a day's pay" amount to half of what the workers would usually get for the week.

That bakkra was also quick to use the whip on people He was one to take pleasure in taking workers before the magistrate. His favourite thing use to be to say, "I'll lick you and the magistrate will jail you." And he could do it, too.

The planters also use to use the militia to keep people in check and the militia would have the back up of the magistrates and the jail-house and the government. No way for us to fight back—it was like worm going against nest of ants—for the bakkra was the militia and the magistrates and the jail-house and the government. Whatever happen to us, we must grunt and bear it. If you didn't have manners, them give you the cat-o-nine and them hang you in jail. Nothing for it. You dead and gone. Them give you coffin and that's that.   (38–46)

· · ·

One of the happiest moments in the life of my family took place in 1888. In that year we built our own house at Freeman's Ville, the second village put up after freedom come. . . . At last we were under our own roof and enjoying, for the first time, family privacy. Estate life was behind our back at last. . . .

That village had less houses in it when I was a boy than shortly after the time of the Emancipation. People couldn't afford to build a house then.

Building houses in the village were slow back in them days. It was real hard to get a house. . . .

You have to keep in mind that in them days there was nobody to speak up for us. Nobody. It seem to me that there was not one single person that have the right to talk up or represent anybody. No, we lived and worked back then as massa say. . . .

We were bound and determined to work the land. Back then, the planters was very well aware that no race work harder than we. If we could work the land, then in process of time we would become self-sufficient or we would be in control of things.

But the bakkra knew very well that was the main artery to independence for we. They was also well aware that if we have land we will have no need to work cheap for them. You see, if we have our own land, this will be the biggest threat to the British Empire, so all the land was massa's own; nega man own nothing. . . .

As time pass, things gradually change. More planters continue to go back to England and, step by step, a larger portion of land became available. There was room for us to build up the villages. . . .   (55–57)

• • •

[Smith works on two other estates, North Sound and Duers.] One of my jobs was to make sure the ploughing was done properly and on time. It was tiresome to keep moving up and down from one end of the field to the other. We hardly would have a break from morning till night, keeping pace behind the plough for twelve hours and more each day. . . .

Nega man would have to find himself behind that plough even if sick. Plenty man drop down dead behind plough because they couldn't stay home when sick. Massa hardly believe when them talk. It was an offence to even complain, so workers was afraid to let massa know they couldn't make it. Neither was there half days for us. Sick or well, we were forced to hold that plough. I held plough for years and never slow up. I was lucky I was never sick.   (89)

• • •

The years was rolling on. I was no longer a thirteen year old boy starting out at North Sound. By the time the Gunthorpes Sugar Factory started up in 1904, I had done seven years hard work at Duers and seven at North Sound. Fourteen years of my young work life had already gone.

Gradually land got to be available and I got a piece of land to work. Along with sugar cane, I use to plant some food. Back then we use to have to work half-land. Now when the bakkra talk of half-land, it did not mean the half we learnt at school. Their half meant that if the nega plant three rows of potatoes, the massa would have the right to two of them three rows. This was the case even after the sugar factory was in operation for some time, but it was still an improvement over what it use to be.   (115)

• • •

The war [World War I] was over and the Gunthorpes Sugar Factory was in full swing. Man, I tell you, the small estate mill was gradually fading out and Old Betty—that's Betty's Hope [estate]—no longer was the great Betty she used to be.

Gunthorpes took the place of Betty's Hope as the biggest employer on the island. The factory was also paying higher wages to its workers than what the estates was paying theirs. . . .

[Antiguan workers begin to unionize in the 1930s.] The war [World War II] was occupying the mind of everybody, but in quick time the union made three great steps ahead. It get a good wage increase and was improving conditions of work for the workers at Gunthorpes. . . . The union made the planters to finish with the half-land farming. Now that was a great thing for small farmers. . . . It was unbelievable what the union got done. . . .

In my mind, 1951 got to be the best year since the end of slavery. What happen that year set the stage for what was going to come. The union was also doing other serious business. It was advancing in politics. . . . That was also when the rule was changed so that you could vote at age twenty-one, whether you could read and write or not. When the Council hold the elections in 1951 and the union got all the elected seats, the two sides really start to square up.

Negas was scoring great gains. The union winning on all sides in 1951 gave a very clear sign that it was just a matter of time before massa have to go back home to England. . . .

During the last years of my working life the planters was finding it harder and harder to get the young generations to work in the fields. Sugar is bull work—slavery. The young people do not know what name bull work [don't know what hard physical work is]. Them definitely scorn field work. . . .

Sugar was on the fade out and the hotels was just starting to come in. The small farmers was starting to have some difficulty to reap the crop and the people wasn't helping the parents in the cane fields anymore. . . . The new generation hate even the name sugar.

In 1962, I finally bow to the wish of my people and I decide to retire. . . .

In 1967, Antigua got home rule from England and as soon as that happen, the planters give up sugar and leave.

Wilfred Jacobs got to be the land's first black governor and V. C. Bird got to be the premier and the first black man to be the chief planter. Remember that he was already the union president. . . .

I hope that you will write down exactly what I am telling you. If you do, the people will see how far down in the mud are we come from. This generation will take care of what is happening to them. I hope that the day will never come again when our people have to suffer indignity like my generation and others have to. I am here to watch and see till the Lord take me home. (127–162)

Scarborough, Ontario, Canada: Edan's Publishers, 1986, 38–46, 55–57, 89, 115, 127–162.

AN INTERVIEW WITH JAMAICA KINCAID

In this document, Jamaica Kincaid compares race relations in the United States and the West Indies today, pointing out that racial attitudes in the two areas are radically different, largely due to the fact that blacks are in the majority in the West Indies and in the minority in the United States. Perhaps the most striking result of the sugar and slave system in Antigua, then, is the ethnic character of Antiguans today—the fact that almost the entire population, like Annie John, is of African descent, aware of the legacy of the slave system and of the African roots of their culture.

FROM MOIRA FERGUSON, "A LOT OF MEMORY: AN INTERVIEW WITH JAMAICA KINCAID" (1994)

I think that American black people seem to feel—almost—that being black is a predestination in some way. They have a kind of nationalism about it that we don't have: black nationalism. Because they are a minority, they are more concerned with their identity being extinct, whereas we don't feel that way. Everybody is black. I mean, we don't think white people are permanent [laughs]. We don't feel permanent, either, but that feeling of "there will always be white people sitting on top of black people"—we don't have, I must say. Black nationalism in this country [United States] is very much because there is an acceptance, in some way, of how the majority of the population have thought about black people. There is very much an internalization of that. Why else have "black pride"? I mean there is no reason to be particularly proud of something you can't help. It is not an effort you made and you became black. It is just the way you are. There is nothing particularly pleasing or displeasing about it. I am speaking as an individual asking a group of people to behave the way I behave. But if you could somehow let them understand that their view of you has nothing to do with you and it remains with them, they are so befuddled. But I believe it's a very West Indian trait. They have never really buckled, maybe because they are a majority. It is still very peculiar to hear West Indians talk about racism because it is all borrowed. There is and was racialism, but on the whole they rejected it. They are sort of strong black people in the West Indies.

Kenyon Review 16, no. 1 (Winter 1994): 164.

STUDY QUESTIONS

1. How did slavery on the sugar plantations differ from what you already know about slave life in the United States? What evidence do historians have to assert that conditions were harsher in the Caribbean?

2. Why do you think there were more slave rebellions in the Caribbean than in the United States?

3. What kind of social hierarchy among whites, coloreds, and blacks do these documents describe?

4. Describe the attitude of John Luffman toward the slaves and the slave system that he observed during his stay in Antigua. In what ways does his attitude seem to differ somewhat from that of the white planter society on the island? In what ways do their attitudes most likely coincide?

5. Describe how Luffman's account differs from and/or coincides with that of Mary Prince, and why.

6. Most modern historians state that the social hierarchy and the economic system remained largely unchanged for quite a long time after emancipation, yet the American Anti-Slavery Society's report asserts that this hierarchy was changing after emancipation and offers a very favorable report. What evidence do they offer? Are there any descriptions in the document that contradict their optimistic assertion?

7. In what ways does Samuel Smith's account of estate life after emancipation differ from that of the American Anti-Slavery Society? How do you account for these differences?

8. Describe the attitude of the commissioners who wrote the report on the conspiracy in Antigua. Do they think the rebellion was in any way justified? What recommendations do they make for the future safety and prosperity of Antigua?

9. Why do you think that African-born slaves, rather than Creoles (born in the New World), were more likely to resist slavery, rebel, or run away? Did the presence of large numbers of slaves from one African ethnic group (such as the Coromantees/Akan/Ghanaians) facilitate rebellion in any way?

10. What were some of the techniques used to control and punish slaves?

11. What roles did women play in resisting slavery in Antigua?

12. Explain some of the arguments—economic, emotional, humanitarian—that Equiano uses to justify the end of the slave trade. What aspect of slavery does Equiano find most reprehensible? What future does he envision for Africa after abolition?

13. In his article about women and slavery in Antigua, Gaspar uses public records, private estate papers, government documents, and private letters and diaries as primary sources. With these kinds of sources, what kinds of facts can we know or speculate about relating to slavery? What kinds of things may we never know about slaves' lives?

TOPICS FOR WRITTEN OR ORAL EXPLORATION

1. Using the documents as evidence, write an essay describing white attitudes toward slaves. How knowledgeable do you think they were about their slaves? What misconceptions did they seem to have?

2. After reading this chapter, do you think that Annie John's comments about slavery are justified? Why or why not?

3. What elements of African culture seem to have survived from the slave past in the Antigua that Annie John describes? What elements of British influence? Is there any evidence of racism in the novel, despite the presence of an overwhelmingly black majority? Write an essay describing the Antigua of *Annie John* as a blend of African and British influences.

4. After reading *Annie John* and these documents, what do you think is the most important legacy of the slave system in Antigua?

5. Write a two-part essay. Imagine that you live in the late eighteenth century. In the first part, assume the role of an Antiguan planter and defend your use of slave labor. In the second part, take the role of a member of an antislavery society and argue for the abolition of slavery. Use your knowledge of the Caribbean slave system to defend each position.

WORKS CITED

"Antigua and Barbuda." *New Encyclopaedia Britannica: Micropaedia.* 15th ed. Chicago: Encyclopedia Brittanica, 1993.

Bonetti, Kay. "An Interview with Jamaica Kincaid." *Missouri Review* 15 (1992): 123–142.

Goveia, Elsa V. *Slave Society in the British Leeward Islands at the End of the Eighteenth Century.* New Haven, Conn.: Yale University Press, 1965.

Hellie, Richard. "Slavery." *New Encyclopaedia Britannica: Macropaedia.* 15th ed. Chicago: Encyclopedia Brittanica, 1993.

Kincaid, Jamaica. *A Small Place.* New York: Plume, 1988.

Knight, Franklin W. "Slavery." *Encyclopedia Americana.* Danbury, Conn.: Grolier, 1994.

Rogozinski, Jan. *A Brief History of the Caribbean: From Arawak and the Carib to the Present.* New York: Meridian, 1992.

Tolson, Richard, David Lawrence Niddrie, and Janet D. Momsen. "The West Indies." *New Encylopaedia Britannica: Macropaedia.* 15th ed. Chicago: Encyclopedia Brittanica, 1993.

Vorda, Allan. "An Interview with Jamaica Kincaid." *Mississippi Review* 20, nos. 1–2 (1991): 7–26. Also in: Vorda, Allan, ed. *Face to Face: Interviews with Contemporary Novelists.* Houston, Tex.: Rice University Press, 1993. 78–105.

SUGGESTED READINGS

See the full text of works excerpted in this section.

Standard References on Slavery in the West Indies in General and in Antigua in Particular

Burns, Sir Alan. *History of the British West Indies.* London: Unwin, 1954.

Craton, Michael, James Walvin, and David Wright, eds. *Slavery, Abolition and Emancipation: Black Slaves and the British Empire.* London: Longman, 1976.

Curtin, Philip D. *The Atlantic Slave Trade: A Census.* Madison: University of Wisconsin Press, 1969.

Gaspar, David Barry. *Bondmen and Rebels: A Study of Master-Slave Relations in Antigua.* Baltimore: Johns Hopkins University Press, 1975.

———. "Slavery, Amelioration, and Sunday Markets in Antigua, 1823–1831." *Slavery and Abolition* 9 (May 1988): 1–28.

———. "Sugar Cultivation and Slave Life in Antigua before 1800." In *Cultivation and Culture: Labor and the Shaping of Slave Life in the Americas*, edited by Ira Berlin and Philip D. Morgan. Charlottesville: University Press of Virginia, 1993.

Goveia, Elsa V. *Slave Society in the British Leeward Islands at the End of the Eighteenth Century.* New Haven, Conn.: Yale University Press, 1965.

Heuman, Gad, ed. *Out of the House of Bondage: Runaways, Resistance and Maroonage in Africa and the New World.* London: Frank Cass, 1986.

Hoetink, H. *Slavery and Race Relations in the Americas: Comparative Notes on Their Nature and Nexus.* New York: Harper and Row, 1973.

Parry, J. H., and P. M. Sherlock. *A Short History of the West Indies.* 2d ed. London: Macmillan, 1965.

Ward, J. R. *British West Indian Slavery 1750–1834: The Process of Amelioration*. Oxford: Clarendon Press, 1988.

Sources on Women and Slavery

Bush, Barbara. *Slave Women in Caribbean Society 1650–1838*. Bloomington: Indiana University Press, 1990.

Mair, Lucille Mathurin. *The Rebel Woman in the British West Indies during Slavery*. Kingston, Jamaica: Institute of Jamaica, 1975.

Other Slave Autobiographies

Adams, Francis D., and Barry Sanders. *Three Black Writers in Eighteenth Century England*. Belmont, Calif.: Wadsworth, 1971.

Cugoano, Ottobah. *Thoughts and Sentiments on the Evil of Slavery*. 1787. London: Dawsons of Pall Mall, 1969.

Katz, William Loren, ed. *Five Slave Narratives*. New York: Arno Press and New York Times, 1968.

3

Spirituality in Antigua: Obeah and Christianity

Religious practices in the Caribbean are a mix of West African and European Christian beliefs, transformed to fit the needs and experiences of the Caribbean people. The majority of slaves came from societies that adhered to African indigenous or "traditional" religion. Although these beliefs are not written down in sacred or doctrinal texts, scholars have been able to study these religions through their practice in West Africa today.

African traditional religion includes the belief that all things have their own power and are related to everything else, and a person interacts with nature as well as with other people. The Supreme Being is omnipresent and mysterious and usually seen as male. This belief facilitated the association among slaves of the Supreme Being with the Christian God. Besides the Supreme Being, there are other gods associated with the environment, such as thunder, hills and mountains, rock formations, snakes. Many West African religions include methods of communicating with these gods, by rituals, divination, dreams, and trances. The purpose is usually to request help in resolving human problems, such as resolving disputes or discovering the cause of personal problems such as illness or infertility. These religions also include a belief in evil and the use of the power of good to overcome it. Many cultures rely on sorcerers, medicine, and charms to ward off evil, along with prayer and ritual.

Ancestors are an important element in African belief systems. They often have spiritual powers to provide help or cause harm, and ancestor worship is practiced in many areas. Some cultures believe that the dead remain spiritual beings and can be reborn in their descendants. Some, particularly those who do evil, become ghosts and are not reborn.

Once in the New World, Africans began to adapt to a new environment. Some transplanted their traditional religion to a new place across the ocean. Many began to believe that water and rocks and mountains and snakes in the New World, as in Africa, are also invested with spiritual power. In addition, many were converted to Christianity, which could confer many social advantages and contains many beliefs that are compatible with African traditional religion, such as the belief in a supreme God, the battle of good and evil, and spiritual survival after death. Christianity, however, did not entirely supplant African beliefs. Often they were combined in a process of amalgamation called *syncretism* (synthesis of beliefs) or as part of a process called *transculturation* (crossover between cultures). In the Caribbean today, many people engage in Christian worship as well as some form of African spiritual practice.

Caribbean religious practices differ from island to island—and even within an island. In Spanish-speaking Cuba, for example, where many slaves were of Yoruba origin (from western Nigeria), many descendants engage in Santería, a religion that worships deities that are combinations of Yoruba gods and Catholic saints. This religion has been transplanted to the United States by Caribbean immigrants, where it is widely practiced in such places as Miami and New York. In French-speaking Haiti, for example, many people engage in a religious cult called voodoo that combines elements of African religions (particularly from Dahomey) and Catholicism. The group participates in ritual dancing, inducement of trances, and animal sacrifices in order to communicate with deities, deified ancestors, and saints ruled by a supreme God. Many of these practices have been transferred to Louisiana, particularly New Orleans, where some elements of voodoo are still practiced today.

The survival of African religions in the British West Indies mostly revolves around the belief in Obeah, which uses magic and sorcery.

There are no priests or priestesses, or group practices, as in Santería or voodoo, but individual practitioners who have been trained by other practitioners. Obeah usually involves the placing of special herbs or other substances or objects in particular locations in order to achieve a desired effect. Often, the desired effect is for something negative to happen to a person, in revenge for some perceived wrong. Obeah can be used to cure illness or to cause illness, even to poison someone. It can help to identify a thief, murderer, or other wrongdoer; keep away thieves or other evils; or even act as a love potion. The clients and the victims usually have deep faith in the effectiveness of Obeah practitioners and believe that the magic works. Often, if someone believes that a negative spell has been cast on him or her, he or she will consult another Obeah practitioner to counteract the black magic with white magic. In *Annie John*, for example, Annie's mother believes that her husband's former lovers are trying to cast bad spirits on Annie and her; she consults with Ma Jolie, a local Obeah woman, for herbs, in this case administered in special baths, to counteract the negative spells.

In the practice of Obeah, a person who wishes something to happen to someone—to have a "fix" or a "spell" or "bad spirits" set on someone—visits an Obeah practitioner to describe the situation and seek out a remedy in exchange for money. Usually, the practitioner gives the client, or has the client find, certain materials, then instructs the client on how to use them. The materials could be special herbs or liquids; animal products; or items from the victim such as hair, clothing, or fingernail clippings. The instructions may include placing the materials in the victim's food or drink or in the victim's house, hanging them in a tree, or burying them in the victim's yard. If the instructions are followed, the desired effect should be achieved.

Obeah can be a very strong force for bringing about positive or negative effects because people believe in the effectiveness of the practice. It serves as a way to maintain control over difficult situations and provides a mechanism to cope with and resolve problems. One can readily see the appeal of Obeah to slaves who lacked any other means of control over their lives; one can also understand the ongoing appeal of this practice today, to people who, owing to economic or social or political circumstances, may have little control over their lives.

Obeah is also related to the belief in the spiritual survival of the dead in the form of ghosts, or "jumbies" or "duppies," and to the practice of bush medicine, or the curing of ailments through the use of herbs. Obeah practitioners may engage in bush medicine, but not all bush doctors use Obeah. Annie John mentions nearly all of these beliefs and practices in her narrative.

Great Britain brought to its Caribbean colonies the belief in Christianity in the form of Protestantism, in this case, the Anglican Church or the Church of England (which broke away from the Catholic Church during the time of Henry VIII). Although it has many members in Antigua today (45 percent of the population), it has been perceived in history as the church for the elites, or for whites. In colonial times, slaves were excluded from the Anglican Church, which left fertile ground for the Methodist (Annie's religion) and Moravian missionaries who followed (now 42 percent of the population; 10 percent, Catholic; 3 percent, other). These denominations, especially the Methodists, were opposed to slavery. John Wesley, the founder of Methodism, penned many famous articles and tracts outlining the reasons to abolish slavery. Due to the resistance of slave owners, missionaries were not permitted to preach these beliefs in the islands, but they did reach out and try to help slaves in the way they thought best—by saving their souls through baptism and conversion to Christianity. The slaves, who had been denied religion and even legal marriage, often became willing and enthusiastic converts. There was a second wave of missionary activity around the time of World War I, as Samuel Smith mentions in his autobiography, excerpted in a later document in this chapter. These denominations are particularly strong in Antigua, even today. In fact, Antigua has been considered the center of Methodism—Annie John's denomination—in the West Indies.

These churches preached against the use of African "superstitions" and discouraged the use of Obeah. Many people abandoned their belief in Obeah, while others feared and avoided it; but many people in Antigua today, like Annie's mother, combine their belief in Christianity with their belief in the effectiveness of Obeah. In the documents that follow, one can see that the Obeah practices described have been passed down over the years to contemporary times.

MEMOIR OF WILLIAM S. BIRGE

Annie John's mother came to Antigua from Roseau, the capital of the island of Dominica, where her own mother was skilled in Obeah practice. Her husband, a Methodist minister, did not approve of Obeah. When their son John (Annie's uncle, her mother's brother) became sick, no Obeah medicine was used. John languished and died. When the mother saw a worm emerge from his leg after his death, she knew that the sickness was the result of an Obeah spell and that a counterspell might have worked. She blamed her husband for her son's death and never spoke to him again. When the Obeah woman on Antigua fails to cure Annie, her mother calls in her own mother from Dominica, and she seems to magically appear, on a day when there is no ferry. It is she who realizes the nature of Annie's illness and cures her by remothering her.

The following excerpt is a description of Obeah on the island of Dominica, as told from the point of view of a man from the United States who visited there around the turn of the century.

FROM WILLIAM S. BIRGE, M.D., *IN OLD ROSEAU: REMINISCENCES OF LIFE AS I FOUND IT IN THE ISLAND OF DOMINICA, AND AMONG THE CARIB INDIANS* (1900)

The superstition which existed in ancient times in the power of talismans, amulets and charms of all kinds, it would seem, finds a parallel in our own amongst the negroes of the West Indian Islands, where it exists in perfection under the name of Obeah or Obi. . . . It would seem, therefore, that this form of fetishism must have been carried to the West Indies by captured negroes in slavery times, and there developed into an oracle and the patron of all kinds of superstitious delusions.

Those who practice fetishism of this kind are called Obeah men or women, for both sexes are supposed to become adept in this mysterious science. Those that attract the most devotion and confidence are such as are old and crafty, and whose hoary heads give them at least an appearance of antiquity. In the town of Roseau one was pointed out to me who was said to be an Obeah man, and whose age was known to be at least ninety-three. He had a peculiarly harsh and forbidding aspect, and not at all calculated to inspire one with awe, but rather fear. He was bent nearly double, and one eye was concealed from view by means of a large black patch. This man's name was Drondeleau, and he was much sought after by the natives of Roseau and the adjoining country, and his talismanic powers were supposed to be unsurpassed.

Most of these creatures, I think, have some knowledge of the native plants of a medical and poisonous species and have qualified themselves sufficiently for successful imposition upon the ignorant and credulous. A professor at Hamilton College, Barbadoes, informed me that it was surprising to find how large a number of natives revere and consult these Obeah men, and what implicit faith they repose in them, whether for the cure of disease, the obtaining of revenge for insult and injury, conciliating the favor of love of the opposite sex, or the prediction of future events. The business of these impostors is said to be quite lucrative, and they sell their Obeis adapted to the various cases at different prices, corresponding to the wants of the individuals. The most of their work is done during the midnight hour, purposely to conceal and keep from discovery by the white people, and also to add a veil of mystery to their actions. The deluded negroes so thoroughly believe in their supernatural power that they become willing accomplices to this concealment. The most courageous native will tremble at the sight of the ragged bundle or the little bunch of bird's claws and feathers that may be hung over the door of the hut to deter marauders. Most of the cases of sudden death that occur in the islands are by the ignorant natives ascribed wholly to the workings of an Obei. Then they will not reveal even a suspicion through a dread of incurring the terrible vengeance of the Obeah man should they betray him. For this reason it is extremely difficult to detect one of these miscreants from any other negro.

When a native has been robbed of any article, he immediately applies to the Obeah man of the neighborhood, and the fact is made known that an Obei is set for the thief, who becomes so terrified that, as an only resource, he applies to the superior skill of some more prominent Obeah man to counteract the workings or spell of the first. If he does not succeed in finding such a one, or his imagination leads him to feel himself still afflicted, the chances are that he soon falls into a condition of complete melancholy, sleep and appetite leave him, his strength rapidly fails, and he is a complete wreck, both bodily and mentally, gradually sinking into the grave.

The Obei is usually composed of a great variety of materials, such as blood, feathers, bird's claws, pieces of bone, hair, teeth of different animals, etc. Dr. Barnham, who practiced medicine in Dominica in the last century, spoke of numerous cases of poisoning by Obeah men that came to the notice of the colonists at that time. In such a secret and insidious manner was the poisoning done, that detection was rendered almost impossible. The murderers were occasionally brought to justice, but it is reasonable to believe that by far the greater number escaped. A singular case occurred in Trinidad a few months ago, which will serve to illustrate to what extent this awful practice is sometimes carried. A man by the name of La Fave, with his family, lived near another negro called Umbredo. The latter had for some years made his living as an Obeah man, and so great was the terror inspired by him that the natives obeyed him implicitly. La Fave alone declined to believe in Umbredo, saying that he could do no more than any other man, and called him a fraud and impostor. This so enraged Umbredo that he declared that all the food the La Fave family ate would henceforth act as poison, and that before the month was out not a member of the family would be living. Two days later the La Fave family, consisting of the father, mother and eight children, grew suddenly ill after dinner. By two o'clock one of the children was dead. By six a second victim was added to the list, and at nine o'clock a third. Instead of going to the authorities in regard to the matter, the La Fave family were now firmly convinced that Umbredo was really possessed of supernatural power and could visit his wrath upon those who offended him; so they determined to keep the whole matter secret, fearing that further vengeance might be wrought upon them. Before the funeral of the three children took place a fourth died, while the six other members of the family were dangerously ill; that forenoon the mother died, and during the evening still another child. The father, who had eaten less heartily than the rest of the family, recovered sufficiently to be about; but his mind was gone, and he would not touch a mouthful of food for fear of being poisoned. Two days later he died in convulsions. In less than a week's time the remaining members of the family were dead, and the Obeah man's prophecy was fulfilled. As soon as the white residents learned the facts, Umbredo was hidden or spirited away by the colored people, and, at last accounts, had never been found.

The following is a narrative respecting Obei in Jamaica during the days of slavery, many years ago:

Upon returning to Jamaica, after a short residence in England, a planter found that a great many of his negroes had died during his absence, and that of such as remained alive at least one-half were debilitated and bloated, and in a deplorable condition. The mortality continued upon his return, and frequently two or three were buried in one day, while others were taken ill and began to decline under the same symptoms. All was done by medicine and the most careful nursing that could be done to preserve the lives of the feeblest; but, in spite of all his endeavors, this depopulation went on for a twelve-month longer, with more or less intermission, and without his being able to ascertain the real cause, though the Obeah practice was strongly suspected as well by himself as by the doctor and other white persons on the plantation. Still, he was unable to verify his suspicions, because the patients constantly denied having anything to do with persons of that order, or any knowledge of them. At length, a negress, who had been ill for some time, came one day and informed him that, feeling it was impossible for her to live much longer, she felt herself bound in duty before she died to impart a very great secret and acquaint him with the true cause of the disorder, hoping that the disclosure might prove the means of stopping the mischief which had already swept away such a number of fellow-slaves. She proceeded to say that her stepmother, a woman more than eighty years of age, but still hale and active, had put Obei upon her, as she had also done upon those that had lately died, and that the old woman had practiced Obei for as many years as she could remember. The other negroes of the plantation no sooner heard of this impeachment than they ran in a body to their master and confirmed the truth of it, adding that she had carried on this business ever since her arrival from Africa, and was the terror of the whole neighborhood. Upon this he repaired directly with six white servants to the old woman's home, and forcing the door open, observed the whole inside of the roof, which was of thatch, and every crevice of the walls stuck with the implements of her trade, consisting of rags, feathers, bones of cats, and a thousand and other articles. Examining further, a large earthen pot or jar, closely covered, was concealed under the bed. It contained a prodigious quantity of round bulk of earth or clay of various dimensions, whitened on the outside, and variously compounded— some with hair and rags, or feathers of all sorts, and strongly bound with twine; others blended with the upper section of the skulls of cats, or stuck around with cat's teeth and claws, or with human or dog's teeth and glass beads of different colors. There were also a great many egg shells filled with a viscous or gummy substance, the properties of which he neglected to examine, and many little bags stuffed with a variety of articles, the particulars of which cannot now be recollected. The house was immediately pulled down, and the whole of its contents committed to the flames, amid the general acclamation of all the negroes. In regard to the old woman, he declined bringing her to trial under the law of the island, which would have punished her with death, but from a principle of humanity delivered her into the hands of a party of Spaniards, who, as she was capable of doing some trifling kinds of work, were willing to carry her with them to Cuba. From the moment of her departure all his negroes seemed to be animated with new life, and the malady spread no further among them. The total loss of life, in the course of about fifteen years previous to the discovery of the Obeah practice, and imputable solely to that, he estimated as at least one hundred negroes.

New York: Isaac H. Blanchard Co., 1900, 42–49.

MEMOIR OF MATTHEW GREGORY LEWIS

A common practice in Obeah is the use of poison, which was one method of resistance to slavery and also a mode of personal revenge. Annie's mother fears the use of Obeah for revenge against Annie and herself by one of her husband's former lovers. The following document describes the use of poison among slaves, then goes on to recount the fate of one Obeah man named Adam on an estate in Jamaica.

FROM MATTHEW GREGORY LEWIS, *JOURNAL OF A WEST INDIA PROPRIETOR, KEPT DURING A RESIDENCE IN THE ISLAND OF JAMAICA* (1834)

There are many excellent qualities in the negro character; their worst faults appear to be, this prejudice respecting Obeah, and the facility with which they are frequently induced to poison to the right hand and to the left. A neighboring gentleman, as I hear, has now three negroes in prison, all domestics, and one of them grown grey in his service, for poisoning him with corrosive sublimate; his brother was actually killed by similar means; yet I am assured that both of them were reckoned men of great humanity. Another agent, who appears to be in high favour with the negroes whom he now governs, was obliged to quit an estate, from the frequent attempts to poison him; and a person against whom there is no sort of charge alleged for tyranny, after being brought to the doors of death by a cup of coffee, only escaped a second time by his civility, in giving the beverage, prepared for himself, to two young book-keepers, to both of whom it proved fatal. It, indeed, came out, afterwards, that this crime was also effected by the abominable belief in Obeah: the woman, who mixed the draught, had no idea of its being poison; but she had received the deleterious ingredients from an Obeah man, as "a charm to make her massa good to her"; by which the negroes mean, the compelling a person to give another every thing for which that other may ask him.   (148–149)

• • •

One of the deadliest poisons used by the negroes (and a great variety is perfectly well known to most of them) is prepared from the root of the cassava. Its juice being expressed and allowed to ferment, a small worm is generated, the substance of which being received into the stomach is of a nature the most pernicious. A small portion of this worm is concealed under one of the thumb-nails, which are suffered to grow long for this purpose; then when the negro has contrived to persuade his intended victim to eat or drink with him, he takes an opportunity, while handing to him a dish or cup, to let the worm fall, which never fails to destroy the person who swallows it. Another means of destruction is to be found (as I am assured) in almost every negro garden throughout the island: it is the arsenic bean, neither useful for food nor ornamental in its appearance; nor can the negroes, when questioned, give any reason for affording it a place in their gardens; yet there it is always to be seen. The alligator's liver also possesses deleterious properties; and the gall is said to be still more dangerous.   (329–330)

• • •

A negro, named Adam, has long been the terror of my whole estate. He was accused of being an Obeah-man, and persons notorious for the practice of Obeah had been found concealed from justice in his house, who were afterwards convicted and transported. He was strongly suspected of having poisoned more than twelve negroes, men and women; and having been displaced by my former trustee from being principal governor, in revenge he put poison into his water jar. Luckily he was observed by one of the house servants, who impeached him, and prevented the intended mischief. For this offence he ought to have been given up to justice; but being brother of the trustee's mistress she found means to get him off, after undergoing a long confinement in the stocks. I found him, on my arrival, living in a state of utter excommunication; I tried what reasoning with him could effect, reconciled him to his companions, treated him with marked kindness, and he promised solemnly to behave well during my absence. However, instead of attributing my lenity to a wish to reform him, his pride and confidence in his own talents and powers of deception made him attribute the indulgence shown him to his having obtained an influence over my mind. This he determined to employ to his own purposes upon my return; so he set about forming a conspiracy against Sully, the present chief governor, and boasted on various estates in the neighbourhood that on my arrival he would take care to get Sully broke, and himself substituted in his place. In the mean while he quarreled and fought to the right and to the left; and on my arrival I found the whole estate in an uproar about Adam. . . . The breeding mothers also accused him of having been the cause of the poisoning of a particular spring, from which they were in the habit of fetching water for their children, as Adam on that morning had been seen near the spring without having any business there, and he had been heard to caution his little daughter against drinking water from it that day, although he stoutly denied both circumstances. Into the bargain, my head blacksmith being perfectly well at five o'clock, was found by his son dead in his bed at eight, and it was known that he had lately had a dispute with Adam, who on that day had made it up with him, and had invited him to drink, although it was not certain that his offer had been accepted. He had, moreover, threatened the lives of many of the best negroes. Two of the cooks declared, that he had severally directed them to dress Sully's food apart, and had given them powders to mix with it. The first to whom he applied refused positively; the second he treated with liquor, and when she had drunk, he gave her the poison, with instructions how to use it. Being a timid creature, she did not dare to object, so threw away the powder privately, and pretended that it had been administered; but finding no effect produced by it, Adam gave her a second powder, at the same time bidding her remember the liquor which she had swallowed, and which he assured her would effect her own destruction through the force of Obeah, unless she prevented it by sacrificing his enemy in her stead. The poor creature still threw away the powder, but the strength of the imagination brought upon her a serious malady, and it was not till after several weeks that she recovered from the effects of her fears. The terror thus produced was universal throughout the estate, and Sully and several other principal negroes requested me to remove them to my property in St. Thomas's as their lives were not safe while breathing the same air with Adam. However, it appeared a more salutary measure to remove Adam himself; but all the poisoning charges either went no further than strong suspicion, or . . . were not liable by the laws of Jamaica to be punished, except by flogging or temporary imprisonment, which would only have returned him to the estate with increased resentment against those to whom he should ascribe his sufferings, however deserved. However, on searching his house, a musket with a plentiful accompaniment of powder and ball was found concealed, as also a considerable quantity of materials for the practice of Obeah: the possession of either of the above articles (if the musket is without the consent of the proprietor) authorises the magistrates to pronounce a sentence of transportation. In consequence of this discovery, Adam was immediately committed to gaol; a slave court was summoned, and to-day a sentence of transportation from the island was pronounced, after a trial of three hours. As to the man's guilt, of that the jury entertained no doubt after the first half hour's evidence; and the only difficulty was to restrain the verdict to transportation. We produced nothing which could possibly affect the man's life; for although perhaps no offender ever better deserved hanging; yet I confess my being weak-minded enough to entertain doubts whether hanging or other capital punishment ought to be inflicted for any offence whatever: I am at least certain, that if offenders waited till they were hanged by me, they would remain unhanged till they were all so many old Parrs. However, although I did my best to prevent Adam from being hanged, it was no easy matter to prevent his hanging himself. The Obeah ceremonies always commence with what is called, by the negroes, "the Myal dance." This is intended to remove any doubt of the chief Obeah-man's supernatural powers; and in the course of it, he undertakes to show his art by killing one of the persons present, whom he pitches upon for that purpose. He sprinkles various powders over the devoted victim, blows upon him, and dances round him, obliges him to drink a liquor prepared for the occasion, and finally the sorcerer and his assistants seize him and whirl him rapidly round and round till the man loses his senses, and falls on the ground to all appearance and the belief of the spectators a perfect corpse. The chief Myal-man then utters loud shrieks, rushes out of the house with wild and frantic gestures, and conceals himself in some neighboring wood. At the end of two or three hours he returns with a large bundle of herbs, from some of which he squeezes the juice into the mouth of the dead person; with others he anoints his eyes and stains the tips of his fingers, accompanying the ceremony with a great variety of grotesque actions, and chanting all the while something between a song and a howl, while the assistants hand in hand dance slowly round them in a circle, stamping the ground loudly with their feet to keep time with his chant. A considerable time elapses before the desired effect is produced, but at length the corpse gradually recovers animation, rises from the ground perfectly recovered, and the Myal dance concludes. After this proof of his power, those who wish to be revenged upon their enemies apply to the sorcerer for some of the same powder, which produced apparent death upon their companion, and as they never employ the means used for his recovery, of course the powder once administered never fails to be lastingly fatal. It must be superfluous to mention that the Myal-man on this second occasion substitutes a poison for a narcotic. Now, among other suspicious articles found in Adam's hut, there was a string of beads of various sizes, shapes, and colours, arranged in a form peculiar to the performance of the Obeah-man in the Myal dance. Their use was so well known, that Adam on his trial did not even attempt to deny that they could serve for no purpose but the practice of Obeah; but he endeavoured to refute their being his own property, and with this view he began to narrate the means by which he had become possessed of them. He said that they belonged to Fox (a negro who was lately transported), from whom he had taken them at a Myal dance held on the estate of Dean's Valley; but as the assistants at one of these dances are by law condemned to death equally with the principal performer, the court had the humanity to interrupt his confession of having been present on such an occasion, and thus saved him from incriminating himself so deeply as to render a capital punishment inevitable. I understand that he was quite unabashed and at his ease the whole time; upon hearing his sentence, he only said very coolly, "Well! I can't help it!" turned himself round, and walked out of court. . . . Once condemned, the marshal is bound under a heavy penalty to see him shipped from off the island before the expiration of six weeks, and probably he will be sent to Cuba. He is a fine-looking man between thirty and forty, square built, and of great bodily strength, and his countenance equally expresses intelligence and malignity. The sum allowed me for him is one hundred pounds currency, which is scarcely a third of his worth as a labourer, but which is the highest value a jury is permitted to mention.   (350–357)

London: John Murray, 1834, 148–149, 329–330, 350–357.

OBEAH: WITCHCRAFT IN THE WEST INDIES

This document, from the late nineteenth century, describes a circumstance similar to that which Annie's mother fears—that one of her husband's former lovers, with whom he has had children, will try to do harm to her and Annie through the use of Obeah. In this case, the former lover succeeded. The same document also describes the use of Obeah for positive, medicinal purposes, much like when the two Obeah women are brought in to help cure Annie John's illness.

FROM HESKETH J. BELL, *OBEAH: WITCHCRAFT IN THE WEST INDIES* (1893)

Notwithstanding Quashie's [the African's] fear of jumbies [ghosts], the influence of Obeah is sometimes strong enough to cause him to disregard the powers of outraged spirits, and gruesome tales are told of graves being desecrated in order to procure the most powerful of all the instruments of Obeah. This is none other than the liver of a human corpse. Two or three years ago, a woman and a child died under suspicious circumstances, in Carriacou, a small island some twenty miles distant from Grenada. A post-mortem examination proved the deaths to be owing to poison of some sort, and after a good deal of inquiry, a barrel of brown sugar was found in the house, and evidently contained a quantity of highly poisonous matter. Further evidence disclosed that this sugar had been sent to the unfortunate woman as a present from another woman in Grenada, who had lived for many years with the present husband of the deceased. It also cropped up that a grave near the residence of the Grenada woman had been disturbed, and on examination, the coffin was found to have been opened and the liver of the corpse extracted. This horrible substance, which has the reputation of being the most powerful of all the instruments of Obeah, had been ground and mixed up with the sugar, and thus had caused the deaths of the woman and child. (144–145)

• • •

If he gets worse, his wife or mother will lay him up and proceed to apply vinegar and brown paper over every inch of his body. Should his ailments not succumb to this favourite remedy, a bush doctor will then be called in. This may be either some old African man or woman with a reputation for Obeah or some Creole quack with a trifling knowledge of bush remedies or such medicines as he has seen used in the case of sick animals. These persons, if successful in a simple case, at once acquire a great reputation, and enjoy more of the confidence of the people than the government medical officer of the district. However, it is most probably that for every cure which they effect, perhaps five unfortunates are hurried to their graves by their attempts at medicine. . . .

Most people affect to consider all bush medicines as rubbish; this is a very erroneous idea, and I feel sure that there exist in the woods of these islands hundreds of plants possessing valuable medicinal properties still unknown to the faculty. There are still some old Africans in Grenada who undoubtedly possess the secret of several wild plants, most valuable in certain diseases, but this knowledge is most difficult to extract from them, and their use is mixed up with so many absurd superstitions and conditions, that it is most difficult to find out where the rubbish leaves off and the truth begins.   (147–149)

London: Sampson, Low, Marston & Co., 1893, 144–145, 147–149.

JAMAICA AS IT IS

In this short excerpt from a book-length description of Jamaica around the turn of the century, the author describes a medicinal bath similar to the ones Annie John describes in the novel.

FROM B. PULLEN-BURRY, *JAMAICA AS IT IS* (1903)

They have a patent treatment for fever, called the "bush bath." This consists of equal proportions of the leaves of the following plants: akee, sour sop, jointwood, pimento, cowfoot, elder, lime-leaf and liquorice. The patient is plunged into the bath when it is very hot, and is covered with a sheet. When the steam has penetrated the skin, the patient is removed from the bath, and covered with a warm blanket, leaving the skin undried. A refreshing sleep is invariably the consequence, and a very perceptible fall in temperature.

London: T. Fisher Unwin, 1903, 140–141.

MORAVIAN MISSIONARIES IN JAMAICA

This document describes the efforts of the Moravian missionaries to convert West Indian slaves to Christianity. In this section, the author criticizes two circumstances that, in his opinion, make conversion much more difficult—the appalling living conditions of the slaves and their belief in the "superstitions" of Obeah.

FROM J. H. BUCHNER, *THE MORAVIANS IN JAMAICA: HISTORY OF THE MISSION OF THE UNITED BRETHREN'S CHURCH TO THE NEGROES IN THE ISLAND OF JAMAICA, FROM THE YEAR 1754 TO 1854* (1854)

It is beyond the power of the missionary to remove the chief obstacles to the free course of God's word in a slave country. No system could be invented more effectually to hinder and oppose the spread of the gospel than slavery. The slaves had no time to hear the word, except when worn out in body and mind by their cruel bondage; and their souls injured by a system which overthrows all morality, and sets at defiance the plainest commands of scripture. How can there be morality where marriage is illegal? where overseers, bookkeepers, and drivers know no bounds, no obstacles to their evil lusts? How is the debased ignorant heathen to be taught the fear of God, and the heinousness of sin, when he finds himself the victim of evil; assassins, and the most unblushing immorality, in those who profess to be his superiors, and when he sees his equals treated as the beasts of the field? The most faithful instructions, the most earnest labours, will be ineffectual, if not accompanied by the grace of God. The influence and teaching of God's holy Spirit must *abound*; must work a change, a conviction in the heart of the individual, strong, thorough, and decided; before a poor slave can say with the apostle, "I am persuaded that neither death nor life, nor angels, nor principalities, nor powers, nor things present, nor things to come, nor height, nor depth, nor any other creature, shall be able to separate me from the love of God which is in Christ Jesus our Lord." Examples of the abounding grace of God were not indeed wanting at this time, among the Negro slaves; still we are not to suppose, even where this change had taken place, that such a one was a pattern of christian perfection. By no means: nevertheless, if the slave was weak and ignorant, yet he learned to love, and was beloved of the Lord. This was his strength. We who have grown up, particularly, in christian families, enjoyed religious instruction from our youth, and are members of those churches in which everything combines to check evil inclinations, and to foster good resolutions, are scarcely able to comprehend the darkness of a heathen's mind. The fortitude, decision, and surrender of the heart to the Saviour, that are requisite to make a slave confess the Lord, by word and action, in the midst of degradation, violence, and cruel depravity, assume in many respects the character of a perpetual martyrdom. If a mission to the Negro slaves really prospers, if instances of such conversions are multiplied, it is a miracle of divine grace, far greater than anything which we meet with in civilized society or christian lands.   (42–43)

• • •

The practices of Obeah and Myalism, formerly so common, become less and less frequent, though to this day they are still followed, and have not lost their power and influence over the minds of those who take part in them. Again and again we have to use all our authority and influence against these devices of the wicked one. Nothing so entirely perverts the mind of man; they uproot christian faith, destroy every sound principle, and being foolish and absurd in the extreme, they ruin at once both soul and body. There is no sin against which a missionary, who knows the consequences, should be more watchful to guard his people. It might prove the ruin of a congregation if not exposed and offenders brought under the strictest exercise of church discipline, as soon as anything tending towards such wickedness makes its appearance. The same fanaticism has shown itself also in our congregations at Nazareth and Bethany as late as 1849 and 1852, though in a somewhat different form. Inflated with pride, some gave themselves out to be prophets, inspired by the Spirit of God, and began to preach; but there were the same immoral practices, the same dances, always connected with it, which stamped it as the same heathenish superstition, decorated with some christian doctrines applied to blasphemous purposes. Offenders of this kind, after having been spoken with and entreated not to grieve the Spirit of God, are, if they persist in their infatuation, publicly excluded from all church privileges, and not re-admitted, until humbly, before the whole congregation, they confess their sin and error, and beg to be pardoned; and then they are again admitted, only upon trial. "From the murdering spirit and devices of Satan;—*Preserve us, gracious Lord and God.*" (141–142)

London: Longman, Brown & Co., 1854, 42–43, 141–142.

THE PRACTICE OF OBEAH

A recent study of Obeah, by two university anthropologists, describes Obeah in more objective terms. Although they are discussing the practice in the Bahamas, it is similar to practices in Antigua during the time in which *Annie John* takes place.

FROM BASIL C. HEDRICK AND JEANETTE E. STEPHENS, *IT'S A NATURAL FACT: OBEAH IN THE BAHAMAS* (1977)

The Practice of Obeah

. . . Obeah is practiced by essentially "ordinary" persons who happen to have the ability to effectively utilize its powers. Practitioners may be either men or women. Outwardly, they usually conduct unobtrusive lives and professions as average members of the society. As a rule, they do not wear any distinctive clothing or other personal items that denote their trade. There are no recognized costumes or insignia distinctive to them. An informant reports, however, that he does know of one Obeahwoman who wears a silver bracelet with supposedly secret magic inscriptions on it as part of her trade, although this does not automatically distinguish her as a practitioner. Obeah practitioners are not manifestly wealthy as a group, although they do at times receive sizable payments for their services (which can amount to hundreds of dollars in difficult cases). The unobtrusive posture of the practitioners reflects the nature of the art: (1) because Obeah has been illegal, its practitioners historically have had to keep their identities a secret for fear of reprisals; and (2) the air of secrecy aids in maintaining the mystery associated with the practice, thereby enhancing the suggestion of it having special powers. An individual's success as a practitioner depends, to a large degree, on his reputation of having strong magical powers and the ability to achieve effective results. The more powerful the person is, the more he is feared and his abilities respected.

Obeah may be learned from several different sources. Some practitioners are said to be "born with the gift," which is discovered during their childhood and is encouraged to develop into a profession. Such individuals, or others who are interested but not inherently "gifted," learn the specifics of the art from older, established practitioners to whom they are "apprenticed." Usually the teacher is a parent, grandparent or other relative, but it may be any person knowledgeable in Obeah. Practitioners may be reluctant to teach their knowledge to others unless they are assured of the latter's sincerity, for fear of divulging "trade secrets" which would diminish the aura of mystery, the prestige and mystique of the practice. Other persons "received their 'power' during adulthood with a 'vision' or, while 'in a trance,' were instructed into their art" (McCartney, 1976:79). . . . Some novice practitioners are reported to have gone to Haiti or Jamaica to learn the art because it is so well-developed there.

Obeah practices are generally initiated by a secret meeting between a prospective client and a practitioner. This usually takes place in the home of the latter. The residences of several practitioners have been described as being well-stocked with the items of their trade. . . .

Obeahmen tend to be skeptical of prospective clients and often refuse to help them or deny an ability to do so, until they are convinced of the person's sincerity and belief in the practice. For that reason, an individual desiring the services of an Obeahman is often introduced to him by a third person who already knows, or is known by, the practitioner. The client-practitioner relationship begins, generally, with the client describing his problem to the Obeahman and asking for the latter's professional help in alleviating it. The practitioner assesses the problem and, once convinced of the client's sincerity, prescribes a cure or performs it himself, in return for a given fee. The client then departs to execute his prescribed tasks and await the results of the Obeah magic.

The actual uses of Obeah, as well as the procedures employed and individual items used, varies considerably in contemporary contexts. Primarily, Obeah revolves around the practice of "setting a fix" on someone or something; that is, casting a spell on him (it). By "fixing" someone, the Obeah practitioner may, for example, cause the "fixed" individual to do what the client requests of him. The "fix" thus refers to the magic itself. The "set" (or "setting a fix") refers to the procedures and materials involved in carrying out a fix. Such procedures are also referred to as "dressing" an item. For example, gardens are said to be "dressed with Obeah" (Bell, 1970:2) to prevent the theft of their contents. When a practitioner is about to perform Obeah, the room in which he works must be "dressed" (prepared), often by placing a candle in each corner. One prepares an item, such as a candle, to make it susceptible to or focused toward the Obeah magic.

An Obeah fix is set through the medium of fetish objects. In contemporary Bahamian practices, important items include: candle wax, "seals" (tablets bearing foreign, "mysterious" inscriptions on them), religious books (particularly the *Bible, The Sixth and Seventh Books of Moses*, and *Master Key*), grave dirt, egg shells, certain herbs, articles of clothing, and items from the victim's person. In addition a vast array of other mundane items may be used in any given instance. Poisons are not, today, heavily employed, although many potions comprised of "bush medicines" are used which may have somewhat deleterious effects on individuals. The objects of constituents are chosen because they are believed to have certain power, themselves, which is harnessed by the Obeahman, or because they are able to act as mediums for the practitioner's own power. Some items are used differently for black or white magic; some are used for either aspect. For example, in the context of black magic, passages from certain books are used, including *Seven Steps to Power, Black Guard, Seven Keys to Power* and *Master Key* (McCartney, 1976:78, 122); whereas in white magic the *Bible* (particularly the Psalms) is used. . . .

The objects take their effect on the victims by being placed in their houses (often under their beds), sprinkled around their houses, buried under or in their walkways so that they step over them when leaving the house, or hung in a tree in their yards. Once the victim comes in contact with the item (whether knowingly or not), he will reputedly be affected by it, and the desired outcome of the fix will thus soon be achieved. In context of negative Obeah (used as black magic), the outcome is said to entail such things as "the loss of hair; unexplained swelling of the limbs or stomach; constant headaches or 'ringing in the ears'; unexplained outbreaks of boils or festering sores that do not respond to medication; the loss of the use of the limbs (not being able to walk, etc.) or deformity of the limbs, loss of sight," (McCartney, 1976:118), or sometimes even death. A common outcome professed for victims is that they will "swell up and burst." To counteract the effects of a fix, individuals generally will consult a second Obeahman or woman and receive a remedy from him/her in the form of curing substances or prescribed actions. Usually, the fix can be effectively countered in this way.

Obeah is used in solving a variety of problems—often in reference to crime dissuasion, romantic disputes, legal problems, revenge, finding lost articles, or curing ailments. A list of the kinds of results that reputedly may be obtained through Obeah is provided by Missick (1975:45):

Gain the love of the opposite sex

Unite people for marriage

Obtain property

Make persons do your bidding

Make persons love you, no matter who

Get any job you want

Make people bring back stolen goods

Make people lucky in any games

Cure any kind of sickness without medicine

Cast a spell on anyone no matter where they are

Get people out of lawsuits, courts or prison

Bring happiness to broken lives

Remove the source of unhappiness

Such applications have been documented in informant interviews and written accounts of persons who have contracted for Obeah fixes or who have been victims of such fixes. The accounts may be used to graphically demonstrate the application of Obeah and its effects on believing individuals. While other, more "rational," explanations can often be given for occurrences attributed to Obeah, they do not diminish the value of Obeah explanations to some people.

Obeah may be employed for detecting criminals, as well as dissuading people from illegal or antisocial activities. The following account is an example of situations in which positive Obeah is credited with bringing about justice:

> After Smith murdered his mistress, he took to the bush. Inagua had a lot of scrubland where the former Turks Islander could hide from his pursuers. An armed search party scoured the bush, but could find no trace of Smith. He thought he was safe.
>
> He was safe from ordinary searchers; but the old woman who attended his sweetheart's funeral told the other mourners that Smith would give himself up after six days.
>
> She told them so just after she had placed a fork, a stick and a stone in the coffin and had muttered a Creole incantation.
>
> Six days later Smith was found sitting on the steps of the courtroom. He was red-eyed and shivering in terror.
>
> "I don' sleep for six day now," Smith complained. "Demon I can't see, he stick me wit' fork, hit me wit' stick and throw rocks at me" (Dupuch and Perfetti, 1966:92, 93).

In the context of romantic relationships and troubles Obeah may effect a negative reprisal against someone (often for revenge), or may be used in a positive, helpful sense. The following account, in which Obeah powers are supposedly involved in seeking revenge on a romantic rival, is paraphrased from a recent Nassau newspaper article (White, 1973:6). The incident began when two women had a heated argument over the claim of one that her husband had been "sweethearting" the other woman. The other woman did not deny the charge, but said that it was the wife's fault for not satisfying her husband. The wife then shouted "Okay you going to get what you asked for. Between this day and tomorrow you ger sleep under the cotton tree . . . that's right, you just as well go inside your house and put your burying gown on." Unknown to the other woman the wife had a reputation of being an Obeahwoman. The police had heard of the incident and were suspicious of the wife, so they kept watch over the other woman's house during the night. She lived alone and they saw no one enter or leave the premises that night. The next morning the woman was found dead in bed, and the cause of her death was unknown, although no obvious foul play was involved. The neighbors all were convinced that it was the wife's Obeah power that had caused the death.

In a more positive context, McCartney (1976:82) relates how an informant applied Obeah to bring about the return of a client's wayward lover. . . .

The use of Obeah to solve romantic troubles may also precipitate the application of counter-Obeah. . . .

The use of Obeah is reported in several incidents in which individuals attempt to use fetishes to obtain favorable verdicts in court. An informant states, for example, that such an outcome can be achieved by three methods. In one, the accused is instructed to walk backward on a grave, write the deceased person's name backward on a piece of paper, then put the paper in his shoe when he goes to court. By pressing on the paper during the trial he will supposedly make the prosecutor become confused and ruin his case. Similar results occur if the accused writes the prosecutor's name backward on a piece of paper, wraps the paper around an egg using new needles to secure it there, places the egg under the armpit or another concealed place, then presses the egg when the prosecutor speaks. Certain oils rubbed on the accused person's body are said to harm the prosecutor's case when he walks near him. Portions of the Bahamian legal statutes that pertain to Obeah make specific reference to the use of such practices in courtrooms, as they are fairly common occurrences. . . .

Obeah Related to Other Beliefs

In the Bahamas, Obeah is closely associated with the use of medicinal folk remedies known as "bush medicine," . . . [which] involves the administering of pharmaceutical plants to heal ailments. In its practice, indigenous Bahamian plants are collected and processed into substances used to prevent, relieve or cure diseases (e.g., heart conditions, kidney disease, chicken pox, diabetes and tuberculosis) and various other disorders (e.g., headaches, muscular aches, boils, coldsores and fevers) (Higg, 1974:5–20). The leaves, bark or other parts of plants may be employed in bush medicine practices. Often the plants are boiled into teas and taken internally. Also, they may be made into salves and applied directly to an ailing area or may be washed over the patient's body. The latter practice is called a "bush bath" and is rather common in the Bahamas. The plants do have genuine curing value, although not always to the degree credited to them. The unjudicious use of some of them may also have distinctly harmful effects. Their effective ability is of the same sort that has been demonstrated for pharmaceutical herbs throughout the world for centuries.

The practice of bush medicine requires an intimate knowledge of local plants, methods of their preparation and effects of their administration. Obeah practitioners tend to be among such knowledgeable people. The practitioners use the plants, which—as mentioned before—often do have actual curing abilities, to aid in achieving desired Obeah results. . . . The use of bush medicine in Obeah thus helps to lend credence to the Obeah practitioner's claims of power through the achievement of verifiable results from the plants. Bush medicine is not synonymous with Obeah, however. While Obeah practitioners may use medicine—since it brings direct results (and thus credibility) to their art—the practitioners of bush medicine are not necessarily Obeahmen and may not use Obeah as a part of their work at all. . . .

Conclusion

In the Bahamas, Obeah provides a useful social function by bringing some measure of control (or attempts at control) to situations that are normally uncontrollable. It provides a means by which ordinary members of society can affect events in their lives, through the application of its practices that are believed to have the power to influence such events. Its validity as a viable course of action rests on the credibility of the Obeah practitioners and their ability to bring about desired results. Their credibility is maintained, in some respects, by their use of bush medicine, which does have actual healing capabilities, and by their ability to perceive and assess their clients' problems and the latters' faith in the results of Obeah. Foremost, Obeah depends on the fact that a certain group of people strongly believe, and want to continue believing, in its power and abilities. There are some contemporary Obeah practitioners who take advantage of their clients' faith, purposely deceiving them with useless (or even harmful) remedies. Other practitioners, however, are sincere about the practice; they believe deeply in their art. For those segments of the society who manifest a strong faith in Obeah, it is a valid and socially useful practice—that is, in its helpful forms. It is certainly an intriguing practice, even to those not quite so faithful.

University of Northern Colorado, Museum of Anthropology *Miscellaneous Series* No. 39, 1977, 15–33.

NINETEENTH-CENTURY MISSIONARIES IN ANTIGUA

Due to its colonization by England, the dominant Western religion on Antigua is Protestantism. The Anglican Church (the Church of England) has the highest number of members, while the other most popular sects make up about the same number of members, if taken together. The two denominations with the highest number of members today, and since colonial times, are the Moravians and the Methodists. In the novel, Annie mentions that she belongs to the Methodist Church. Why are these two denominations so popular even today? The reason can be traced back to the time of slavery, when missionaries from these two groups went to Antigua to convert the slaves. They had great success on this island; as a matter of fact, for many years Antigua was the center of Methodist missionary work in the British West Indies. These two sects were particularly successful with the slaves for several reasons. First, they sympathized with the plight of the slaves. They were opposed to slavery but had to be careful of what they said on the plantations in order to avoid the ire of the plantation owners. In fact, some plantation owners in Jamaica forbade the Methodists to preach there, believing that they fomented unrest among the slaves. The Moravians and Methodists also preached that all people are human beings and equal in the eyes of God. This sentiment would be highly appealing to people who were treated as beasts of burden by most whites. In addition, the slaves were taught that every person had a soul that could be saved with the belief in Jesus Christ as the saviour and that there was a beautiful afterlife in heaven. This belief helped to comfort suffering slaves and did not contradict African spiritual beliefs. The Moravians and the Methodists were particularly zealous in their efforts to convert "heathens" in the British West Indies. Their letters and journals reveal their enthusiasm and hard work, which bore fruit, as these groups are still particularly popular in Antigua even today.

The following document, from an important early account of Antigua by a white woman later identified as Mrs. Lanaghan, describes the arrival of missionaries on the island and the state of religion in Antigua in the mid-nineteenth century. She reveals that many of the missionaries, although not suffering as much as the black laborers, also endured hardships, both physical and social, in order to spread the gospel. They were relatively few in number, with great numbers of followers, and often had to travel from plantation to plantation, often working long hours. They also had to placate nervous plantation owners and other whites who did not agree with their teachings; even if they believed, they often did not agree with the teaching of slaves. For example, the missionaries preached monogamy and marriage to the slaves, which the plantation owners discouraged or forbade to them. The proprietors also feared unrest, especially if the slaves began to believe in their dignity and rights as human beings.

FROM [MRS. LANAGHAN], *ANTIGUA AND THE ANTIGUANS* (1844)

The next building to be mentioned is, the new Ebenezer Chapel, belonging to the Methodist society. The cornerstone of this edifice was laid by the Honourable Nicholas Nugent (then speaker of the house of assembly, but who now resides in England as the colonial agent) in 1837. A religious service was first held in the old chapel, and then, forming into a procession, consisting of ministers of the different sects in Antigua, some of the aristocrats of the island, the leading members of the Methodists, and the scholars of their Sunday-schools, they marched to the spot appointed for the erection of their new place of worship. A bottle containing the customary inscription was placed in the cavity, the stone lowered to its proper situation, the three blows of the mallet struck, addresses delivered, and the ceremony was over.

It is a spacious building, the front being constructed of free-stone, the gift of the Honourable and Rev. Nathaniel Gilbert. . . . The ground-floor is appropriated to the use of the infant and Sunday schools, as also their "teaparties," held for charitable purposes; above is the chapel, which is approached by an outward flight of stone steps. The interior is fitted up in the usual plain style; but boasts a smart display of blue and white paint. . . . Altogether, the chapel is an excellent building, superior to anything of the kind I have seen in the West Indies, and makes a good and commanding outward appearance, particularly when lighted up of an evening; but to my eye it looks more like reading rooms, or a philosophical institution, than a place of worship.

Methodism was first established in Antigua in 1760, by the Honourable Nathaniel Gilbert, speaker of the house of assembly. In 1758, Mr. Gilbert visited England, carrying with him some of his negro servants; and during his stay there, he formed an acquaintance with the Rev. John Wesley, the venerable founder of Methodism, who baptized two of the negroes. Upon Mr. Gilbert's return to Antigua, he signified to those individuals who resided near him, that he should feel happy in meeting them at his house on certain evenings, when he would expound the word of God to them, and endeavour to enlighten their minds upon religious subjects. This invitation was eagerly accepted by many of the negroes and coloured people, and Mr. Gilbert was led to increase his views, and form a regular organized society, which in a short time amounted to two hundred members.

This proceeding of Mr. Gilbert produced the greatest astonishment among the inhabitants of Antigua. A man in his rank of life to herd with negro slaves, and their coloured offspring, who, although perhaps they might be free, bore about with them the marks of their despised race!— oh! wondrous! incomprehensible!—the man must be mad, thought they. But when he, unmindful of their censure, proceeded in his acts of love towards these poor outcasts from the pale of society, their wonder knew no bounds; their feelings took another turn, and what at first was surprise, gave way to reproach and contempt. Mr. Gilbert, however, was not to be moved by what mankind said of him; he knew the consequence before he commenced his labours; and reckless of scorn or reprehension, he steadily pursued the path he had chalked out, knowing full well in whom he trusted. Thus he proceeded, until death called him from this world, and summoned him to reap his reward in heaven; when, strong in faith, he left his infant society without a shepherd to watch over its welfare. . . .

Unpromising as the state of this little society might seem, the good seed already sown was not destined to perish. The Great Shepherd cared for it; and when least expected, raised another pastor in the person of a Mr. John Baxter, a native of England. Mr. Baxter was a man who moved in humble life, and who worked in the capacity of shipwright, in Chatham Dockyard; but he was justly esteemed by all who knew him, a patter to the society to which he belonged, and a highly-respected leader among Mr. Wesley's sect. In 1777, a proposal was made him by some of the directors of the Chatham Dockyard, to sail for Antigua, and work as foreman of the calkers in the naval establishment of the island. To this Mr. Baxter assented; but not so his friends: they made use of every argument in their power to make him forego his purpose—representing, in the most glowing colours, the distance he would be from all he loved; the dangers of the ocean, oer which he must pass; and the difference, perhaps insalubrity, of climate he would have to contend with. But all without avail; he felt an unconquerable desire to visit that portion of the globe, and accordingly, bidding his friends farewell, he left England, and arrived in Antigua on the 2nd of April, 1778.

As might be expected, he found the infant Methodist Society in a very languishing state. Upon hearing of his arrival, and of his being a member of the same sect as their beloved benefactor, the little band waited upon him, and after welcoming him to their shores, begged him to tell Mr. Wesley he had many children in Antigua whom he had never seen, but who were earnestly desirous of his aid. On the following Sabbath, Mr. Baxter met them in the services of religion, and from that day constituted himself their pastor; which office he performed until his death, assembling them together on Sundays, and performing the full service, as in England, and on the other week-days, after his labours in the dockyard were over, visiting the different estates, and teaching the poor slaves the road to salvation.

His exertions were greatly blessed; and by the following year, 1779, six hundred negroes were joined to the congregation. He now contemplated the erection of a chapel, and for that purpose instituted collections among his people, and adopted every other consistent method to acquire funds to carry out his plans.

Mr. Baxter's situation was productive of great discomfort to himself; his duties to be performed in the naval-yard were very laborious; and after a long day's work, his evenings were spent in traveling from plantation to plantation, the harbinger of Gospel news. He had no one to assist him in his self-appointed task, but for some years laboured on alone. In 1782, he mentions in a letter to a friend, "There is no white person in the congregation but myself. At St. John's thirty coloured persons receive the Lord's Supper."

Assistance, however, was not so far off as he supposed. About this time an Irish family (who were all members of Mr. Wesley's sect) were persuaded by an unprincipled captain of a trading vessel, to sell all their little property, and emigrate with him to America. Deceived by his plausible manners and fair speeches, they acquiesced in his proposals; and turning all their goods into money, the whole family, consisting of an elderly father and mother, a son, and some daughters, embarked on board his vessel, and sought with him their better fortune in a far-off land. But their false friend having inveigled them into his power, under various pretenses, robbed them of their little all, and then deserted them, in a strange country. After suffering many and bitter privations, they found their way to Antigua, where they eventually became valuable assistants to Mr. Baxter.

In the meantime, Mr. Baxter's great object, the erection of a Methodist chapel in St. John's, was rapidly being accomplished; and on the 8th of November, 1783, that worthy man, with an overflowing heart, had the happiness of preaching his first sermon in it, to a full and serious audience. In the space of the three following years, the society increased to 2000 persons.

In 1786, Dr. Coke, the Wesleyan missionary and historian, left England, for the purpose of spreading gospel tidings in America. Meeting, however, with violent gales, the ship in which he took passage was unable to make her destined port; and after encountering a series of disasters, as a last and only resort, was obliged to put into Antigua, in distress. Dr. Coke was delighted to find the Wesleyan society in that island in so satisfactory a state—a circumstance he was unprepared for; and in his letters to England, expresses in warm terms his pleasure upon the subject.

The first conference was held at Antigua, in the year 1787; but the annual conferences, or district meetings, were not established until 1793, when, on the returns being made, the society was found to consist of 6570 members; out of which there were 36 white, and 105 coloured persons. Although the Methodist Society had progressed so far, and embraced so many members, yet its proceedings were reviled and insulted by the greater part of the white inhabitants. All kinds of petty insults were heaped upon its pastors; while their place of worship was made the scene of vulgar waggeries and ribald jests. One favourite amusement of many of the young men of that period was, to procure a live goat, and after hampering with its legs, fling it into the midst of the assembly, while engaged at their devotion at the Methodist chapel. At other times, in order to vary the sport, the goat was secured against the chapel door; and as the minister pronounced the amen, or the members raised their hymns of praise to God, the poor animal was beat and kicked until it joined in chorus with its deep and unharmonious cries, which were received with burst of applauding laughter by its foolish captor.

Mr. Baxter, although a very good man, was not, I have understood, possessed of very superior talents; and accordingly, many of his discourses produced much merriment among that class of persons who frequented his chapel for the sake of passing criticisms, as well as killing time. He had a favourite servant living with him, whose name was John Bott, and who attended to the lighting up of the chapel, as well as performing his home duties. Upon one occasion, John neglected to snuff the candles; an omission which caused his master so much uneasiness, that, after endeavouring in vain to read the portion of Scripture selected, he was fain to interrupt himself in the midst of a passage—"And Nathan said unto David—John Bott, snuff the candles!" This intervention, as may be supposed, caused a tumult of laughter; nor (said an ear-witness) could his own people restrain their risible faculties. But to return. About 1793, Dr. Coke paid Antigua another visit, and preached upon many plantations; one of which was Sir George Thomas's at North Sound. The old chapel at Parham was erected in 1802; the returns of the society made that year were, 4000 persons. . . .

Since Mr. Baxter's death [in 1805], the Wesleyan society has been rapidly progressing, not only in Antigua, but in all the other West India Islands, although Antigua is still looked upon as the parent church; and in 1842, the society in that island consisted of about 2700 members. Besides the chapel in St. John's, they have places of worship at Parham, English Harbour, Willoughby Bay, and elsewhere.

Thus, for a small beginning—from a few black slaves gathered together by night beneath the roof of a white man—this society has spread far and wide, like some huge wave, until now it boasts a vast increase of number, of every variety of shade, from the ruddy son of Britain, down to the jetty offspring of Afric's soil. Great success has attended the preaching of this sect; and although an episcopalian myself, and consequently more attached to that form of worship, I cannot let the opportunity pass me without offering my mite of praise to the character of their undaunted and fervent ministers, and, at the same time, expressing my firm belief that they have, through God, been the means of preventing much crime, and saving many, very many, from the fearful retribution, the inevitable attendant on a misspent life.

From this view of the Methodist Chapel and Methodism, I proceed to mention the Moravian settlement. The Moravians, or rather, "United Brethren," as many of my readers may be aware, revived under the celebrated Count Zinzendorf, a native of Germany, who, with some of his followers, visited England in the reign of George II, and formed several settlements of their sect in different parts of that kingdom. They also established colonies in Greenland, Labrador, and other parts of North America, and in South America.

In 1731, Count Zinzendorf visited Denmark, for the purpose of attending the coronation of Christian VI, who, by the death of his father, was called to the throne of that kingdom. During his residence at that court, some of his domestics became acquainted with a negro, named Anthony, from one of the Danish islands. This man related many instances of the moral darkness in which the West Indies were enveloped, and of the distressed state of the negroes; which being repeated to the count, he felt an invincible desire to send missionaries to that part of the world, to proclaim the "tidings of great joy" to those poor benighted negroes.

In 1732, this desire was carried into effect; and two missionaries were dispatched from "Hernhult," (the principal Moravian station, in Lusatia, Germany,) to St. Thomas. Other missionaries followed them; and in 1733, they planted their standard in St. Croix. In 1754, the society in London sent missionaries to Jamaica, who were followed by some of the brethren from America; and in 1756, Samuel Isles, a true and exemplary Christian, came from St. Thomas, where he had been residing as missionary for eight years, and established the first Moravian settlement in Antigua.

Their labour of love was at first very slow in its progress; but they succeeded, in 1761, in raising a chapel, for the accommodation of the negroes, on a spot of land, purchased for the purpose, in St. John's. Still their society rather decreased than flourished, until, about 1768, there were only fourteen members in the church at St. John's. Disheartening as these circumstances were, like true soldiers of the Cross, they would not lay down their arms; and at length, their faith and patience met with their reward. A wonderful revival took place, and in 1775 "the number of their stated hearer amounted to 2999; and never a month elapsed without an addition to the church of ten or twenty by baptism."

By the year 1787, 5465 negroes were admitted into the church. Their first settlement was situated at St. John's; but in 1782, they had formed another at Grace Hill, or, as it was first termed, Bailey Hill; a delightful spot, about ten miles from the capital. The number baptized at St. John's in 1789, was 507; while at Grace Hill, 217 were admitted into the church by that ceremony. By this time, five preachers were settled in Antigua; and in the course of the two following years, the society enrolled 7400 members. At the present period, 1842, the number may be estimated at 11,000.

Their settlement at St. John's is situated in Spring Gardens, at the extreme north end of the town, and looks the very picture of neatness and domestic comfort. The present chapel, erected in 1773, is a plain building—devoid of any great architectural beauty, it is true, but interesting from its very simplicity, and from being built by the negroes in times of slavery. The rapid increase of their numbers, already mentioned, rendered it necessary to provide a larger place of worship; which fact being mentioned to their negro converts, they immediately commenced procuring some of the materials, by each bringing a few stones with them, when they came to their evening meetings in the week. Those of them who were masons and carpenters worked with the greatest energy "in their free hours, after their daily tasks were done; and those who could not assist in the labour provided victuals for the workmen." Since that period, the chapel has had many enlargements and alterations made to it. The dwellings of the preachers are gathered around it; and their neat, cheerful-looking burying-ground, in which grows many a beautiful tree, bounds the settlement to the east. Everything about them looks green, and fresh, and lovely; and their wives, in their neat caps, and Quaker-like style of dress, and the often very pretty, but quiet contour of their features, appear in perfect harmony with the other parts of the picture. I must say, I like the Moravians: they seem to have so much open-heartedness about them—such patriarchal simplicity of manners. Among themselves they are ever kind and courteous, forming, as it were, one large family of affectionate brothers and sisters. They have done much good among the black race, for whose welfare the mission was particularly intended; and many happy deaths among them attest the truth. Besides their settlement in St. John's, they have several in other parts of the island; namely, at Grace Hill, Grace Bay, Newfield, Cedar Hall, Lebanon, Gracefield, and Five Islands.

London: Saunders and Otley, 1844, 141–154.

METHODISM IN COLONIAL ANTIGUA

The following document, a history of the West Indies, was written by a prominent Methodist missionary during colonial times, so the emphasis is on the history of missionary efforts in the West Indies, particularly by the Methodists. The following excerpt is from the section on Antigua, where Methodism has its strongest roots in the Caribbean. Thomas Coke paints a rather rosy picture of missionary success in Antigua and emphasizes its positive effects on the behavior of the converted slaves.

FROM THOMAS COKE, *A HISTORY OF THE WEST INDIES*
(1808–1811)

Antigua became the primary scene of action. In this island the work began first to take root. From hence a variety of branches spread themselves into other colonies; and the event has been, that thousands have been savingly converted to God. As this island must be considered as the parent church in this Archipelago, it behooves us, in this place, to give a brief, but full, account of the manner in which the gospel was first established, together with the instruments through which it was effected. By these means we may trace the conduct of Almighty goodness, in those displays of mercy which he has so abundantly manifested towards multitudes of the swarthy inhabitants of the torrid zone. . . .

Mr. Baxter thus fully employed, and laboring both for the bread which perishes, and for that which endures unto everlasting life, after having resided in the island a little more than one year, gives the following account, both of his prospects in religion and himself.

"We labor under great hardships in this island, as the hand of God seems to be upon us. We have had no rain for some months, therefore the ground is parched up. There have been hardly any crops these three years, so that all the proprietors of estates are nearly ruined. We have expected rain every full and change of the moon, but still the windows of heaven are shut against us. As to the poor negroes, they have not even water to drink; and having nothing allowed them to eat but a pint of horse-beans a day, their case is truly deplorable."

"But I hope their extremity is God's opportunity; for they seem ripe for the gospel. *Six hundred* of them have joined the society; and if using the means of grace be any proof, we may conclude they are in earnest.

As an evidence of their sincerity, some of them come three or four miles after the labors of the day, that they may be present at eight o'clock at night to hear the word; and on Sundays, many come seven or ten miles barefooted to meet their classes.

The distresses of the island, we flattered ourselves, would have constrained the legislature to appoint a day of fasting and prayer; but as they neglected it, we thought it our duty to do it among ourselves; and we appointed Friday, the 28th of May, for that purpose. It is remarkable, that while we were assembling for prayer, the Lord granted our request by sending rain in abundance. And at the same time that he was pouring out floods upon the dry ground, the times of refreshing came from his presence in such a manner, that many were constrained to cry, *my cup runs over*. Some strangers also joined us, who acknowledge the power of God. . . ."

The influence of the gospel upon the lives of the negroes, in general, through this island, was so conspicuous, even at this early period, as to render military law, which had been formerly enforced at Christmas, when several days of recreations were allowed the negroes, wholly unnecessary. The members of society formed a part of those whose lives had, evidently, been reformed; they were, indeed, the little leaven which was leavening the lump; and the light that shone in them not only formed a contrast with the darkness which others manifested, but diffused a lustre through almost every corner of the colony. . . .

From such a society it is natural to infer, that the congregations were both large and well behaved, which in reality was the case. That of St. John's and one in the country which I had the pleasure of addressing, would not have disgraced even those parts of England in which we have met with the greatest success. Decency, solemnity, and attention, were not only visible, but predominant features in their general character. The life of genuine and vital Christianity beamed in the countenances of many, from that internal principle which had been planted in the heart. . . .

Our blessed Lord, before he quitted earth for heaven, gave to his followers a new commandment, namely, *that they should love one another*; and, perhaps, we can find but few places in which this command has been more punctually obeyed, than in the island of Antigua. In times of sickness the members of our society visit each other in their respective neighborhoods, with the most affectionate solicitude. And even in those cases where medical assistance is required by a patient who is unable to provide it, it is instantly procured without any regard to the expense. It may be said, that they love like brethren, that they are pitiful and tenderhearted, and melt in sympathy at each other's woe.

Those riots and robberies, which were viewed as preludes to insurrection and revolt, have disappeared; insomuch that those precautions which in former periods were so necessary for the preservation of order, were now become nothing more than empty and unmeaning parade. Many, who had been turbulent lions, were now become peaceable lambs; and from a conviction of duty, endeavored to promote the interest of their masters, whom in former days they deemed it a virtue to injure. Such were some of those changes through the instrumentality of two faithful men. . . .

The work of God, evidently, appeared to be deepening throughout the island. . . . And, as a proof of the peaceable demeanor which they had uniformly manifested, the conduct of their masters must be an unexceptionable witness. For so far satisfied were the planters and other respectable inhabitants, with the conduct of the Missionaries, and so conscious of the political as well as religious advantages resulting from their labors, that they supported the work by voluntary contributions and subscriptions. . . .

It was on the 8th of February 1793, that the author for the last time visited this island; and in company with those Missionaries which were established in different colonies, we began our annual Conference for these parts. . . .

By the returns which were made at this Conference from the different islands, we found that our total number of members in society amounted to six thousand five hundred and seventy souls; and out of this number two thousand four hundred and twenty resided in Antigua. Of this company in Antigua, thirty-six only were whites, one hundred and five people of color, and the rest were blacks. The blacks, indeed, through all the islands, almost uniformly make the chief part of the converts that are to be found; they are the people who, in general, pay the greatest attention to the word delivered; and the Almighty has been graciously pleased to bless it to their souls.

These negroes, throughout the various islands, had either in a greater or less degree been brought out of heathenish darkness to a knowledge of God. Their outward sins, so far as observation could reach, they had abandoned. Even the practice of polygamy itself, their besetting evil, divine grace had given them fortitude to resist; and a considerable part of them gave so clear and rational an account of their conversion, and of the influence of religion upon their hearts and lives, as was sufficient to prove it genuine, and to animate the Missionaries to still new exertions in behalf of others.

Liverpool: Nutthall, Fisher & Dixon, 1808–1811, 427–444.

MEMOIRS OF SAMUEL SMITH

In these excerpts from Samuel Smith's autobiography, this Antiguan black man from the working class discusses the use of herbs, based on African practices, to cure common diseases, much as they are used in *Annie John*. He also comments on the role of the Christian church in Antigua. It is interesting to note that, like Annie, he has a rather wary and cynical attitude toward institutions. In this case, he critiques the church, particularly the Anglican Church, and white Antiguans in general, particularly what he perceives as their racism, snobbery, and hypocrisy.

FROM KEITHLYN B. SMITH AND FERNANDO C. SMITH, *TO SHOOT HARD LABOUR: THE LIFE AND TIMES OF SAMUEL SMITH, AN ANTIGUAN WORKINGMAN, 1877–1982* (1986)

Disease was indeed a problem. Now very few trained doctors was around and they were not interested to attend to poor black people, so we just have to make up our minds to live without them and use our own means to make life more easy. For example, there was always a local village doctor. Now whether it was by accident or by design, I don't know, but the local village doctor was always a woman. I can't remember even one man that know very much local remedy. These women doctors knew the local remedy for all kinds of things, the best bush for the particular sickness. Some people was cured, others wasn't. The important thing was them women sure try. Them did their best to help.

The bush syrup, for colds and so on, was made up of manger dagger, eucalyptus, sage and cattle tongue leaves along with bark mixed up with sugar. Sissle, bamboo bush and French thyme was also capital for colds. To clean the blood you would take and boil white head broom and law lavington bush together with bitter mint and inflammation bush. The sixty-six bush was also a good blood cleaner. And tizan bush tea and tanbrana root water were use by men to keep them cross [to ensure male potency]. We indeed use to love and cherish them bush.

There was also the blood pressure bush and the love bush that the blessed bush doctor usually give you for kidney and liver sickness. And the heart bush was capital for heart problems. The human milk was the remedy for sore eyes.

The women also knew to boil up the root of the powerful doctor dull-dull bush for the painful monthly things. And later it was found that maiden blush bush was good for blood pressure and headaches and that brackish jelly water will serve for rheumatism and arthritis. The friendly and helpful village doctor also have what was the best cure for insect bites and stings—rub the spot with three different kinds of bush—and that too was capital. The sweetheart and inflammation bushes was the remedy use for the stoppage of water, for men use to suffer regularly from the various kinds of venereal diseases. That inflammation bush was well-known to all the men. So too women use vervine tea to clean them when pregnant and sage tea was for baby gripe. But the amazing cure to stop nagging belly gripe was to put the person across the doorway to lie down, put your foot in the belly and quarrell. The belly gripe would then stop.

Roast potatoes and salt butter was the remedy for mumps. The worm grass was for worms and you would use turpentine for boils and heat. Senna and epsom salts was the remedy for almost everything. For a fact, epsom salts was over-used and sometimes people dead from it. Soap and sugar was for poultice and castor leaf bush was to cool down fever and blood pressure. Aloes mixed with gin was the cure for sugar [diabetes].

The leaves of the large pain killer tree at North Sound Estate was to cure pain. Whoever pick the leaves must pay the tree, either with a coin or a ten-penny nail. People say that if you did not pay the tree, the leaves would be of no effects and the pain would not get better. Back then the people truly believe in that story and pay the tree at all times. The nails and coins are still there for all to see.

The best village doctor also have the knowledge to refit dislocated ribs back into the right place. The bakkra [white] doctors wasn't competent in this. Them never could do that job better than the women that serve as village doctors. Them women do everything to lessen the sufferings of our poor people. "There is a tree to cure every sickness and a tree to suit every purpose"—that was our belief. God bless them. . . .

Mark you, there was no undertakers back then. Everybody have to bury them dead and the dead have to stay in the house until the next day. Maybe that was the main reason for "wakes."

A bunch of grass would be placed on the belly of the dead to keep it from rising. People had to bear the dead from their homes to the church. All the houses would be closed down where the funeral procession was passing. In similar manner, women use to turn their dresses over their head when walking at nights and men use to turn their shirts on the wrong side. The bearers of the coffin have to carry six gravel stones to keep the dead from putting too much weight on them.

If there would be a young picknee [child] living in the house, the parents would usually have a ritual. Two people would stand on each side of the dead and the child would then be toss over the dead three times to keep the jumbie [ghost or spirit] from coming back to interfere with the picknee.

The people in my days was superstitious to the proper. On the first day of each month, before my old people got out of bed, they use to shout "Rabbit, Rabbit, Rabbit!" to bring them some kind of good luck—at least for the remainder of the month. And that was the way almost all the people was behaving back then. People use to be mortally afraid of black cats. Whenever one would run across the road, or whenever people met up with them, they would get very disturbed, for they were of the belief that was bad luck for sure.

Children were warned against counting stars, for if they did, the belief was that not less than three people from the village will die in a short time. It was also a serious matter to turn back; back then people seldom turn back for anything. It would have to be something that was of extreme importance to get a person to turn back and if you was forced to turn back, you must then spin around three times in the road to prevent the sure bad luck that was destined to meet you.

You would never find a single woman sitting on a table. She was also certain to get out of the way if somebody was sweeping for the broom must not touch her feet. The belief was that if any of these things happen, she would never get a husband. And back then, it was also the case that a pregnant woman would never be found around a butcher's stall when an animal was being killed or the picknee would be born with some defects. If the animal was a goat, the babe would have the face of a goat. She must also not feel sorry for anything for that would also affect the babe.

In the old days, anybody that was throwing away a piece of bread first must soak that bread in water. If that wasn't done, bad luck would follow the person for a long time. So too, it was said that if a person throw away salt that person must wet the place, or throw one of the grains behind without looking back, or else bad luck was sure to befall that person.

And you know, I think that even up to now some people are still of the belief that the first person you see in the morning will determine the kind of day you will have. You see, it was the belief that if you see a lazy man first thing in the morning, then you will feel lazy throughout the day. The opposite will be the case if the first person you see is jolly and hardworking. But it was a happy thing when a cock crew more than once in front of the door for a good visitor was bound to show up.

If a window be converted to a door, then the head of the house must kill a cock as a sacrifice, or somebody in that house was sure to die. Also, if a hen crows it is a bad sign and the owner of that hen must destroy it.

It was also the belief that if a huckster [vendor in an open-air market] leave home without selling something, that huckster may not have a good selling day. She would have the same fate if an enemy happen to be the first to buy from her in the morning.

Whenever a dog would hound [howl] at night it was definite that somebody's spirit was walking. In similar manner people would say that if somebody whistle in the night, that person was calling a spirit.

Every village would have its obeah man or woman. I remember there was the coffee woman [fortune teller] that people use to check out to know what was going on or what would happen in the future. It was not a joke. The people believed in the superstition and the rituals. (63–69)

• • •

[Around the time of World War I] the frustration was building up. The food was rationed and the lines was long. The change of attitude went over the whole island. Then the Englishmen get smart all of a sudden and religion come in.

No longer them try to stop us from going to church. The priests and the parsons was in every home preaching the gospel to nega [negro] people. Them say we go to church or we would be going to hell; if we would not harken to the voice of God, we would not see His face. Them give us Bible and the hymn books and told us we must be obedient to our massas for Christ was obedient to death. I think there was hardly one Englishman in this land that was not telling the nega people how good was heaven and what we must do to get there.

Although the massas' preachermen ram them religion down our throat, them never change from doing wickedness to black people. Massa work still come first, anything else—well, that was after. The nega was still working for nothing and still going to jail when he didn't show up for work. It was still jail or licks, for religion didn't have nothing to do with that. The priests and the parsons never preach that was wrong. The most they use to do was to go to the magistrate to beg off some time from the jail or some strokes if the order was the cat-o-nine, and only if they happen to know you. Mind you, although religion didn't change the misery and the hardships, nega drink it in. The doctrine take hold early.

The priests get to be very powerful, more powerful even than the planters. Anything the priests want the people to do, it was absolute certainty that the people would do it. It seem to me, if the priests and the parsons ever wanted the injustices against black people to stop, that would be bound to happen. If the priests and the parsons wanted the people to stand up against hunger and starvation, that would have happened. If them wanted even the slightest improvement in our living conditions, it would have happened. A nar two people soak in the doctrine [in a very short time the people were swayed].

The people that was as old as I was or older was less convinced about the thing. I went along living my life. I had too much experience about what the church was like for me to hear them. A good many of the preachers was planters and them was wicked, wicked, wicked. I didn't have nothing to do with any church. That's not to say I don't believe in God, but when the bakkra preachers use to tell us that if we don't obey God, hell will be our portion, I knew there couldn't be a hell hotter than North Sound [a sugar estate]. No hell could be hotter than what was going on in this land against nega people.

I remember an Anglican priest that make it absolutely clear that the Anglican church wasn't built for nega people. Nega must go to church, but they must please keep out of St. George's. That priest was right. The Anglican Churches in Antigua that wasn't built before our relations reach to this land was built when we was in chains like cattle out in the pasture. They was also built far away from the plantations and even up to now some are still out of bounds to us.

It's only nowadays that the bakkra don't swap animals on Sundays after service. I remember the first time I went to Valley Church was to follow Massa Affie one Sunday to swap horse after the service. The English planters use to love to go to church on Sundays to trade. Don't let them fool you at all [don't think religion was the only reason they went to church]. The god them serve was they money and nega must slave to get that money for them. The honest planter would never be afraid to tell you that his money was his god.

Priest after priest, parson after parson use to go see my mother to try and get me to go to church. She was against them all. She use to argue with them. . . .

During the war years [World War I] wherever there was a group of white people, you would be right if you guess they would be talking about how was the war going. Any little gathering of planters, the topic was sure to be the war. News didn't come by so quickly back then and they was anxious to know what was happening. They use to get into the churches and pray to them God and sing songs for the Mother Country like "Rule Britannia, Britannia rule the waves, Britannia never, never shall be slaves." . . . The churches use to be full up with them. Some could hardly work a day, for the war was on their mind.

The nega people was in sympathy with the massas. We love the Mother Country and we wanted her to win. We use to sing another song that goes like this at the end, "And love the land that bore you, But the Empire best of all." All the people accept that. We did love the Empire best of all. We didn't stop to think how they were treating us.

During and after the war people nearly ate one another. There seem to be no end to the hunger and starvation. The priests and parsons was all keeping things quiet. More and more people start to go to church and many of them couldn't go on Sundays would go to the open air services at nights. Any time the moonlight was up there would be two and three services in the week. And in the midst of the preaching the people all around was dying from all manner of diseases. Every week, small as our village was, somebody dead. Ever so often you would find dead bodies in the guts [ditches] and ponds around the place. . . .

The war slowed down everything, even cricket. Gov. Heskette Bell spent a lot of time afterwards starting up cricket again. The islands use to compete for the Heskette Bell trophy, but no cricket could be played during the war years. Cricket was my favourite sport. Even after I get married, I use to play a little cricket. The bat was made from village wood and the ball was made from cloth knit with twine.

It was around the time of the war that the churches start to christen black people picknee, but never would they do it at the same time with the white people. The rule was wedlock christen on Sundays and bastards during the week. And all the bastards was for black people. The massas knew that. Up to 1914 most of the men was just living with the women.   (121–125)

Scarborough, Ontario, Canada: Edan's Publishers, 1986, 63–69, 121–125.

CONTEMPORARY SURVIVAL OF OBEAH PRACTICES

The following interview, between the author of this book and Michael Porobunu, a citizen of the southeastern region of Nigeria, who has been trained in West African traditional religious practices, took place after Mr. Porobunu had read the other documents in this chapter. He was questioned about similarities between Obeah practices as described in the British West Indies and spiritual practices in West Africa that he has observed. Perhaps the most striking result of this interview is the similarity of practices in both places, suggesting that they were transferred to the New World intact and survive to this day in the Caribbean among the descendants of African slaves, as they did in Annie John's family.

INTERVIEW WITH MICHAEL POROBUNU, OF NIGERIA (1997)

DM: Mr. Porobunu, you have done me the courtesy of reading most of this chapter. When you read the documents pertaining to Obeah in the British Caribbean, did you see any similarities between the practices described here and the practices that you know of in West Africa?

MP: Yes, there are a lot of similarities. As you are well aware, these were Africans taken from Africa and they actually came over there with the African traditional beliefs and I don't think they've lost them over the years. There are a lot of practices here that are similar, but if you would be more specific I would be willing to talk more in detail about them.

DM: Okay, let me ask you about a few of them here. In one of them, a woman talks about putting a fix on another woman so that she and her daughter will be killed. The woman is jealous because the other woman is now living with her ex-lover. Is such a thing really possible? Could someone cause someone else to die?

MP: Yes, it is possible in some instances. In Africa you find most of these conflicts in polygamous families where you have two wives struggling to be the favorite of the husband. So you have struggles like these, and they consult a priest, or what we call the traditional religious leaders. In this book, you call them the Obeah practitioner.

DM: What do you call them?

MP: There are different names all across Africa for this type of people, but in my own particular village we call them *nzor*. They are very skilled at what they do, and most of it is actually based on fear more than anything else. If you tell somebody that something is going to happen to them, the fear is carried over, but in other instances it's been cases of pure poisoning rather than through any divine intervention or use of spirits.

DM: So if this person, this Obeah man or woman, says that something is going to happen, fear, or the psychological aspect, can make it happen? If the person hears that they are going to become sick, then the fear of becoming sick will make them sick?

MP: Yes. You can also look at the psychology of this from the Western point of view. If someone tells you they're calling the cops, the fear of being arrested and sent to jail affects your actions; you might do something that you wouldn't normally think of doing. For instance, if you can get over your fear you can get your lawyer before you get arrested. Back in Africa, when someone tells you, "I'm going to a juju priest" (because that is what the white man calls it—juju), one of the things you do is to go to a juju priest yourself, if you know any. Or you tell your relatives and your relatives will take you to a juju priest who is perceived to be of a greater power than the other person's juju priest. So there is that element of fear in everything. It's very powerful in African society.

DM: So if you hear that somebody's putting a fix on you with a juju priest, you would try to see a more powerful juju priest to try to undo whatever the other one has done?

MP: Certainly, because you're talking about a psychological game being played here. And it's not being played on you alone, but on your family. The pressure is being put on you by members of your family, telling you that if you don't take care of yourself, you will be dead, then you are under that pressure to find a juju priest who is more powerful to undo whatever danger might come to you.

DM: So it's not just a case of an individual against an individual, but the family is very involved if they hear about it.

MP: Yes, because you have to understand the African family structure. A member of the family is not an isolated part. In fact, what you call family here is quite different from the African concept of family. Your family here is your immediate family—you, your husband, your kids—but back in Africa your family includes your relatives. You are just a household within the family. When you talk about family in Africa you're talking about brother's wives and children, aunts and uncles, cousins, grandparents. And we do not distinguish between cousins and siblings. We call them all brothers and sisters.

DM: So a cousin is like a brother or sister and a niece or nephew is like a daughter or son?

MP: Yes. The sheer fear of the family losing someone through juju always puts the pressure on the individual involved to seek protection against the juju of the other person.

DM: So if I were to see a juju person, what would she/he do?

MP: It depends on what you're asking the practitioner to do for you. If you want a beautiful woman that you just met to fall in love with you, you tell the practitioner what you want done and he tries to achieve that for you.

DM: Are the practitioners usually men or women?

MP: There are women practitioners and there are men practitioners.

DM: Say I want a certain man to fall in love with me, what kinds of things would the practitioner do? Would he tell me to do certain things or would he have me drink something, or have the other person drink something? What exactly would he do?

MP: It could be a combination, depending on the access you have to the person you want to fall in love with you. If you have access to the person, the practitioner might be able to give you a potion that you can give to the person without her/him knowing. Or you might get some oils that you are supposed to bathe in. If you know when this person is coming from farm or from fishing, when you walk by the person she/he becomes attracted to you.

DM: If you have access to the person, might the practitioner ask for something like hair or fingernail clippings or a piece of clothing?

MP: Yes. They might use one of those things to work the magic.

DM: What's the usual thing that they would ask for?

MP: They usually ask for the hair or a piece of cloth that the person wore.

DM: And this could be used to make a person fall in love with you or to concoct a poison?

MP: Basically to fall in love with you. To concoct a poison is an entirely different thing. Africans are very skilled in poisons. They know the trees in the forest and the fruits that are poisonous.

DM: So some of these things seem strictly psychological. How could

someone fall in love with you just because you bathed in a certain
oil? How does that work?

MP: I haven't done that myself, so I don't know exactly how it works,
but people believe in it enough to do it, and in some cases there are
people who say it worked for them, and there are some cases where
it hasn't worked. So it's a mixed bag.

DM: Can you tell me a little about the African skill in poisons?

MP: One of the things I read in this chapter is about the arsenic beans.
In the southeastern region of Nigeria there is a tree called the calabar
tree that is known among Africans and even European doctors. It's
supposedly the most poisonous fruit in Africa. If it touches anything
that you eat, it can kill you. There is no antidote to it. Besides the
calabar tree there are other trees and plants that are very poisonous.
Only people who are very skilled know in what combination or with
what quantity you can do harm to the person.

DM: What about the cassava root mentioned in this chapter?

MP: There are different types of cassava and some of them are poisonous.
The roots are poisonous; the tuber is not. It is usually concocted
with something else to render it poisonous, so you have to be skilled.
Merely taking the root alone, except in a very excessive quantity, is
not going to kill you, but if it is taken in conjunction with some other
plant, yes, it will kill you.

DM: So the practitioner would know these things. Would the practitioner
also know an antidote?

MP: Yes.

DM: Have you ever heard of a practitioner proving his/her skill by making
someone appear to be dead in a ceremony and then later having
them wake up, like they've come back to life?

MP: I have heard of those cases but I have not been present when that
kind of skill has been performed. But yes, there are instances when
that has happened. Basically, what you have here is someone who
has knowledge of how to use certain types of fish bladders, or certain
chemicals from fish, used in combination with certain plants. When
taken in certain quantities, which only the practitioner knows, it has
an anesthetic effect on you. It renders you unconscious for a certain
period of time, until it begins to wear off. You don't even look like
you're breathing. But when you're lying down still, whether you're
breathing or not, the mere fact that you're lying down still produces
a degree of fear in the people that they are not able to go down and
touch the person to verify what actual state the person is in, whether
he is dead or alive. You have the priest who is standing there, boast-

ing that he has done it, and so you fear that if you even touch the person, it will bring the wrath of the priest on you. So you don't touch the person. You stand aside in fear, just to observe what is going on. Because the practitioner knows what he is doing, he knows the amount of time that must elapse before he administers the antidote. He knows the timing of all of this, so he is able to do it cleverly without the people knowing what he has actually done.

DM: So if you wanted to poison someone, you might be able to find a practitioner who would give you a poison and instructions on how to use it?

MP: Yes, if you have the right amount of money.

DM: In what form would the poison most likely be in?

MP: It could be a powder or the calabar fruit. For you to be able to do this, you have to know the kind of food this person is going to eat, what he likes. You have to know his behaviors and have access to the person you intend to poison for these things to work.

DM: One of the documents mentions that some people allow a fingernail to grow long and keep a poisonous paste under their fingernail. When they hand the person a drink, they dip their finger in the drink, the poison dissolves, and the person is killed. Have you ever heard of such a practice?

MP: Yes. It's a very common practice among Africans, especially among Nigerians in the Niger delta. The practitioners grow their nails long enough to be able to put some poison underneath their nails, and if you watch during a ceremony, they usually sit close to the victim. That is, someone drinks the wine and passes the gourd to the other person. He drinks and passes the gourd to the next person. The person who is going to poison you will make sure that he has drunk down the wine so much that when he gives you the gourd, you will have to finish the entire thing. So you can watch by the way people hold their calabash or gourd. Depending on what fingernail has the poison in it, that finger is always above the glass. But they are so skilled, that just tapping your finger on top of the gourd will allow the poison to drop from your nails without actually dipping you finger into it. They practice these things, and they know how to do it.

DM: So they would make sure that they were drinking before the victim, drink it down so the victim would have to finish it and nobody else would get it, and while they were holding the gourd, tap their finger so the poison falls into the gourd?

MP: Yes, if you intend it for only one specific person. In most cases, after the victim has taken the drink, the practitioner usually breaks the gourd, making it look like an accident, so that someone else would not use it. At many ceremonies people bring their own drinking gourds so that they do not have to share it, making it impossible for poisoning.

DM: So this is a fairly common practice, if people bring their own cups.

MP: Yes.

DM: Have you ever known people who were poisoned, or suspected of being poisoned?

MP: Yes. Basically, when you have a disagreement with another fellow over a piece of land, or because he's seeing your wife, or you don't want your daughter to marry the person, but usually it's over property that people usually poison over. There was a case of a close relative of mine being poisoned while drinking in the company of someone with whom he had a dispute. Luckily, he didn't die, because he had other people around who recognized what happened and immediately administered the antidote.

DM: How did they know what type of poison it was?

MP: Because when the person fell down in the midst of other people, they knew he was a healthy man and he was in the presence of someone with whom he had a dispute. So they immediately suspected poison and questioned the man, who told them what kind of poison it was and gave them the antidote. Afterwards, the poisoner is usually punished by the village, by society. In this case, his sanction was not to practice his art within the community again.

DM: These documents also mention that people are able to locate stolen articles through the use of a practitioner. Have you ever heard of that?

MP: Yes. As a matter of fact, that is one of the most common reasons why people go to those practitioners. They tell you that they can see into the past and the future. There have been cases where people go to these practitioners to recover their missing property. The practitioner would be able to tell you who stole it and where it was.

DM: Have you ever heard of a murderer being revealed through Obeah?

MP: Yes. Some members of my family have experienced that. When one member of my family died, some other members wanted to find out who killed him. So he went to this priest, who had a bowl of water in which, after invoking certain spirits and giving the client a potion, the water begins to look like a mirror, which we call a looking glass, where the priest is able to see who did it. Or the dead relative appears in the looking glass and he tells you who did it. The process of punishing the murderer is not a jungle justice kind of thing. You take your case to the chief of your village, who will launch an investigation to make sure that your allegation against the man is right. And then you will call the priest you went to, who will testify that he saw the guilty person. If the murderer denies it, you have to produce evidence that he did it, because the punishment is death, usually by tying stones around their legs and dumping them into the sea.

DM: What kind of evidence is accepted?

MP: If the juju man comes in to prove that this is how the murderer killed the person, this is accepted. There need not be any physical evidence. But it has to be shown beyond a reasonable doubt, so that the murderer will admit that he did it. It cannot be just your word against mine. If he continues to deny it, he's forced to take an oath administered by a more powerful juju practitioner. It is believed that the juju oath will kill him after a specified period of time if he is lying. Moreover, the person becomes an outcast from society, which is almost a fate worse than death.

DM: Have you ever heard of any practices regarding eggs?

MP: Eggs and chickens are always common instruments of Obeah. In fact there is a saying among the easterners of Nigeria, that if you have wine and a chicken in your hands, the voice of God and the voice of man are in agreement. If you are going to the Obeah man to seek a favor, you must show some appreciation of what the spirits are doing for you. The wine and chicken are a gift to the spirits. They are sacrificed for the spirit. The blood of the chicken is always in the ground and some libation [spilling] of the wine that you gave as a supplication to the gods.

DM: So if you asked the Obeah man to concoct a poison, you might also invoke the spirits while you were doing that?

MP: Yes. Africans believe as strongly in spirits as the Westerner does. You can see the similarities between the Catholic Good and Evil, the God and the Devil, and the African beliefs. They believe in Good and Evil too. If you want something good to happen, you go to the god of Good; if you want something evil to happen, you go to the god of Evil. The Obeah man can invoke either one. He can invoke the god of Good to bring you good luck, and he can invoke the god of Evil to bring you bad luck.

DM: Do you see any other similarities between what you read in these documents and practices in Africa?

MP: Everything you see in this chapter is based on African religious beliefs. The West Indian religious beliefs are like the African beliefs. It is a direct transplantation from Africa to the Caribbean. Some plants were also brought over from Africa with the slaves, and other plants in the Caribbean were similar because of the similar climate. And people who are inquisitive will always find an alternative to whatever plants they need. And there may have been a disproportionate number of Obeah practitioners sent to the New World, because they were often punished in Africa by being sent into slavery, especially when they are considered a threat to the rulers of the society. So many of these practitioners ended up in the Caribbean.

DM: How do you explain the fact that these practices survived almost intact in the Caribbean, but not in the United States, except in places where there has been Caribbean immigration?

MP: The only explanation I have is the latitude of freedom the slaves were given in the Caribbean, such as being allowed to have a garden plot and grow whatever they like. There is a tendency to grow things that you know will be useful to you, even arsenic or bitter cassava. It's like you, being a college professor. You will always find where the bookstore is around you so you can use it.

DM: Do you think the difference in climate was a factor?

MP: It would have to be a factor, because certain plants and trees that would grow in a tropical area would never grow in a temperate area.

DM: I think we've covered most of the information on Obeah, but I did want to ask you a question about missionaries. Part of this chapter deals with missionary activities in the British West Indies, especially the Moravians and the Methodists in Antigua. Did you see a similar kind of activity with missionaries of other denominations in your part of West Africa? Was Christianity attractive to West Africans?

MP: The acceptance of foreign religion was imposed. If you see how the missionaries were able to convert Africans to Christianity, you will see that there is always the psychological use of fear. If you do this, you will go to hell, which is the same thing the Obeah man uses. If you do this, you will suffer the consequences. So Western religion was not readily accepted, because it forced Africans to distance themselves from ancestral worship, but over time it became an acceptable thing, because you didn't really have much choice. But over time there has been some integration of the two religions. You leave church and go straight to the Obeah man's house. I am a Catholic myself, but I have gone to some of these traditional religious leaders. There really isn't a contradiction. Before the white man came, Africans believed in God, in a Supreme Being, before Christianity came in. The two religions are actually compatible.

DM: So Annie John's mother going to the Methodist church on Sundays and seeing an Obeah woman later is not a contradiction?

MP: No, it is not a contradiction, and it is quite common in the Caribbean and in Africa. I practice it. Until 1960, for example, drums were not allowed in Catholic churches, because it was believed that the drums invoked the devil. But now drums are used in the churches. The line between the two religions is now blurred.

DM: Can you talk a little about the healing, the good things, that these practitioners do?

MP: Before Westerners came to Africa with their doctors, we had our own doctors. The white men call them "bush doctors," and the practice, "bush medicine." Like in the Caribbean, some Obeah men are healers, but not all healers are Obeah men. These healers—so-called bush doctors—have knowledge of plants with medicinal values, and some are able to combine them with good or evil purposes, so some healers also make very good juju priests or Obeah masters.

DM: What kinds of illnesses can they cure?

MP: Malaria is a common disease. You can bathe in a certain combination of plants and roots that is supposed to wash that illness out of you. I had that bath when I had malaria. It helped by reducing my fever. There are also plants that can heal broken bones by making a paste after setting the bone. These plants can also cure other illnesses. You can drink them or bathe in them, as prescribed by the healer.

DM: It sounds to me like there are many similarities between what we see in the Caribbean and West African practices. What we see in these documents was something that was transplanted directly from Africa.

MP: Well, to that I can only say that they took them out of Africa but they did not take Africa out of them. No matter how long they have been out of Africa, they are still Africans.

Interview with author, Haverhill, Mass., October 5, 1997.

STUDY QUESTIONS

1. Describe the attitudes toward Obeah expressed by the white writers who describe these practices. Why do you think they were skeptical? What were the attitudes of missionaries? Does the document written by the anthropologists coincide with or contradict the earlier descriptions of Obeah?

2. The Nigerian interviewee confirms that many of the practices described in these documents are similar to West African practices. Why do you think so many beliefs, among oppressed slaves, survived for hundreds of years, across the ocean in the New World? Why have they survived in the Caribbean and not in the United States (except in places with large Caribbean immigrant populations)?

3. Why do you think Christianity caught on so well in the Caribbean among the black population? What beliefs would be particularly appealing to this population?

4. How does Samuel Smith's view of organized religion differ from that of the white Protestants? What are the grounds for his criticisms? Do you agree with him? Why or why not?

TOPICS FOR WRITTEN OR ORAL EXPLORATION

1. Research information on other African-based religious practices, such as Santería and voodoo, and compare them to Obeah. What are the significant similarities and differences? What African beliefs is each system based on?

2. How do you think it is possible for Annie John's mother, and many others, to adhere to beliefs in both Christianity and Obeah? Do they contradict each other? How can one reconcile the differences?

3. Research information on herbal remedies used here in the United States. Are any of them similar to "bush medicine" as described in these documents? See if you can find information on the study of plants that can be used for pharmaceutical purposes. Do you think there are many other plants, in such places as the Amazon rainforest, that are currently unknown to the Western world but that may have medicinal properties?

4. Do you notice any similarities between beliefs described in these documents and popular "superstitions" here in the United States? Give a few examples.

5. Do you think the Obeah beliefs have any validity? Do you think they work? Why or why not?

6. Discuss the pros and cons of missionary work, of trying to convert people to a different religion. What do the missionaries gain or lose? What do the converts gain or lose? For example, why do you think the Moravian missionary emphasizes that the converted slaves are more docile and better behaved? Is this a positive result?

SUGGESTED READINGS

See the full text of works excerpted in this section. This list includes general works on religion in the Caribbean, as well as a sampling of works on West African religion, African-American religion, voodoo, Santería, and Christianity.

Baer, Hans A., and Merrill Singer. *African American Religion in the Twentieth Century*. Knoxville: University of Tennessee Press, 1992.

Barrett, Leonard E. *Soul Force: African Heritage in Afro-American Religion*. Garden City, N.Y.: Anchor Press/Doubleday, 1974.

Bastide, Roger. *African Civilisations in the New World*. Translated by Peter Green. New York: Harper and Row, 1971.

Cooper, Donald B. *The Establishment of the Anglican Church in the Leeward Islands*. Stillwater: Oklahoma State University Press, 1966.

Courlander, Harold. *The Drum and the Hoe: Life and Lore of the Haitian People*. Berkeley: University of California Press, 1985.

Ferguson, Moira, ed. *The Hart Sisters: Early African Caribbean Writers, Evangelicals, and Radicals*. Lincoln: University of Nebraska Press, 1993. Contains a history of Methodism in Antigua.

Gonzalez-Wippler, Migene. *The Santeria Experience*. Englewood Cliffs, N.J.: Prentice-Hall, 1982.

Haskins, James. *Witchcraft, Mysticism and Magic in the Black World*. Garden City, N.Y.: Doubleday, 1974.

Laguerre, Michel. *Voodoo Heritage*. Beverly Hills, Calif.: Sage Publications, 1980.

McCartney, Timothy. *Ten, Ten the Bible Ten: Obeah in the Bahamas*. Nassau, Bahamas: Timpaul Publishing Company, 1976.

Murphy, Joseph M. *Santeria: African Spirits in America*. Boston: Beacon Press, 1992.

———. *Working the Spirit: Ceremonies of the African Diaspora*. Boston: Beacon Press, 1994.

4

A Colonial Education: The Christopher Columbus Controversy

In the 1960s, when Annie John was in school, Antigua followed the British educational system designed for its West Indian colonies. Annie's curriculum emphasized European history and culture, particularly of Great Britain, and British literature, such as Milton's *Paradise Lost*. Children studied West Indian history from a British colonial perspective. Children were taught to revere Christopher Columbus as a great man and the founder of their island, despite the fact that their ancestors were victims of the slave trade initiated in the Caribbean by Columbus and his followers. This disparity between the official lessons learned in school and the popular, oral knowledge of roots and heritage can lead to confusion in the minds of bright young girls like Annie John. What is at stake here is not just the interpretation of history but the values imparted by the educational system and their impact on the formation of identity in young people like Annie.

One important purpose of education is the socialization of the child, that is, the child's initiation into his or her culture. Through education, children learn who they are and their place in their society. When foreign values and perspectives are taught and respected, rather than native ones, the native culture comes to be seen as somehow inferior—and by extension, the native people as well. So a colonial education can establish strong feelings of inferiority within a child's psyche, as well as the sense that his or her own culture is inferior to the one taught in school (in this case, the British culture). Annie John's rebellion in school, particularly her defacing of the Columbus illustration, can be seen as a rebellion against a system that does not recognize its students' own history, culture, and values. One critic of colonial education succinctly explains the effects of a colonial education system that "transmits foreign cultural values of the imperial power to the native population: In a colonial society the purpose of education, the initiation of a child into his culture, became distorted since it was the values of a foreign culture which had to be taught while the native tradition was derided or ignored. Colonial education separated people from their environment, taught them dependence and destroyed their self-worth" (Drayton, viii).

The Columbus incident at Annie's school is a case in point. Schoolchildren everywhere, Annie included, have been taught that Columbus was a great hero, an exceptional navigator and explorer, and the discoverer and founder of the New World. During the lesson on Columbus's second voyage, the English student, Ruth, does not know the date that Columbus discovered the island of Dominica. Schoolchildren in the West Indies would have been taught this fact many times in their classes on West Indian history, just as Americans learned the important names and dates in U.S. history. The difference in Ruth's education leads Annie to contemplate the injustices of slavery visited upon them by the British and her own confusion over the contradiction between her own view of history and that of the school. She thinks that she cannot tell the side on which she really belongs, the masters or the slaves, because now everyone celebrates Queen Victoria's birthday (and by extension, European history, including Columbus), even the descendants of slaves, who are well aware of their origins as victims of that history. This contradiction between the official values taught in the schools and the popular values of the people, "who knew quite well what had really happened" (Kincaid, 76), culminates in Annie's dislike of Columbus, despite what her teachers and the official textbooks say. When she sees the picture of Columbus being brought back to Spain in chains after his third voyage, Annie is happy to see Columbus, usually pictured as triumphant, humbled and brought down. To Annie, it seems a just punishment for the explorer, whose travels resulted in the extermination of the

Caribs (her mother's heritage) and in Caribbean slavery, to no longer be able to "just get up and go" (Kincaid, 78).

Her punishment for defacing the textbook, and for the arrogance and blasphemy of defaming the great Columbus, exemplifies the European colonial values the school emphasizes—Annie is made to copy long portions of a famous work of British literature, *Paradise Lost*. There are two ironies at work in Annie's punishment. Often the Caribbean is seen as a "paradise lost" since the arrival of Columbus, and Milton's Lucifer character offers Annie a prime example of defiance and rebellion. (Jamaica Kincaid has remarked that she named the main character of her next book Lucy after the Lucifer of *Paradise Lost*. This novel is often regarded as a sequel to *Annie John*, after the girl leaves Antigua and travels to New York rather than England.)

Christopher Columbus is used in the book as a symbol of the contradictions of a colonial education. Annie is taught the official, positive attitude toward Columbus in school, despite widespread negative attitudes in the Caribbean. Now, thirty years have passed since Annie was a student in a colonial Antigua. Since then Antigua has gained its independence from Great Britain, and the educational system has been slowly changing to reflect Caribbean values. On the eve of the 500th anniversary of Columbus's arrival in the Caribbean, one journalist remarked that one important aspect of independence is local control of the curriculum in the schools, because

> Caribbeans want to put history right. One of the benefits of independence that is deeply valued by many Caribbeans is control of the school systems. Until independence, Jamaican schoolchildren learned more about England and France than they did about Trinidad and Barbados. They learned little about that fact that . . . there was a slave rebellion, or at least the very real threat of one, almost every year. These things are part of their oral tradition, the stories children are told at night, but there was little of them in schools. . . . Caribbeans were taught that while Europeans were doing great things, their own ancestors were working in the fields. Many saw their only choices to be either rejecting education entirely or being molded by a colonial education that rejected their own world. . . . It was an education designed to make the students feel inferior. They learned that they were underlings, that greatness was elsewhere, in France and England and Spain. Important things were

always achieved by white foreigners. Caribbeans were expected to admire men who had owned and traded their ancestors. (Kurlansky, 14–15)

So is Columbus a hero or a villain, or somewhere in between? Whose point of view do we believe? In the years surrounding the Columbus quincentennial of 1992, the figure of Columbus became controversial in the United States as well as the Caribbean for many of the reasons alluded to in *Annie John*. Spain led the move to celebrate what came to be politely and euphemistically called "the encounter" between cultures, while others began to call it a "holocaust"; still others wanted to keep the traditional, European-oriented word *discovery* despite the fact that there were millions of indigenous people in the New World who had already "discovered" it and settled there long before Columbus. This time period is rich with articles analyzing the impact of Columbus's voyages, with a wide range of opinions and interpretations.

Before beginning to examine the documents to determine the significance of Annie's attitude, it would be helpful to summarize the less controversial historical facts surrounding Columbus's life.

Christopher Columbus was born in Genoa, Italy, in 1451 and became an accomplished sailor and navigator. Columbus formulated the idea that one could reach the Far East by sailing west. He called this project the "Enterprise of the Indies" and looked for a sponsor to finance the trip. After several years, he received support from Queen Isabella of Spain. In exchange for making this voyage, Spain agreed to give Columbus extensive rewards. He was to become Admiral of the Ocean Sea and Viceroy and Governor-General over whatever lands he discovered. He was to receive 10 percent of any treasures obtained—such as gold, silver, pearls, spices—tax free. He was to be allowed to make a one-eighth investment in future voyages to the new lands. All of these titles and privileges would be hereditary.

On October 12, 1492, Columbus arrived in the Caribbean and encountered the local inhabitants, who were called Arawaks (sometimes called Taínos). Columbus named them Indians because he thought he had reached the East Indies. In December he reached the island of Hispaniola and met a helpful Indian leader, or cacique, Guacanagari. When the *Santa María* ran aground, Columbus decided to use the wood to build a settlement, left some Spaniards behind, then returned in triumph to Spain.

Six months later, in 1493, Columbus began his second voyage with explicit instructions: to convert the natives to Christianity, to establish a trading colony, and to determine if Cuba was the eastern portion of Asia. On this voyage, Columbus sighted the islands mentioned in Annie's history lesson—Dominica, Montserrat, Antigua, Nevis, St. Kitts, forty-six of the Virgin Islands, Marie Galante, Guadeloupe, St. Croix, and Puerto Rico. On St. Croix, they fought with the natives, leaving one Spaniard and one Carib killed. When they reached Hispaniola, they found the settlement at Navidad destroyed and all the Spaniards dead. According to some friendly natives, the Spaniards had left the settlement and had become extremely aggressive, taking gold and women. A local cacique named Caonabo had taken his revenge, killing all the Spaniards from the settlement. Now mutual suspicion grew between the natives and the Spaniards.

Before sailing off to explore Cuba and leaving his brother Diego in charge of Hispaniola, Columbus established a new settlement and an inland fort, left under the command of Pedro Margarit and, later, Alonso de Hojeda. These two men further damaged relations with the locals. Hojeda cut off the ears of one native for stealing some clothes, while Margarit roamed around, capturing boys as slave labor and girls as sex slaves for his men.

After exploring Cuba and concluding that it was, indeed, Asia, Columbus returned to Hispaniola to find trouble brewing. Margarit was angry at Columbus's brother Diego for trying to stop his depredations against the natives. Margarit was joined by priest Fray Buil who returned to Spain to give the Queen a negative report on Columbus.

Columbus was having trouble finding gold, so to compensate, he decided to enslave the natives. Five hundred were shipped to Spain. Two hundred died at sea; the others were sold in Seville. The remaining captives who were not chosen for the voyage scrambled to escape, with some mothers even abandoning their infants in their haste. Over the next year, the Spaniards fought battles against the natives and consolidated their control over them. After the natives were pacified, the Spaniards instituted a gold tribute to be found and delivered every three months. Any native who did not comply was subject to having his or her hands cut off. There was little gold, so it was impossible to meet the tribute, and natives' lives were made miserable. Many tried to starve the Spaniards out by refusing to grow crops and hiding in the mountains. But the Spaniards received supplies from abroad while the natives starved. Many were hunted down by vicious dogs and either killed or recaptured. Others committed suicide, principally by drinking the poisonous bitter cassava root (which the slaves who arrived later were also to use). It has been estimated that Hispaniola's native population declined by one-third to one-half between 1494 and 1496 (and within fifty years the natives disappeared). Columbus returned to Spain with thirty slaves, including Caonabo, who died at sea.

In 1498, two years later, Columbus made his third voyage and arrived in Hispaniola to face a rebellion by Francisco Roldán and other men. Eventually, Columbus granted them amnesty, but many negative reports about Columbus reached the Queen's ears. She sent Francisco de Bobadilla to investigate the situation, giving him full authority, even over Columbus. When Bobadilla reached Hispaniola in 1500, he saw seven executed Spaniards on the gallows, with five more executions scheduled, all for rebellion and atrocities. Columbus's brother Diego was in charge, while Columbus and his brother Bartholomew were off exploring. Bobadilla arrested Diego, then Columbus and Bartholomew as well, and had them all put in chains and shipped home to Spain.

On Hispaniola, the Spaniards began the system of *repartimiento*, later called *encomienda*, in which the settlers were given control over land and all the natives on it, to use however they pleased. The natives accepted it because they wished to be released from paying the gold tribute.

Columbus successfully defended himself to the Queen and made a fourth voyage in 1502, but the monarchs had ended Columbus's political authority in Hispaniola by appointing Nicolás de Ovando as governor of the islands. (Jamaica Kincaid published a scathing story about this man called "Ovando.") After being marooned off Jamaica for some months, Columbus was reluctantly received by Ovando in Hispaniola, then returned to Spain in 1504. He died in 1506 (see Wilford; the summary of the life of Columbus is based on his book).

Columbus's status as a great man and explorer has shifted over the years since his death. After his first voyage, he was a great hero.

After subsequent voyages, his reputation became somewhat tarnished. Around 1692, the British colonists in North America began to praise Columbus, although there was no formal celebration. In the eighteenth century, the District of Columbia and Columbia University were named after Columbus, and the tricentennial was celebrated in several places. Washington Irving's praise of Columbus began the rise in Columbus's reputation in the nineteenth century. There were widespread celebrations in 1892 in the United States—even a move to confer sainthood on Columbus in France (which was squelched because Columbus never married his son Ferdinand's mother, Beatriz Enríquez de Haraña).

In the twentieth century, with the decline of European colonialism, the negative aspects of Columbus the hero and Columbus the explorer have been expressed more and more frequently, in both the United States and the newly independent Caribbean. Many of the descendants of the original native tribes (although they are few—mostly Caribs in Dominica, like Jamaica Kincaid's mother) and the descendants of slaves (like Annie John) have been strongly opposed to the glorification of Columbus.

In the Caribbean, as in the United States, the debate over Columbus continues. The documents that follow present many sides of this issue and help to explain the educational environment in which Annie lived as well as her attitude toward Columbus and the Eurocentric view of Caribbean history taught in her school.

A TRADITIONAL VIEW OF COLUMBUS

The first document is a short excerpt from an old history textbook. It shows the traditional approach to Columbus, like the one that Annie John would have read in her West Indian history textbooks. Notice the laudatory attitude mixed with regret that Columbus was not compensated adequately in his lifetime for his remarkable feat. This writer also mentions Washington Irving's biography of Columbus, which greatly influenced nineteenth-century attitudes toward Columbus, an attitude that filtered its way down to history textbooks for the next hundred years.

FROM GEORGE BANCROFT, *HISTORY OF THE UNITED STATES, FROM THE DISCOVERY OF THE AMERICAN CONTINENT* (1841)

The enterprise of Columbus, the most memorable maritime enterprise in the history of the world, formed between Europe and America the communication which will never cease. . . .

Imagination had conceived the idea, that vast inhabited regions lay unexplored in the west; and poets had declared, that empires beyond the ocean would one day be revealed to the daring navigator. But Columbus deserves the undivided glory of having realized that belief. During his lifetime he met with no adequate recompense. The self-love of the Spanish monarch was offended at receiving from a foreigner in his employ benefits too vast for requital; and the contemporaries of the great navigator persecuted the merit which they could not adequately reward. Nor had posterity been mindful to gather into a finished picture the memorials of his career, till the genius of Irving, with candor, liberality, and original research, made a record of his eventful life, and in mild but enduring colors sketched his sombre inflexibility of purpose, his deep religious enthusiasm, and the disinterested magnanimity of his character. . . . The magnificent achievement of Columbus, revealing the wonderful truth, of which the germs may have existed in the imagination of every thoughtful mariner, won the admiration which was due to an enterprise that seemed more divine than human, and kindled in the breasts of the emulous a vehement desire to gain as signal renown in the same career of daring.

Boston: Charles C. Little and James Brown, 1841, 1: 5–8.

WASHINGTON IRVING'S VIEW OF CHRISTOPHER COLUMBUS

Washington Irving, the famous American author of such works as "The Legend of Sleepy Hollow," also wrote an influential, three-volume biography of Christopher Columbus, calling him intrepid, constant, heroic, and courageous. Published in the mid-nineteenth century, Irving's work reflects the positive attitudes toward Columbus mixed with the antislavery attitudes of that time period. Irving elaborates, in detail, many of the cruelties visited upon the natives but tries to rationalize Columbus's actions by comparing them to the dominant European values of the time, particularly those regarding slavery.

This work had a great influence on attitudes toward Columbus for the next few decades and influenced many interpretations of Columbus to be found in history textbooks. These attitudes were most likely similar to those expressed in Annie's history textbooks as well.

FROM WASHINGTON IRVING, *THE LIFE AND VOYAGES OF CHRISTOPHER COLUMBUS; TO WHICH ARE ADDED THOSE OF HIS COMPANIONS* (1868)

It is the object of the following work to relate the deeds and fortunes of the mariner who first had the judgment to divine, and the intrepidity to brave the mysteries of this perilous deep; and who, by his hardy genious, his inflexible constancy, and his heroic courage, brought the ends of the earth into communication with each other. The narrative of his troubled life is the link which connects the history of the old world with that of the new. (1:11)

• • •

[On the second voyage] . . . it was determined, therefore, to send home his brother Diego, to attend to the wishes of the sovereigns, and to take care of his interests at court. At the same time, he exerted himself to the utmost to send by the ships satisfactory proofs of the value of his discoveries. He remitted by them all the gold that he could collect, with specimens of other metals, and of various fruits and valuable plants, which he had collected either in Hispaniola or in the course of his voyage. In his eagerness to procure immediate profit, and to indemnify the sovereigns for those expenses which bore hard upon the royal treasury, he sent, likewise, about five hundred Indian prisoners, who, he suggested, might by sold as slaves at Seville.

It is painful to find the brilliant renown of Columbus sullied by so foul a stain. The customs of the times, however, must be pleaded in his apology. The precedent had been given long before, by both Spaniards and Portuguese, in their African discoveries, wherein the traffic in slaves had formed one of the greatest sources of profit. In fact, the practice had been sanctioned by the Church itself, and the most learned theologians had pronounced all barbarous and infidel nations, who shut their ears to the truths of Christianity, fair objects of war and rapine, of captivity and slavery. If Columbus needed any practical illustration of this doctrine, he had it in the conduct of Ferdinand himself, in his late wars with the Moors of Granada, in which he had always been surrounded by a crowd of ghostly advisers, and had professed to do everything for the glory and advancement of the faith. In this holy war, as it was termed, it was a common practice to make inroads into the Moorish territories and carry off *cavalgadas*, not merely of flocks and herds, but of human beings, and those not warriors taken with weapons in their hands, but quiet villagers, laboring peasantry, and helpless women and children. These were carried to the mart at Seville, or to other populous towns, and sold into slavery. The capture of Malaga was a memorable instance, where, as a punishment for an obstinate and brave defense, which should have excited admiration rather than revenge, eleven thousand people of both sexes, and of all ranks and ages, many of them highly cultivated and delicately reared, were suddenly torn from their homes, severed from each other, and swept into menial slavery, even though half of their ransoms had been paid. These circumstances are not advanced to vindicate, but to palliate the conduct of Columbus. He acted in conformity to the customs of the times, and was sanctioned by the example of the sovereign under whom he served. Las Casas, the zealous and enthusiastic advocate of the Indians, who suffers no opportunity to escape him of exclaiming in vehement terms against their slavery, speaks with indulgence of Columbus on this head. If those pious and learned men, he observes, whom the sovereigns took for guides and instructors, were so ignorant of the injustice of this practice, it is no wonder that the unlettered admiral should not be conscious of its impropriety.   (2:39)

• • •

Having been forced to take the field by the confederacy of the caciques [Indian leaders], Columbus now asserted the right of a conqueror, and considered how he might turn his conquest to most profit. His constant

anxiety was to make wealthy returns for Spain, for the purpose of indem-
nifying the sovereigns for their great expenses; of meeting the public
expectations, so extravagantly excited; and above all, of silencing the cal-
umnies of those who had gone home determined to make the most discouraging representations of his discoveries. He endeavored, therefore,
to raise a large and immediate revenue, by imposing heavy tributes on
the subjected provinces. In those of the Vega, Cibao, and all the region
of the mines, each individual above the age of fourteen years was required to pay, every three months, the measure of a Flemish hawks'-bell
of gold dust. The caciques had to pay a much larger amount for their
personal tribute. Manicaotex, the brother of Caonabo, was obliged individually to render in, every three months, half a calabash of gold, amount-
ing to one hundred and fifty pesos. In those districts which were distant
from the mines, and produced no gold, each individual was required to
furnish an arroba (twenty-five pounds) of cotton every three months.
Each Indian, on rendering this tribute, received a copper medal as a
certificate of payment, which he was to wear suspended round his neck:
those who were found without such documents were liable to arrest and
punishment. . . .

In this way was the yoke of servitude fixed upon the island, and its
thralldom effectually insured. Deep despair now fell upon the natives
when they found a perpetual task inflicted upon them, enforced at stated
and frequently recurring periods. Weak and indolent by nature, unused
to labor of any kind, and brought up in the untasked idleness of their
soft climate and their fruitful groves, death itself seemed preferable to a
life of toil and anxiety. They saw no end to this harassing evil, which had
so suddenly fallen upon them; no escape from its all-pervading influence;
no prospect of return to that roving independence and ample leisure, so
dear to the wild inhabitants of the forest. The pleasant life of the island
was at an end; the dream in the shade by day; the slumber during the
sultry noontide heat by the fountain or the stream, or under the spreading palm-tree; and the song, the dance, and the game in the mellow
evening, when summoned to their simple amusements by the rude Indian drum. They were now obliged to grope day by day, with bending
body and anxious eye along the borders of their rivers, sifting the sands
for the grains of gold which every day grew more scanty; or to labor in
their fields beneath the fervor of a tropical sun, to raise food for their
taskmasters, or to produce the vegetable tribute imposed upon them.
They sank to sleep weary and exhausted at night, with the certainty that
the next day was but to be a repetition of the same toil and suffering. Or
if they occasionally indulged in their national dances, the ballads to which
they kept time were of a melancholy and plaintive character. They spoke
of the times that were past, before the white men had introduced sorrow,

and slavery, and weary labor among them; and they rehearsed pretended prophecies, handed down from their ancestors, foretelling the invasion of the Spaniards; that strangers should come into their island, clothed in apparel, with swords capable of cleaving a man asunder at a blow, under whose yoke their territory should be subdued. These ballads, or areytos, they sang with mournful tunes and doleful voices, bewailing the loss of their liberty, and their painful servitude. . . .

Finding how vain was all attempt to deliver themselves by warlike means from these invincible intruders, they now concerted a forlorn and desperate mode of annoyance. They perceived that the settlement suffered greatly from shortness of provisions, and depended, in a considerable degree, upon the supplies furnished by the natives. The fortresses in the interior, also, and the Spaniards quartered in the villages, looked almost entirely to them for subsistence. They agreed among themselves, therefore, not to cultivate the fruits, the roots and the maize, their chief articles of food, and to destroy those already growing; hoping, by producing a famine, to starve the strangers from the island. They little knew, observes Las Casas, one of the characteristics of the Spaniards, who, the more hungry they are, the more inflexible they become, and the more hardened to endure suffering. They carried their plan generally into effect, abandoning their habitations, laying waste their fields and groves, and retiring to the mountains, where there were roots and herbs and abundance of utias for their subsistence.

This measure did indeed produce much distress among the Spaniards, but they had foreign resources, and were enabled to endure it by husbanding the partial supplies brought by their ships; the most disastrous effects fell upon the natives themselves. The Spaniards stationed in the various fortresses, finding that there was not only no hope of tribute, but a danger of famine from this wanton waste and sudden desertion, pursued the natives to their retreats, to compel them to return to labor. The Indians took refuge in the most sterile and dreary heights; flying from one wild retreat to another, the women with their children in their arms or at their backs, and all worn out with fatigue and hunger, and harassed by perpetual alarms. In every noise of the forest or the mountain they fancied they heard the sound of their pursuers; they hid themselves in damp and dismal caverns, or in the rocky banks and margins of the torrents, and not daring to hunt, or fish, or even to venture forth in quest of nourishing roots and vegetables, they had to satisfy their raging hunger with unwholesome food. In this way, many thousands of them perished miserably, through famine, fatigue, terror, and various contagious maladies engendered by their sufferings. All spirit of opposition was at length completely quelled. The surviving Indians returned in despair to their habitations, and submitted humbly to the yoke. So deep an awe did they conceive of their conquerors, that it is said a Spaniard might go singly and securely all over the island, and the natives would even transport him from place to place on their shoulders.   (2:47–53)

· · ·

The tidings that a new governor had arrived, and that Columbus was in disgrace, and to be sent home in chains, circulated rapidly through the Vega, and the colonists hastened from all parts to San Domingo to make interest with Bobadilla. It was soon perceived that there was no surer way than that of vilifying his predecessor. Bobadilla felt that he had taken a rash step in seizing upon the government, and that his own safety required the conviction of Columbus. He listened eagerly, therefore, to all accusations, public or private; and welcome was he who could bring any charge, however extravagant, against the admiral and his brothers. . . .

No sooner did Bobadilla hear of his arrival, than he gave orders to put him in irons, and confine him in the fortress. This outrage to a person of such dignified and venerable appearance, and such eminent merit, seemed, for the time, to shock even his enemies. . . .

Columbus conducted himself with characteristic magnanimity under the injuries heaped upon him. There is a noble scorn which swells and supports the heart, and silences the tongue of the truly great, when enduring the insults of the unworthy. Columbus could not stoop to deprecate the arrogance of a weak and violent man like Bobadilla. He looked beyond this shallow agent, and all his petty tyranny, to the sovereigns who had employed him. Their injustice or ingratitude alone could wound his spirit; and he felt assured that when the truth came to be known, they would blush to find how greatly they had wronged him. With this proud assurance, he bore all present indignities in silence. . . .

It has been questioned whether Bobadilla really had authority for the arrest and imprisonment of the admiral and his brothers; and whether such violence and indignity was in any case contemplated by the sovereigns. He may have fancied himself empowered by the clause in the letter of instructions, dated March 21st, 1499, in which, speaking of the rebellion of Roldan, "he is authorised to *seize the persons, and sequestrate the property* of those who appeared to be culpable, and then to proceed against them and against the absent, with the highest civil and criminal penalties." This evidently had reference to the persons of Roldan and his followers, who were then sent in arms, and against whom Columbus had sent home complaints; and this, by a violent construction, Bobadilla seems to have wrested into an authority for seizing the person of the admiral himself. In fact, in the whole course of his proceedings, he reversed and confounded the order of his instructions. His first step should have been to proceed against the rebels; this he made the last. His last step should have been, in case of ample evidence against the admiral, to have superseded him in office; and this he made the first, without waiting for evidence. Having predetermined, from the very outset, that Columbus was in the wrong, by the same rule he had to presume that all the opposite parties were in the right. It became indispensable to his own justification to inculpate the admiral and his brothers; and the rebels he had been sent to judge became, by this singular perversion of rule, necessary and cherished evidence to incriminate those against whom they had rebelled.

The intentions of the crown, however, are not to be vindicated at the expense of its miserable agent. If proper respect had been felt for the rights and dignities of Columbus, Bobadilla would never have been intrusted with powers so extensive, undefined, and discretionary; nor would he have dared to proceed to such lengths, with such rudeness and precipitation, had he not felt assured that it would not be displeasing to the jealous-minded Ferdinand.

The old scenes . . . were now renewed with tenfold virulence, and the old charges revived, with others still more extravagant. From the early and never-to-be-forgotten outrage upon Castilian pride, of compelling hidalgos [prominent men], in time of emergency, to labor in the construction of works necessary to the public safety, down to the recent charge of levying war against the government, there was not a hardship, abuse, nor sedition in the island, that was not imputed to the misdeeds of Columbus and his brothers. Besides the usual accusations of inflicting oppressive labor, unnecessary tasks, painful restrictions, short allowances of food, and cruel punishments upon the Spaniards, and waging unjust wars against the natives, they were now charged with preventing the conversion of the latter, that they might send them slaves to Spain, and profit by their sale. This last charge, so contrary to the pious feelings of the admiral, was founded on his having objected to the baptism of certain Indians of mature age, until they could be instructed in the doctrines of Christianity; justly considering it an abuse of that holy sacrament to administer it thus blindly.

Columbus was charged, also with having secreted pearls, and other precious articles, collected in his voyage along the coast of Paria, and with keeping the sovereigns in ignorance of the nature of his discoveries there, in order to exact new privileges from them: yet it was notorious that he had sent home specimens of the pearls, and journals and charts of his voyage, by which others had been enabled to pursue his track.

Even the late tumults, now that the rebels were admitted as evidence, were all turned into matters of accusation. They were represented as spirited and loyal resistances to tyranny exercised upon the colonists and the natives. The well-merited punishments inflicted upon certain of the ringleaders, were cited as proofs of a cruel and revengeful disposition, and a secret hatred of Spaniards. Bobadilla believed, or affected to believe, all these charges. He had, in a manner, made the rebels his confederates in the ruin of Columbus. It was become a common cause with them. He could no longer, therefore, conduct himself towards them as a judge. Guevara, Requelme, and their fellow-convicts, were discharged almost without the form of a trial, and it is even said, were received into favor and countenance. Roldan, from the very first, had been treated with confidence by Bobadilla, and honored with his correspondence. All the others, whose conduct had rendered them liable to justice, received either a special acquittal or a general pardon. It was enough to have been opposed in any way to Columbus, to obtain full justification in the eyes of Bobadilla.

The latter had now collected a weight of testimony, and produced a crowd of witnesses sufficient, as he conceived, to insure the condemnation of the prisoners, and his own continuance to command. He determined, therefore, to send the admiral and his brothers home in chains, in the vessels ready for sea, transmitting at the same time the inquest taken in their case, and writing private letters, enforcing the charges made against them, and advising that Columbus should on no account be restored to the command, which he had so shamefully abused.

San Domingo now swarmed with miscreants just delivered from the dungeon and the gibbet. It was a perfect jubilee of triumphant villainy and dastardly malice. Every base spirit which had been awed into obsequiousness by Columbus and his brothers when in power, now started up to revenge itself upon them when in chains. The most injurious slanders were loudly proclaimed in the streets; insulting pasquinades and inflammatory libels were posted up at every corner; and horns were blown in the neighborhood of their prisons, to taunt them with the exultings of the rabble. When these rejoicings of the enemy reached him in his dungeon, and Columbus reflected on the inconsiderate violence already exhibited by Bobadilla, he knew not how far his rashness and confidence might carry him, and began to entertain apprehensions for his life. . . . When [Villejo] arrived with a guard to conduct the admiral from the prison to the ship, he found him in chains in a state of silent despondency. So violently had he been treated, and so savage were the passions let loose against him, that he feared he should be sacrificed without an opportunity of being heard, and his name go down sullied and dishonored to posterity. . . . [When Villejo tells Columbus they are to embark for Spain], with these words the admiral was comforted, and felt as one restored from death to life. . . .

The caravels set sail early in October, bearing off Columbus, shackled like the vilest of culprits, amidst the scoffs and shouts of a miscreant rabble, who took a brutal joy in heaping insults on his venerable head, and sent curses after him from the shores of the island he had so recently added to the civilized world. Fortunately the voyage was favorable, and of but moderate duration, and was rendered less disagreeable by the conduct of those to whom he was given in custody. The worthy Villejo, though in the service of Fonseca, felt deeply moved at the treatment of Columbus. The master of the caravel, Andreas Martin, was equally grieved: they both treated the admiral with profound respect and assiduous attention. They would have taken off his irons, but to this he would not consent. "No," said he proudly, "their majesties commanded me by letter to submit to whatever Bobadilla should order in their name; by their authority he has put upon me these chains, I will wear them until they shall order them to be taken off, and I will preserve them afterwards as relics and memorials of the reward of my services."

"He did so," adds his son Fernando; "I saw them always hanging in his cabinet, and he requested that when he died they might be buried with him!"

The arrival of Columbus at Cadiz, a prisoner and in chains, produced almost as great a sensation as his triumphant return from his first voyage. It was one of those striking and obvious facts, which speak to the feelings of the multitude, and preclude the necessity of reflection. No one stopped to inquire into the case. It was sufficient to be told that Columbus was brought home in irons from the world he had discovered. There was a general burst of indignation in Cadiz, and in the powerful and opulent Seville, which was echoed throughout all Spain. If the ruin of Columbus had been the intention of his enemies, they had defeated their object by their own violence. One of those reactions took place, so frequent in the public mind, when persecution is pushed to an unguarded length. Those of the populace who had recently been loud in their clamor against Columbus, were now as loud in their reprobation of his treatment, and a strong sympathy was expressed, against which it would have been odious for the government to contend. . . .

When [Columbus's letter to the sovereigns] was read to the noble-minded Isabella, and she found how grossly Columbus had been wronged and the royal authority abused, her heart was filled with mingled sympathy and indignation. . . .

However Ferdinand might have secretly felt disposed against Columbus, the momentary tide of public feeling was not to be resisted. He joined with his generous queen in her reprobation of the treatment of the admiral, and both sovereigns hastened to give evidence to the world, that his imprisonment had been without their authority, and contrary to their wishes. Without waiting to receive any documents that might arrive from Bobadilla, they sent orders to Cadiz that the prisoners should be instantly set at liberty, and treated with all distinction. They wrote a letter to Columbus, couched in terms of gratitude and affection, expressing their grief at all that he had suffered, and inviting him to court. They ordered, at the same time, that two thousand ducats should be advanced to defray his expenses.   (2:294–309)

3 vols. New York: G. P. Putnam and Son, 1868, 1: 11, 2: 39, 47–53, 294–309.

A REVISIONIST VIEW OF COLUMBUS

The following document, published in the year of the Columbus quincentennial, offers a revisionist view of the history of Columbus's "discovery," focusing on the annihilation of the Native Americans that was initiated by Columbus's arrival and calling it an "American Holocaust." In the eloquent prologue to the book, David Stannard outlines the reasons why this history is so important. In this document, he echoes Annie John's attitude toward Columbus's arrival and spells out the reasons why he holds this point of view.

FROM DAVID E. STANNARD, *AMERICAN HOLOCAUST: THE CONQUEST OF THE NEW WORLD* (1992)

[From the Prologue:]

In the darkness of an early July morning in 1945, on a desolate spot in the New Mexico desert named after a John Donne sonnet celebrating the Holy Trinity, the first atomic bomb was exploded. J. Robert Oppenheimer later remembered that the immense flash of light, followed by the thunderous roar, caused a few observers to laugh and others to cry. But most, he said, were silent. Oppenheimer himself recalled at that instant a line from the Bhagavad-Gita:

I am become death,
the shatterer of worlds.

There is no reason to think that anyone on board the *Niña*, the *Pinta*, or the *Santa María*, on an equally dark early morning four and a half centuries earlier, thought of those ominous lines from the ancient Sanskrit poem when the crews of the Spanish ships spied a flicker of light on the windward side of the island they would name after the Holy Saviour. But the intuition, had it occurred, would have been as appropriate then as it was when that first nuclear blast rocked the New Mexico desert sands.

In both instances—at the Trinity test site in 1945 and at San Salvador in 1492—those moments of achievement crowned years of intense personal struggle and adventure for their protagonists and were culminating points of ingenious technological achievement for their countries. But both instances also were prelude to orgies of human destructiveness that, each in its own way, attained a scale of devastation not previously witnessed in the entire history of the world.

Just twenty-one days after the first atomic test in the desert, the Japanese industrial city of Hiroshima was leveled by nuclear blast; never before had so many people—at least 130,000, probably many more—died from a single explosion. Just twenty-one years after Columbus's first landing in the Caribbean, the vastly populous island that the explorer had renamed Hispaniola was effectively desolate; nearly 8,000,000 people—those Columbus chose to call Indians—had been killed by violence, disease, and despair. It took a little longer, about the span of a single human generation, but what happened on Hispaniola was the equivalent of more than fifty Hiroshimas. And Hispaniola was only the beginning.

With no more than a handful of generations following their first encounters with Europeans, the vast majority of the Western Hemisphere's native peoples had been exterminated. The pace and magnitude of their obliteration varied from place to place and from time to time, but for years now historical demographers have been uncovering, in region upon region, post-Columbian depopulation rates of between 90 and 98 percent with such regularity that an overall decline of 95 percent has become a working rule of thumb. What this means is that, on average, for every twenty natives alive at the moment of European contact—when the lands of the Americas teemed with numerous tens of millions of people—only one stood in their place when the bloodbath was over.

. . . The destruction of the Indians of the Americas was, far and away, the most massive act of genocide in the history of the world. That is why, as one historian aptly has said, far from the heroic and romantic heraldry that customarily is used to symbolize the European settlement of the Americas, the emblem most congruent with reality would be a pyramid of skulls.

Scholarly estimates of the size of the post-Columbian holocaust have climbed sharply in recent decades. Too often, however, academic discussions of this ghastly event have reduced the devastated indigenous peoples and their cultures to statistical calculations in recondite demographic analyses. It is easy for this to happen. From the very beginning, merely taking the account of so mammoth a cataclysm seemed an impossible task. Wrote one Spanish adventurer—who arrived in the New World only two decades after Columbus's first landing, and who himself openly reveled in the torrent of native blood—there was neither "paper nor time enough to tell all that the [conquistadores] did to ruin the Indians and rob them and destroy the land." As a result, the very effort to describe the disaster's overwhelming magnitude has tended to obliterate both the writer's and the reader's sense of its truly horrific human element.

In an apparent effort to counteract this tendency, one writer, Tzvetan

Todorov, begins his study of the events of 1492 and immediately thereafter with an epigraph from Diego de Landa's *Relación de las cosas de Yucatán*:

The captain Alonso López de Avila, brother-in-law of the adelantado Montejo, captured, during the war in Bacalán, a young Indian woman of lovely and gracious appearance. She had promised her husband, fearful lest they should kill him in the war, not to have relations with any other man but him, and so no persuasion was sufficient to prevent her from taking her own life to avoid being defiled by another man; and because of this they had her thrown to the dogs.

Todorov then dedicates this book "to the memory of a Mayan woman devoured by dogs."

It is important to try to hold in mind an image of that woman, and her brothers and sisters and the innumerable others who suffered similar fates, as one reads Todorov's book, or this one, or any other work on this subject—just as it is essential, as one reads about the Jewish Holocaust or the horrors of the African slave trade, to keep in mind the treasure of a single life in order to avoid becoming emotionally anesthetized by the sheer force of such overwhelming human evil and destruction. . . . We must do what we can to recapture and to try to understand, in human terms, what it *was* that was crushed, what it *was* that was butchered. It is not enough merely to acknowledge that much was lost. So close to total was the human incineration and carnage in the post-Columbian Americas, however, that of the tens of millions who were killed, few individual lives left sufficient traces for subsequent biographical representation. The first two chapters to follow are thus necessarily limited in their concerns to the social and cultural worlds that existed in North and South America before Columbus's fateful voyage in 1492. We shall have to rely on our imaginations to fill in the faces and the lives.

The extraordinary outpouring of recent scholarship that has analyzed the deadly impact of the Old World on the New has employed a novel array of research techniques to identify introduced disease as the primary cause of the Indians' great population decline. As one of the pioneers in this research put it twenty years ago, the natives' "most hideous" enemies were not the European invaders themselves, "but the invisible killers which those men brought in their blood and breath." It is true, in a plainly quantitative sense of body counting, that the barrage of disease unleashed by the Europeans among the so-called "virgin soil" populations of the Americas caused more deaths than any other single force of destruction. However, by focusing almost entirely on disease, by displacing responsibility for the mass killing onto an army of invading microbes, contemporary authors increasingly have created the impression that the eradication of those tens of millions of people was inadvertent—a sad, but both inevitable and "unintended consequence" of human migration and progress. This is a modern version of what Alexander Saxton recently has described as the "soft-side of anti-Indian racism" that emerged in America in the nineteenth century and that incorporated "expressions of regret over the fate of Indians into narratives that traced the inevitability of their extinction. Ideologically," Saxton adds, "the effect was to exonerate individuals, parties, nations, of any moral blame for what history has decreed." In fact, however, the near-total destruction of the Western Hemisphere's native people was neither inadvertent nor inevitable.

From almost the instant of first human contact between Europe and the Americas firestorms of microbial pestilence *and* purposeful genocide began laying waste the American natives. Although at times operating independently, for most of the long centuries of devastation that followed 1492, disease and genocide were interdependent forces acting dynamically—whipsawing their victims between plague and violence, each one feeding upon the other, and together driving countless numbers of entire ancient societies to the brink—and often over the brink—of total extermination. In the pages that lie ahead we will examine the causes and the consequences of both these grisly phenomena. But since the genocidal component has so often been neglected in recent scholarly analyses of the great American Indian holocaust, it is the central purpose of this book to survey some of the more virulent examples of this deliberate racist purge, from fifteenth-century Hispaniola to nineteenth-century California, and then to locate and examine the belief systems and the cultural attitudes that underlay such monstrous behavior.

• • •

History for its own sake is not an idle task, but studies of this sort are conducted not only for the maintenance of collective memory. In the Foreword to a book of oral history accounts depicting life in Germany during the Jewish Holocaust, Elie Wiesel says something that befits the present context as well: "The danger lies in forgetting. Forgetting, however, will not affect only the dead. Should it triumph, the ashes of yesterday will cover our hopes for tomorrow."

To begin, then we must try to remember. For at a time when quincentennial festivities are in full flower to honor the famed Admiral of the Ocean Sea—when hot disputes are raging, because of the quest for tourist dollars, over whether he first actually landed at Grand Turk Island, Samana Cay, or Watlings Island—the ashes of yesterday, and their implications for all the world's hopes for tomorrow, are too often ignored in the unseemly roar of self-congratulation.

Moreover, the important question for the future in this case is not "can it happen again?" Rather, it is "can it be stopped?" For the genocide in the Americas, and in other places where the world's indigenous peoples survive, has never really ceased. As recently as 1986, the Commission on Human Rights of the Organization of American States observed that 40,000 people had simply "disappeared" in Guatemala during the preceding fifteen years. Another 100,000 had been openly murdered. That is the equivalent, in the United States, of more than 4,000,000 people slaughtered or removed under official government decree. . . .

Almost all those dead and disappeared were Indians, direct descendants—as was that woman who was devoured by dogs—of the Mayas, creators of one of the most splendid civilizations that this earth has ever seen. . . . And many of the detailed accounts from contemporary observers read much like those recorded by the conquistadors' chroniclers nearly 500 years earlier. . . .

Reminders are all around us, if we care to look, that the fifteenth- and sixteenth-century extermination of the indigenous people of Hispaniola, brought on by European military assault and the importation of exotic diseases, was in part only an enormous prelude to human catastrophes that followed on other killing grounds, and continue to occur today— from the forest of Brazil and Paraguay and elsewhere in South and Central America, where direct government violence still slaughters thousands of Indian people year in and year out, to the reservations and urban slums of North America, where more sophisticated indirect government violence has precisely the same effect—all the while that Westerners engage in exultation over the 500th anniversary of the European discovery of America, the time and the place where all the killing began.

Other reminders surround us, as well, however, that there continues among indigenous peoples today the echo of their fifteenth- and sixteenth-century opposition to annihilation, when, despite the wanton killing by the European invaders and the carnage that followed the introduction of explosive disease epidemics, the natives resisted with an intensity the conquistadors found difficult to believe. "I do not know how to describe it," wrote Bernal Díaz de Castillo of the defiance the Spanish encountered in Mexico, despite the wasting of the native population by bloodbath and torture and disease, "for neither cannon nor muskets nor crossbows availed, nor hand-to-hand fighting, nor killing thirty or forty of them every time we charged, for they still fought on in as close ranks and with more energy than in the beginning."

Five centuries later that resistance remains, in various forms, throughout North and South and Central America, as it does among indigenous peoples in other lands that have suffered from the Westerners' furious wrath. Compared with what they once were, the native peoples in most of these places are only remnants now. But also in each of these places, and in many more, the struggle for physical and cultural survival, and for recovery of a deserved pride and autonomy, continues unabated.

All the ongoing violence against the world's indigenous peoples, in whatever form—as well as the native peoples' various forms of resistance to that violence—will persist beyond our full understanding, however, and beyond our ability to engage and humanely come to grips with it, until we are able to comprehend the magnitude and the causes of the human destruction that virtually consumed the people of the Americas and other people in other subsequently colonized parts of the globe, beginning with Columbus's early morning sighting of landfall on October 12, 1492. That was the start of it all. This book is offered as one contribution to our necessary comprehension.

[*He'eia, O'ahu*   D.E.S]
[*January 1992*   (ix–xv)]

[From the last page of the book:]
The Columbian Quincentennial celebrations have encouraged scholars worldwide to pore over the Admiral's life and work, to investigate every rumor about his ancestry and to analyze every jotting in the margins of his books. Perhaps the most revealing insight into the man, as into the enduring Western civilization that he represented, however, is a bland and simple sentence that rarely is noticed in his letter to the Spanish sovereigns, written on the way home from his initial voyage to the Indies. After searching the coast of all the islands he had encountered for signs of wealth and princes and great cities, Columbus says he decided to send "two men upcountry" to see what they could see. "They traveled for three days," he wrote, "and found an infinite number of small villages and people without number, but nothing of importance."

People without number—but nothing of importance. It would become a motto for the ages.   (258)

New York: Oxford University Press, 1992, ix–xv, 258. (Footnotes are not included here. For full citations, refer to original book.)

AFRICAN-AMERICAN RESISTANCE TO
COLUMBUS DAY

The following article illustrates the resistance to celebrating the Columbus "encounter," much like Annie John's in school, by present-day African Americans. Like Annie, they are aware that Columbus's arrival in the New World heralded the beginning of the African slave trade in the New World and that they are the descendants of those people.

J. ZAMGBA BROWNE, "REJECT COLUMBUS DAY?: THE PEOPLE SPEAK" (1993)

A grassroots effort is underway in African-American communities across the city to scrap the annual observance of Columbus Day in honor of Christopher Columbus, the so-called discoverer of America. Dr. John H. Clarke, a noted African-American historian, said Blacks would be crazy to honor Columbus on October 11. "We should be mourning on that day, and all flags in our community should fly at half mast," Clarke declared. In addition, the noted historian suggested that services be held in Black churches across the city for those who died as a result of Columbus, who did not discover America, but opened up the Americas and the Caribbean for exploitation by Europe. "This exploitation led to a massive slave trade to rescue the economy of Europe," Clarke explained. "Modern capitalism was born through this slave trade," Clarke declared in a telephone response concerning this year's celebration.

Meanwhile, calling for the holiday to be abolished or renamed Indigenous People's Day, a group of New York City residents began fasting Oct. 1, leading up to the official Columbus Day celebration. In addition to the New York fasters, there are also groups across the country who have been fasting since Oct. 1. The fast was initiated by individuals who were part of last year's 42-day People's Fast for Justice and Peace in the Americas.

Some critics of the observance said just as Jews wouldn't dream of celebrating Hitler's birthday or Irish the Queen of England's birthday or White Americans the Japanese attack on Pearl Harbor, no one should expect Blacks to honor Columbus. "Columbus had no more discovered the people and lands he claimed than a rapist has discovered the women he rapes," said one critic. According to Dr. Jack Felder, the White Western world loves Columbus. "The U.S. ruling class have named cities, counties, towns, rivers, colleges, parks, streets and even their capital after Columbus," he continued, "now they are organizing a global celebration in his honor."

Dr. Ivan Van Sertima, professor of African Studies at Rutgers University, said the Columbus period needs total reappraisal because he definitely did not discover America as detailed in the history books. "It is important to note that Columbus merely set in motion the enslavement of African and Caribbean peoples. We have to abandon the notion that Columbus was a man of progress as featured by some historians," said Sertima.

Dr. Gwendolyn C. Baker, head of the U.S. Committee for UNICEF, feels that the holiday shouldn't be scrapped, but rather use the opportunity to educate the masses that Columbus did not discover America because people were living on these shores when he arrived. "The holiday should not be celebrated in the traditional sense that makes people believe Columbus is being honored because he discovered America, but help people understand the true story," said Baker, former president of the Board of Education.

Michael Simmonds, student government president at Medgar Evers College in Brooklyn, also agreed that Columbus did not discover America. "I just don't believe that Columbus deserves all the honor he has been receiving through the years," said Simmonds. Like Baker, Simmonds called for seminars and symposia to debate the Columbus controversy and come up with appropriate means to educate the masses, especially Black people, about the real story.

The A. L. Crawford Memorial Division of the Universal Negro Improvement Association and African Communities League (UNIA and ACL), founder Marcus Garvey, will commemorate the Second African Holocaust Day on Tuesday, October 12, with a Parade and Commemorative Service in Brooklyn, cosponsored by the African Peoples Christian Organization (APCO). Assemble at Douglas Street between Nevins and Bond Streets, at 6 p.m. The route is along Douglas Street to Bond Street, North to Atlantic Avenue, to the House of the Lord Church.

A commemorative service is scheduled for 7:30 p.m., The House of the Lord Pentecostal Church, 415 Atlantic Ave., Brooklyn. The parade and commemorative service will remember the 140 million Africans who perished in the Western and Eastern slave trade.

New York Amsterdam News, October 9, 1993, 34.

THE MYTH OF COLUMBUS

Much as Columbus has sparked controversy in some localities in the West Indies, small communities in the United States have felt the effects as well. The following editorial, from a local newspaper in Haverhill, a small city in northern Massachusetts, responds to an incident that occurred in city council there in 1992. On the night that the city council was to vote to rename a park after Christopher Columbus, in honor of the quincentennial, a local Native American stood up at the meeting to speak against the proposal, arguing that Columbus should not be honored because of the destruction of the indigenous cultures that followed his arrival. City councilors were surprised but listened to his arguments. In the end, this person was one lone voice, and the council voted to rename the park. A local columnist responded to this sequence of events with an editorial, in which he cites the latest history of Native Americans after the arrival of Columbus, David Stannard's *American Holocaust*, excerpted in an earlier document. The small controversy engendered by Annie John's resistance in her school now has its counterparts in many communities in the New World.

MARK KOSINSKI, "MYTH OF COLUMBUS IS HARD TO DISPEL" (1992)

When City Council voted two weeks ago to rename the park at Railroad Square after Christopher Columbus, little did the councilors know it would spark a larger controversy, namely, the debate on whether or not Columbus initiated an era of genocide against thousands of native peoples of the New World.

The case against naming the park in honor of Columbus was made by Ronald Canns, a Native American who works out of an office in City Hall.

Heard the Argument

Surprised, somewhat taken aback, but firm in their resolve to go ahead with the motion, the council listened to Mr. Canns' argument. "Christopher Columbus doesn't need honoring," he claimed. "There are all kinds of folks that could be honored. Columbus was right up there with Mussolini, Hitler, Sadam Hussein and other despots."

Mr. Canns rightfully draws attention to an issue that, until recently, has been largely ignored by our culture—the devastating impact of the European intrusion into the New World. This question has been ignored for a long time because historians who have written about Columbus have chosen to interpret his life in exclusivistic terms—namely, from a white, European point of view. To them, Columbus' "discovery" of the New World was simply the beginning of the progressive acquiescence of inferior cultures to the dominant civilization of Western Europe.

But now historians are challenging this version as a pernicious myth. For example, a recent book on Columbus appears to support much of what Mr. Canns said to City Councilors. I'm referring to *American Holocaust: Columbus, Christianity, and the Conquest of the Americas*, by David Stannard, an historian at the University of Hawaii.

Arrival Brought Disaster

Stannard argues that the arrival of Spanish and other Europeans brought about a demographic disaster of incredible proportions. Disease, depredation, as well as enslavement and outright massacre resulted in mass genocide of native peoples over the period of European exploration.

Stannard's book is provocative and worth reading because it is carefully researched, well written, and based on some of the latest sources. From the standpoint of acknowledging Columbus' 500th anniversary of arriving in the Americas, this approach does not mean, as some have perhaps suggested, abandoning attention to Columbus' influence. On the contrary, it strengthens the case that we need to take a more inclusive and unflinching view of how his presence in the New World had a profound impact on native cultures.

A reconceptualization of Columbus' "discovery" of America is leading to a drastic change of conventional interpretations. The very term "discovery," as I have already suggested, looks quite different from the standpoint of native culture, and suggests we need to seriously reflect on the persistent myths such a term carries about Columbus' persona.

Undoing Damage Not Easy

Of course undoing these prevailing images of Columbus' "discovery" doesn't just mean adding a previously excluded perspective; it requires a disturbance of the internal security of European cultural tradition in America's history.

Maybe that's why there was a mood of uneasiness in City Council chambers when Mr. Canns rose to oppose the renaming of Railroad Square. Mr. Canns not only challenged the council, he drew attention to the value of other cultures and other world views that are in conflict with the dominant culture of European tradition.

Before we get too busy celebrating the European "discovery" of America, perhaps we should heed the words of Mr. Canns, who reminds us that American history is also the story of the destruction of Native-American culture, which in the final analysis was essential to the political invention of "America."

Editorial, *Haverhill Gazette* (Mass.), September 14, 1992, 4.

AN ARGUMENT FOR CELEBRATING THE QUINCENTENARY

In the next document, the vice chairman of the Christopher Co-lumbus Quincentenary Jubilee Commission of the United States, a historian, offers some reasons why the quincentenary should be celebrated, especially the fact that two worlds are now one. Unlike Annie John, who cannot forget the injustices of the past and cannot celebrate it, this historian and government official urges us to celebrate individuals who can "make a difference."

WILLIAM H. MCNEILL, "WHY CELEBRATE THE QUINCENTENARY?" (1992)

Editor's Note: There has been much talk during the past year about how Christopher Columbus and his voyages should be taught. We've heard from some teachers that they are considering not teaching Colum-bus at all for fear of being called politically incorrect by one faction or another. Although we believe revisionist interpretations of Columbus must stand or fall on their historical merits, we think Professor McNeill makes a strong case for the significance of the Columbian voyages in U.S. and World History courses and what all students should know about Columbus, apart from any conclusions about his personal integrity or of the European civilization from which he came.

The 500th anniversary of Columbus' famous voyage to America in 1492 will be celebrated for different reasons by different people. Americans of Italian descent will celebrate the fact that an Italian commanded the three little ships that went from Spain to America and back again. Some His-panics will celebrate the fact that it was Spanish rulers who sent Colum-bus across the ocean. And people in Columbus, Ohio will shout hurrah for the man their city is named after.

But there are two very good reasons for celebrating the quincentenary that all of us can share.

First is the fact that Columbus' voyage marks the beginning of the One World in which we live. Before 1492 people lived in many separate worlds. The oceans were empty spaces, too big to cross. As a result, people in Europe and Africa did not know that America existed. People on islands only knew their own small part of the earth.

Columbus' voyage changed that by bringing Europe into contact with

America. And once he had shown the way, others soon sailed across all the other oceans. Within thirty years, ships from Europe began to visit the shores of all the places where large numbers of people lived. As a result, Europeans, Asians, Africans and American Indians all had to get used to living together in One World.

We are still getting used to living in a world where what happens in one part of the earth affects what happens everywhere else. On the whole, world-wide exchanges helped human beings to gain in knowledge, wealth and power. But these gains were very unevenly distributed. Some profited, others suffered great disasters. The Indians of America were the biggest losers; the biggest gainers were Europeans. But even those who suffered most are now beginning to benefit from the new skills, knowledge and inventions of the past five hundred years.

We are all here together, after all. What we share is worth celebrating, rather than what divides us. And perhaps the most important thing we share is the One World created by modern communications. That world dates back to Columbus. That, then, is what we all should celebrate.

In addition, we can also think about how a single person, by acting on an idea, and overcoming obstacles, changed the world. Columbus did not arrive on the coast of Asia, as he expected. Instead he stumbled on something entirely unforeseen. Yet it was his action and his knowledge of the pattern of oceanic winds that made it easy to come and go across the Atlantic. As a result, others followed after him, and forever connected the Old World with the new. No single man, and no single event ever affected the lives of so many people. That, too, is worth celebrating for it shows us how even a single person can sometimes make a difference and change the world.

For both these reasons, then, everyone can and should celebrate the quincentenary. It reminds us of who we are: human beings caught up in a single world, who, as individuals, can still make a difference—sometimes great, as with Columbus, sometimes small, as for most of us: but a difference all the same.

William H. McNeill is Vice Chairman of the Christopher Columbus Quincentenary Jubilee Commission of the United States. He is also a Trustee and Vice Chair of NCHE [National Council for History Education, Inc.] and author of the world history, The Rise of the West.

History Matters! National Council for History Education, Inc. 5, no. 1 (September 1992): 1, 5.

POSITION OF THE NATIONAL COUNCIL FOR THE SOCIAL STUDIES

The last document in this chapter is an official response by an educational association to the controversy surrounding the 1992 quincentennial. This group of scholars tries to set the facts straight and to summarize the legacy of Columbus, including both positive and negative aspects of 1492. In this piece, Annie John's position, echoed by many others in 1992, is not ignored but placed in its historical context.

"THE COLUMBIAN QUINCENTENARY: AN EDUCATIONAL OPPORTUNITY" (1991)

The Columbian Quincentenary

An Educational Opportunity

Nineteen ninety-two is the 500th anniversary of Columbus' first voyage to the Americas. The voyage of Columbus is a much too significant event in human history for the nation's schools and colleges to ignore or to treat romantically or trivially. The most fitting and enduring way in which educators can participate in commemorating the quincentenary is to examine seriously the available scholarship to enhance our knowledge about 1492 and, in turn, to enhance the knowledge of our students. Specifically, educators should

help students comprehend the contemporary relevance of 1492, and

provide students with basic, accurate knowledge about Columbus' voyages, their historical setting, and unfolding effects.

Sixty years after Columbus' first landfall in the Americas, Francisco Lopez de Gomara wrote: "The greatest event since the creation of the world (excluding the incarnation and death of Him who created it) is the discovery of the Indies." In the year the thirteen English colonies declared their independence from Britain, Adam Smith observed: "The discovery of America, and that of a passage to the East Indies by the Cape of Good Hope, are the two greatest and most important events recorded in the history of mankind."

Although these two famous assessments of the significance of 1492 in human history may be overstatements, it is certainly true that the world as we know it would not have come to be were it not for the chain of events set in motion by European contact with the Americas.

The Contemporary Relevance of 1492

One of the most significant and visible features of the contemporary United States is its multiethnic and culturally pluralistic character. Scholars describe the United States as one of history's first universal or world nations—its people are a microcosm of humanity with biological, cultural, and social ties to all other parts of the earth. The origin of these critical features of our demographic and our civic life lives in the initial encounters and migrations of peoples and cultures of the Americas, Europe, and Africa.

Another significant feature of the United States is the fact that the nation and its citizens are an integral part of a global society created by forces that began to unfold in 1492. Geographically, the Eastern and Western Hemispheres were joined after millennia of virtual isolation from one another. Economically, the growth of the modern global economy was substantially stimulated by the bullion trade linking Latin America, Europe, and Asia; the slave trade connecting Africa, Europe, and the Americas; and the fur trade joining North America, western Europe, and Russia. Politically, the contemporary worldwide international system was born in the extension of intra-European conflict into the Western Hemisphere, and establishment of European colonies in the Americas, and the accompanying intrusion of Europeans into the political affairs of Native Americans, and the Native Americans' influence on the political and military affairs of European states. Ecologically, the massive transcontinental exchange of plants, animals, microorganisms, and natural resources initiated by the Spanish and Portuguese voyages modified the global ecological system forever.

Basic Knowledge about the Historical Setting and Effects of Columbus's Voyages

Educators should ensure that good contemporary scholarship and reliable traditional sources be used in teaching students about Columbus's voyages, their historical settings, and unfolding effects. Scholarship highlights some important facets of history that are in danger of being disregarded, obscured, or ignored in the public hyperbole that is likely to surround the quincentenary. Particular attention should be given to the following:

1. *Columbus did not discover a new world and, thus, initiate American history*.

Neither did the Vikings nor did the seafaring Africans, Chinese, Pacific Islanders, or other people who may have preceded the Vikings. The land that Columbus encountered was not a new world. Rather, it was a world of peoples with rich and complex histories dating back at least fifteen thousand years or possibly earlier. On that fateful morning of October 12, 1492, Columbus did not discover a new world. He put, rather, as many historians have accurately observed, two old worlds into permanent contact.

2. *The real America Columbus encountered in 1492 was a different place from precontact America often portrayed in folklore, textbooks, and the mass media.*

The America of 1492 was not a wilderness inhabited by primitive peoples whose history was fundamentally different from that of the peoples of the Eastern Hemisphere. Many of the same phenomena characterized, rather, the history of the peoples of both the Western and Eastern Hemispheres, including: highly developed agricultural systems, centers of dense populations, complex civilizations, large-scale empires, extensive networks of long-distance trade and cultural diffusion, complex patterns of interstate conflict and cooperation, sophisticated systems of religious and scientific belief, extensive linguistic diversity, and regional variations in levels of societal complexity.

3. *Africa was very much a part of the social, economic, and political system of the Eastern Hemisphere in 1492.*

The Atlantic slave trade, which initially linked western Africa to Mediterranean Europe and the Atlantic islands, soon extended to the Americas. Until the end of the eighteenth century, the number of Africans who crossed the Atlantic to the Americas exceeded the number of Europeans. The labor, experiences, and cultures of the African-American people, throughout enslavement as well as after emancipation, have been significant in shaping the economic, political, and social history of the United States.

4. *The encounters of Native Americans, Africans, and Europeans following 1492 are not stories of vigorous white actors confronting passive red and black spectators and victims.*

Moreover, these were not internally homogeneous groups but represented a diversity of peoples with varied cultural traditions, economic structures, and political systems. All parties pursued their interests as they perceived them—sometimes independently of the interests of others, sometimes in collaboration with others, and sometimes in conflict with others. All borrowed from and influenced the others and, in turn, were influenced by them. The internal diversity of the Native Americans, the Africans, and the Europeans contributed to the development of modern American pluralistic culture and contemporary world civilization.

5. *As a result of forces emanating from 1492, Native Americans suffered catastrophic mortality rates.*

By far the greatest contributors to this devastation were diseases brought by the explorers and those who came after. The microorganisms associated with diseases such as smallpox, measles, whooping cough, chicken pox, and influenza had not evolved in the Americas; hence, the indigenous peoples had no immunity to these diseases when the Europeans and Africans arrived. These diseases were crucial allies in the European conquest of the Native American. The ensuing wars between rival European nations that were played out in this hemisphere, the four centuries of Indian and European conflicts, as well as the now well-documented instances of genocidal and displacement policies of the colonial and postcolonial governments further contributed to the most extensive depopulation of a group of peoples in the history of humankind. Despite this traumatic history of destruction and deprivation, Native American peoples have endured and are experiencing a cultural resurgence as we observe the 500th anniversary of the encounter.

6. *Columbus's voyages were not just a European phenomenon but, rather, were a facet of Europe's millennia-long history of interaction with Asia and Africa.*

The "discovery" of America was an unintended outcome of Iberian Europe's search for an all-sea route to the "Indies"—a search stimulated in large part by the disruption of European-Asian trade routes occasioned by the collapse of the Mongol Empire. Technology critical to Columbus's voyages such as the compass, sternpost rudder, gunpowder, and paper originated in China. The lateen sail, along with much of the geographical knowledge on which Columbus relied, originated with or was transmitted by the Arabs.

7. *Although most examinations of the United States historical connections to the Eastern Hemisphere tend to focus on northwestern Europe, Spain and Portugal also had extensive effects on the Americas.*

From the Columbian voyages through exploration, conquest, religious conversion, settlement, and the development of Latin American mestizo cultures, Spain and Portugal had a continuing influence on life in the American continents.

The Enduring Legacy of 1492

Certain events in human history change forever our conception of who we are and how we see the world. Such events not only change our maps of the world, they alter our mental landscapes as well. The event of five hundred years ago, when a small group of Europeans and, soon after, Africans, encountered Native Americans is of this magnitude. Educators contribute to the commemoration of the quincentenary in intellectually significant and educationally appropriate ways when they assist students in becoming knowledgeable about this event and about its critical role in shaping contemporary America as a universal nation within an interdependent world.

An official position statement developed by the National Council for the Social Studies, October 1991.

Official Position Statement Developed by the National Council for the Social Studies, Washington, D.C., October 1991.

STUDY QUESTIONS

1. Summarize the reasons why Europeans might consider Columbus a hero, whereas residents of the Caribbean might hold the opposite opinion. Why do you think there were few celebrations of the October 12, 1992, quincentenary in the Caribbean?

2. How do the writers who are sympathetic to Columbus try to explain or justify his behavior? Give several examples.

3. The opinions about Columbus's achievements may depend on whether he is being considered (a) as a a man who performed certain deeds, held certain values, and made certain mistakes or (b) as a symbol of the history of the New World after the arrival of Europeans. How does each point of view influence a possible assessment of Columbus?

4. Now that you have read several conflicting views of Columbus, do you sympathize more, or less, with Annie's point of view in the novel? Explain why.

5. After reading these documents, how do you think the history and impact of Columbus should be taught in the schools? How is it taught in your school? Is there anything about your school's curriculum on Columbus that you would change?

TOPICS FOR WRITTEN OR ORAL EXPLORATION

1. Make a list with two columns. On one side, list Columbus's strengths; on the other side, list his flaws. While looking at the data on your list, how would you make your final assessment of Columbus? Do you think Columbus was a great man, or do you think his flaws prevent him from being considered one?

2. Now make another list with two columns. On one side, list the benefits of the Europeans' arrival in the New World; on the other side, list the disadvantages. What final assessments can you make about the Europeans' arrival in 1492 and after? With your assessments from questions 1 and 2 in mind, how do you think Columbus Day should be observed?

3. Divide into two groups, pro and con, and debate the following resolution: "Columbus' glory is not that he discovered America, but that he set in motion the highest flowering of the Western idea ['that all men are created equal']." (Quoted from an editorial by Jeff Jacoby, *Boston Globe*, October 9, 1997.)

4. Imagine that you are in Annie's school in Antigua, studying British

history and literature and West Indian history from the British point of view. You are reading poems about plants and flowers and other natural occurrences that do not exist on your island, and you are reading stories about the great achievements of people who enslaved your ancestors. What kind of alternative curriculum would you design?

WORKS CITED

Drayton, Kathleen. "Education Perspectives for a New Caribbean." In *Moving into Freedom*, edited by K. Davis. Bridgetown, Barbados: Cedar Press, 1977.

Kincaid, Jamaica. *Annie John*. New York: Farrar, Straus and Giroux, 1985.

Kurlansky, Mark. *A Continent of Islands: Searching for the Caribbean Destiny*. Reading, Mass.: Addison-Wesley, 1992.

Wilford, John Nobel. *The Mysterious History of Columbus: An Exploration of the Man, the Myth, the Legacy*. New York: Knopf, 1991.

SUGGESTED READINGS

Works on Christopher Columbus

Bradford, Ernle. *Christopher Columbus*. London: Michael Joseph, 1973.

Bushman, Claudia L. *America Discovers Columbus: How an Italian Explorer Became an American Hero*. Hanover, N.H.: University Press of New England, 1992.

Duff, Charles. *The Truth about Columbus and the Discovery of America*. New York: Random House, 1936.

Greenblatt, Stephen. *Marvelous Possessions: The Wonder of the New World*. Chicago: University of Chicago Press, 1991.

Jane, Cecil, trans. *The Journal of Christopher Columbus*. New York: Clarkson N. Potter, 1960.

Keen, Benjamin, trans. *The Life of the Admiral Christopher Columbus by His Son Ferdinand*. New Brunswick, N.J.: Rutgers University Press, 1959.

Koning, Hans. *Columbus: His Enterprise. Exploding the Myth*. 1976. New York: Monthly Review Press, 1991.

Morison, Samuel Eliot. *Admiral of the Ocean Sea: A Life of Christopher Columbus*. New York: Oxford University Press, 1942.

———, trans. and ed. *Journals and Other Documents on the Life and Voyages of Christopher Columbus*. New York: Heritage Press, 1963.

Newsweek: Columbus Special Isssue. "1492–1992. When Worlds Collide.

How Columbus's Voyages Transformed Both East and West." Fall–Winter 1991.

Paolucci, Anne, and Henry Paolucci, eds. *Columbus, America, and the World*. New York: Council on National Literatures, Griffon House Publications, 1992.

Phillips, William D., Jr., and Carla Rahn Phillips. *The Worlds of Christopher Columbus*. Cambridge: Cambridge University Press, 1992.

Provost, Foster. *Columbus: An Annotated Guide to the Scholarship on His Life and Writings, 1750–1988*. Detroit: Omnigraphics, 1991.

Vorsey, Louis de, Jr. *Keys to the Encounter: A Library of Congress Resource Guide for the Study of the Age of Discovery*. Washington, D.C.: Library of Congress, 1992.

Wilford, John Noble. *The Mysterious History of Columbus: An Exploration of the Man, the Myth, the Legacy*. New York: Knopf, 1991.

Education in the British West Indies

Davis, K., ed. *Moving into Freedom*. Bridgetown, Barbados: Cedar Press, 1977.

Gordon, Shirley. *A Century of West Indian Education: A Source Book*. London: Longmans, 1963.

Massiah, Joycelin, ed. *Women and Education*. Cave Hill, Barbados: Institute of Social and Economic Research, University of the West Indies, 1982.

Williams, Eric. *Education in the British West Indies*. New York: University Place Bookshop, 1968.

5

Social Context: Family Life in Antigua

Because Antigua and the other Caribbean islands have a different history from the United States, family life there also differs. Annie's father is quite a bit older than her mother, and early in the book Annie mentions that her father has loved many women in his life, women that he did not marry but with whom he had children. These women may harbor a grudge against Annie's mother, who did marry him. In Antigua, it is quite common for men to have several children with different women before finally marrying, often later in life. In fact, about 80 percent of the children born in Antigua are "illegitimate," that is, have parents who are not married to each other. A number of historical and social reasons explain why this situation frequently occurs in Antigua and other Caribbean islands.

West Africans, in general, have very strong family ties, not just to the immediate family but to a much larger extended family that includes grandparents, aunts and uncles, cousins, even distant relatives. In some parts of West Africa, men may take more than one wife and often have many children with different mothers. In addition, some societies still operate under a traditional double standard—men may have relationships with other women outside marriage, but women may not. Often, West African families live in large compounds, a set of houses grouped together for the various wives and relatives, situated in a larger village setting. The adults have steady companionship, usually with those of the same sex. Children grow up surrounded by relatives and other children and by villagers from the same tribe who have known them all their lives. These social patterns are quite organized and offer security and continuity for the people.

With slavery, and transplantation to the New World, some customs survived, and other family patterns were broken. The plantation owner's best interest was in getting as much labor as he could out of his expensive property; he had little interest in the slaves' family ties. Family members were often separated and sold to different estates, and people of different African tribes, with different languages and customs, were often grouped together and mixed in with Creole slaves (born in the New World). A mother always had to be wary of the fact that the master could sell one or all of her children away from her, at any time. The father's ties were weakened by the constant threat of separation and by the lack of marriage among the slaves. As one document mentions, the children were considered to belong to the master, not to the father, and were often named by the master as well. Due to separations and the absence of marriage, relationships between men and women were shorter, more tenuous; people's partners often changed over a lifetime. The slaves were viewed as property, meant to perform labor, and not as people whose family ties should be encouraged and strengthened.

Nevertheless, the ties among family members often remained strong, particularly those between a mother and her children. In one document to follow, an Antiguan workingman relates how his grandmother, after emancipation, searched for a daughter who had been sold to another estate so the mother and three daughters could be reunited. Years later, in *Annie John*, we see the same strong ties between mother and daughter.

With the arrival of missionaries, particularly the Methodists and the Moravians, marriage began to be permitted and even encouraged among slaves on some estates. These missionaries, who preached Christian monogamy and marriage, were often confronted with the problem of how to treat new converts who were involved in polygamous relationships. The Moravians, for example, devised a set of rules for dealing with such relationships, as can be seen in another document to follow.

With the conversion to Christianity in the West Indies, marriage and monogamy came to be seen as the ideal but has been adhered to by people to various degrees. Often, commitment to this social ideal depends on class. The upper and middle classes tend to emphasize marriage and family ties more strongly—the upper classes because they often need to prove white ancestry, and the middle classes because they often wish to improve their social status. Among the poorer rural classes, men often defer marriage until later in life, when they can afford a house and a fancy wedding and support a wife who does not work. Young men rarely have enough resources to marry under these circumstances and often engage in a series of long term relationships that result in children before finally deciding to marry. Despite the high rate of illegitimacy, 80 percent of British West Indians are, or have been, married.

Despite the fact that illegitimacy and mother-centered homes are accepted by the people, until quite recently (1986), and during the time that Annie John was growing up, illegitimate children were often discriminated against. Legitimate children often had more advantages, a higher social status, and more educational opportunities. Legitimate children were baptized on Sundays, at a church service; illegitimate ones were baptized separately during the week. Illegitimate children were often denied entrance to the better schools on the island and thus had fewer educational and vocational opportunities. Fathers had difficulty establishing legal paternity and often could not obtain the proper papers to allow their children to join them in other countries after emigration. In 1986, a law was passed in Antigua that prohibited discrimination against illegitimate children; it also gave them equal rights to inherit property from their fathers, even if the father had died without a will. One document that follows describes family patterns in Antigua and explains the significance of this new law.

With this background knowledge in mind, one can see that Annie John is somewhat privileged in comparison with many other Antiguan children of that time. Her father, typically, is older, with several previous relationships and children, but married to her mother, which gives Annie and her mother increased social status. Her mother does not work outside the home; her father is able to support them through his carpentry work, and they are able to live in town, in St. John's. Annie attends school, even high school. Only a small percentage of Antiguan children (4.5 percent in 1970) were able to graduate from high school around that time. Annie's mother is quite concerned with social status and closely monitors Annie's education, her religious upbringing, and her public behavior. She wishes to avoid the risk of Annie engaging in early sexual relationships outside marriage, which we now understand to be common at that time. Some aspects of Annie's upbringing, therefore, demonstrate a desire for some upward social mobility in Antiguan society.

As mentioned earlier, another feature of West Indian family life is the particularly strong relationship between mothers and their children. This tie is often closer than that between the parents, whose social lives and leisure time are usually spent with other people of the same sex. Young men often stay at home with their mothers until their twenties or thirties and thus have little motivation to marry early. Children are considered blessings, whether born inside or outside marriage, and are expected to care for their parents when they are old. Daughters are close to their mothers, who train them for their future lives. One can readily see the enormity of the break between mother and daughter in *Annie John*, why Annie does not wish the other girls to know about it, and why it causes Annie's illness. This kind of adolescent breaking away, which is perceived as common in the United States, is much less common in the family life of Antigua in the 1960s.

CHRISTIAN ATTITUDES TOWARD POLYGAMOUS RELATIONSHIPS IN THE CARIBBEAN

This excerpt from a history of the Moravian missionaries in the British West Indian island of Jamaica describes the provisions made for the treatment of polygamous relationships in the Caribbean. These customs were in direct conflict with church teachings, and yet the missionaries did not wish Christian conversion to break up long-term, established relationships with children. The situation described here was equally true for the island of Antigua and helps to demonstrate how the marriage and monogamy of Annie's family came to be considered the ideal in the British West Indies.

FROM J. H. BUCHNER, *THE MORAVIANS IN JAMAICA: HISTORY OF THE MISSION OF THE UNITED BRETHREN'S CHURCH TO THE NEGROES IN THE ISLAND OF JAMAICA, FROM THE YEAR 1754 TO 1854* (1854)

I shall conclude this chapter by a brief statement of the regulations adopted by the Brethren's Church to direct her missionaries in their practice towards the Negro slave particularly with regard to polygamy and marriage.

It has been stated already, that the labours of the missionaries, from the year 1770 until 1809, were not accompanied with such demonstrations of the Holy Spirit and power upon many as would enable them to rejoice in their work, though they were encouraged to persevere by seeing occasionally some proof of their labours in the conversion of a few. To teach these the commandments of the Lord, and to maintain a Christian conduct, was their earnest desire. But here again, they met with almost insurmountable difficulties, of which one, common to all slave countries, may be mentioned. Polygamy was the usual practice among the slaves, indeed it was forced upon them by the circumstances in which they were placed. Marriages were illegal. Nevertheless, the members of the congregation were solemnly joined in matrimony at a meeting of the Christian Negroes, when they gave one another the hand and promised faithfulness. These unions were justly considered binding in the church, though not recognized by the laws of the land. And if the husband or the

wife proved unfaithful, they were publicly excluded from the congregation. But it was by no means uncommon for one or the other to be sold
to a distant part of the island, without any prospect of ever meeting again.
In such cases, it was difficult to know how to decide; those rules recognized in all Christian lands as binding, were often inapplicable, and impossible to be carried out. The rules referring to polygamy and marriage
among heathen converts adopted by the Synod of the Brethren's Church,
and which served for the direction of the missionaries in such cases, were
the following, which we believe to be according to scripture, though
perhaps, those who have never considered the matter before, may not
be able at once to satisfy their own minds on the subject. "When a Negro
man or woman applies to be baptized, or to be received into the congregation, strict enquiry is to be made concerning every circumstance
attending his or her situation and connexion in life. If it is found that a
man has more than one wife, the question arises, how the Brethren have
to advise him in this particular. St. Paul says, 'If any brother has a wife
that believeth not, (one that is yet a heathen) and she be pleased to dwell
with him, let him not put her away.' (1 Cor. vii.12) But again, he says, 'A
bishop must be blameless, the husband of one wife.' (1 Tim. iii.2) In
these passages we have the teaching of the holy scriptures concerning
this subject; the Brethren are therefore of opinion that the missionaries
should keep strictly to the following regulations.

1st. That they should not compel a man, who had, before his conversion, taken more than one wife, to put away one or more of them, without her or their consent.

2nd. But yet, that they would not appoint such a man to be a helper
or servant in the church.

3rd. That a man who believeth in Christ, if he marry, should only take
one wife in marriage, and that he is bound to keep himself only to that
woman till death part them.

4th. If by the sale of Negroes, wives are torn from their husbands, and
husbands from their wives, and carried off to distant parts, though the
Brethren cannot advise, yet they cannot hinder a regular marriage with
another person, especially if a family of young children, or other circumstances, seem to make a help-meet necessary, and as is mostly the case,
no hope remains of the former ever returning."

London: Longman, Brown & Co., 1854, 43–45.

MARRIAGE CUSTOMS IN NINETEENTH-CENTURY ANTIGUA

This piece describes marriage customs among the black population of Antigua after emancipation. Written by a white British resident of Antigua, we can see her amused, yet critical, attitude toward the loose adherence to the monogamous ideal among the black population, even though the white men on the island often engaged in similar practices. This document demonstrates the significance of Annie's family situation in determining her status and opportunities in life.

FROM [MRS. LANAGHAN], *ANTIGUA AND THE ANTIGUANS* (1844)

The next point to be considered is polygamy—and here, again, we see the demoralizing effects of slavery. It has been before remarked that there was no legal marriage rite for slaves, such unions being merely transitory. It is true by what has been called the "Melioration Act," rewards were held out to such slaves who should preserve their fidelity in such contracts; and those persons who had the management of negroes were forbidden to encourage immorality among the women by their own example. But, alas for Antigua! when were these regulations put in force? No European can imagine to what extent such vices were carried in former days, vices which will still be painfully felt by society for many, many years to come—at any rate, until this generation shall have passed away; and, even then, the plague-spot will, perhaps, show its taint. When the light of day began to dawn upon this benighted part of the globe by the introduction of Christianity among the negroes, they were encouraged by the Moravians and Methodists to choose a partner from among the other sex, and, in the face of the congregation, vow to each other fidelity and love. Although, of course, such marriages were not held binding by law, it was hoped that it would in some measure check the increase of immorality; and, in some instances, it might have done so, but the greater part violated those vows without compunction, or held them only until a fresh object gained their attention. It has been frequently known for a man thus married to maintain his wife and his mistress in the same house, which arrangement occasioned frequent domestic broils; and in such cases, the man, being applied to as umpire, has settled the dispute

by remarking to his mistress; "That she must not quarrel with her companion, who was *his wife*, and that if she did, he would turn her away";
and then, addressing the aggrieved wife, tell her, for her consolation,
"That *she* must not mind, because she was *his wife already!*"

After the negroes were freed from the thrall of slavery in 1834, and the
same privileges open to them as to the rest of the British subjects, it was
their pride to be married at the established church. In many instances,
they had already been joined by the Moravian and Methodist preachers,
but wishing to get rid of their partners, who had borne with them the
brunt of slavery, they privately paid their addresses to some of the young
ladies already mentioned, carried them to the altar, and there married in
direct opposition to their former vows, which were as binding and sacred
in the eyes of God as if his grace the Archbishop of Canterbury had pronounced the nuptial benediction. Among such an immense number of
negroes, it is almost impossible to discover the offenders in this respect
against common decency, although the clergymen are generally indefat-
igable in their exertions to discover the truth. Still, vigilant as they are,
they have been deceived; and instances are known, where parties have
been twice married, even in the episcopal church. In some cases, a
wedding-party have assembled within the sacred walls, the intended bride
and bridegroom waiting at the altar until the lips of the presiding minister
shall have made them one; when, as that solemn charge has been given,
"If either of you know any impediment why ye may not be lawfully joined
together in matrimony, ye do now confess it," those important words, "I
do," have been suddenly heard, and (as in most cases) a female has come
forward declaring that herself and the guilty beau had been long ago
married at the chapel. When such circumstances have occurred, and the
clergyman refused to re-marry them, it has been no unfrequent practice
for the parties to embark on board a small vessel, and proceeding to
Monserrat, or some other island, there to procure the completion of their
unhallowed purpose.

Another evil to be deplored is, that even when parties are lawfully
joined in the bands of wedlock, they pay such little regard to the solemnity of the act. The smart dresses (for which often they commit an un-
lawful deed), the plentiful breakfast, or lunch, the gilded cake, and the
driving about in borrowed gigs, is much more thought of by them than
the serious, the important promise of loving one another in sickness and
in health, and, forsaking all others, cleave only unto them who, by the
ordinances of God and man, are made one flesh. From this want of regard
to the serious part of the ceremony, great mischief ensues. As soon as
the novelty has worn off, the husband forgets his honour which he is
bound to protect. The old leaven cleaves about them, and throwing off
all shame, they follow the bad example of their parents, (who indeed are

less faulty than themselves, not having had such means of instruction;) and by these means, give to the country, instead of an honest peasantry, a race of idle illegitimate children. I would by no means take upon myself to state, that of the many weddings which weekly take place among this "sober-hued" people, none remember to keep their marriage-vows unstained; on the contrary, no doubt many find it what it should be—a state "ordained for the mutual society, help, and comfort, that the one ought to have of the other, both in prosperity and adversity."

London: Saunders and Otley, 1844, 166–169.

MEMOIR OF FAMILY TIES IN THE CARIBBEAN

The next document describes the strong family ties among people of African descent in the Caribbean, even during slavery and right after emancipation. Despite the forced separation of families during slavery, many sought to find their loved ones after emancipation. This story shows the particularly strong ties between mothers and daughters, as we can see in *Annie John*.

The second section is a description of family life by a male Antiguan workingman who may be only a few decades older than Annie's father. His family patterns are similar to those of Annie's father, with several early relationships that produced children, then marriage later in life.

FROM KEITHLYN B. SMITH AND FERNANDO C. SMITH, *TO SHOOT HARD LABOUR: THE LIFE AND TIMES OF SAMUEL SMITH, AN ANTIGUAN WORKINGMAN, 1877–1982* (1986)

I have no doubt that my race was brought here from Africa. When it comes to Africa—the mother land—my family could not give me the slightest idea of how life was up there. Absolutely nothing. I was surprised that my family did not know head nor tail of the place where their generations was from. But I can't blame them, for up to today—with all the education—very few people in Antigua know much about Africa. You see, slaves wasn't allowed to know where they come from or even what was the fate of their family on other estates. So I don't know anything about the land of my roots.

I believe that planting sucker follow the root [a belief that family members take after each other, a belief in heredity]. I wanted to know for sure when my family was brought to the West Indies. I wanted to hear from the horse's mouth how was the journey from Africa to this side of the world, how rough it was, what cause them not to die before they reach here. I wanted to know which island the ship landed first with them; if Antigua was not the first island, where was that? I wanted to know if they were living in another West Indian island before they were shipped to Antigua, I wanted my parents to tell me if they knew anything of the capture, if they knew how did it happen. I wanted to know what my family was like in Africa. I wanted to know from what tribe my family came and if tribal leaders come from my family. After slavery end, almost every Antiguan did not want to hear anything about slavery. Nothing whatsoever. They were ashamed. But I wanted to know.

One of Antigua's big shots, Mr. R. S. D. Goodwin—he was an estate owner and big wheel among the politicians—told me that my people come from the west coast of Africa. Mr. Goodwin was a bright man, but that's all he could tell me. Maybe that's all he knew about any of the slaves—from the west coast—and where, he could not say. I did not even get the feeling that he was sure of what he was saying. . . .

I know from my mother that when slavery end, her great-grandmother Rachael could hardly speak English; she could only mumble a word or two of the language. My mother also said that after slavery end Rachael pick up a few words, but nothing much to speak about. This give me the idea that my mother family did not come to the West Indies too long before the bakkra [whites] stop bringing slaves. You see, if Rachael was born in Antigua, I think that she would be able to talk the language. So from my own calculation, I reckon that Rachael reach Antigua sometime close to the year 1800.

I do know for sure that Rachael was owned by the Old Road Plantation. She had three gal picknee [children]—Minty, Fanny and Barba.

One day Minty owner went and sold her to another slave massa. Poor Rachael was well shook up, she bawl plenty [she wept for a long time] and so did Fanny and Barba. But slaves have to keep them bawling to themselves. (When a slave disappear, that was that. Massa was the owner and he do what he like for they was his property.) Mother Rachael did not know who it was that bought Minty. She didn't see them; or even what way the slave cart went. That's how it was when Minty was sold and gone away from her people.

Minty was young and did not get to have a child yet. Day in and day out, the family lament over her. But nobody else but she was sold. Emancipation day come and meet the rest of the family living together at Old Road. Then the owners didn't have the headache to provide food for slaves. The slaves do the work in them own garden and feed themselves after slavery end. . . .

Now the old slave massas at Old Road was trick and smart people. After slavery end they wanted the strong slaves they sell or swap off during slavery to come back to work on their plantation. Them thought them have proper luck: slavery was all over and they wouldn't even have to buy them back. They would have both the slaves and the money. So the bad-minded slave massas at Old Road Plantation make sure they tell everybody where their people can be found. All the families say how they give thanks to massa for his great interest, but everybody have in mind not to return to Old Road. People badly want to unite with the family—particularly the womenkind. I hear that the women was furious and desperate to find their people.

That's how Rachael learnt where Minty was for the first time and who bought her. Minty was sold to the Sandersons plantation owners. Rachael could not understand very well what massa was saying so she take her bigger daughter for him to explain about the whereabouts of Minty. Rachael understood then that Minty was at Sandersons Estate, but neither Rachael nor her gals knew where Sandersons was for they never put foot off the Old Road Plantation. But wherever Sandersons was, they was determined to go. Massa, he did not hesitate to explain again and again how they could reach Sandersons. He wanted Minty back; now she was free to work the old estate.

The two sisters, Fanny and Barba, and Mother Rachael got ready to journey to Sandersons in search of Minty. They want a man to follow them, but the man—he was one of the stud or server [a slave used to breed other slaves] of the plantation—said no. Still and all, them women was so bound and determined to find Minty only death could stop them. The plan was that they would leave Old Road very early in the morning, when moon carry day. Moonlight must be bright like a goo'back [the Bible: the moon must shine as brightly as the words in the Good Book for them to see the way] before them leave Old Road. The time come and they start traveling in the north-easterly direction, by way of Fig Tree Hill, through Follies, then on to All Saints and to Sandersons.

Now Fig Tree Hill be less than a mile from Old Road, but the women never know what that hill was like, for during their entire life as slaves they had never gone that far. That morning, when they set out to find Minty, was the first time they was traveling to Fig Tree Hill, the short way to Sandersons—they was told by massa.

It was not too long before trouble start. Mother Rachael couldn't climb Fig Tree Hill. She had a bad foot and the road was rugged and steep, made up of all flintstones [small, sharp stones] and she was afraid she would fall in the gully. She got all the help and push from Fanny and Barba, but the old lady could not climb that hill. That was bad luck, but old Rachael could not see the way. All the glee suddenly turn into pain.

After staying at the bottom of the hill for some time, they decide pride no feel no pain and they would just have to brave whatever bad luck there was. So they turn back and take another route. There was no suggestion of leaving Rachael behind because them gals love them mother: no search for Minty without Rachael. Anyway, they dine, she go supper [they will be together all the time].

The very next morning, Rachael, Fanny and Barba set off again in the

bright moonlight to go to Sandersons. This time it was the twenty mile
journey. . . .

By the time it was broad daylight they were making friends. . . . There
wasn't many people around the estate-works that could give them news
of Minty, but the women were confident that Minty was there so them
patiently wait until the gangs finish working at the end of the day.

When that time come they were well-disappointed. The people at Sandersons know Minty, but she was no longer at that plantation. She was
sold to the massas at Betty's Hope. On hearing that news, Mother Rachael
bust into tears and so did little sister Barba. Them nearly have fit. Would
they find Minty after all? It was like Bible days—Rachael wept. Fanny
again was the comforter, the person with the heart. Fanny too was well-
disappointed, but she was a determined person, not the kind that give
up easily. It was night then and they decide to stay over at Sanderson.
Them never sleep that night for worry about Minty.

As day clear, they drink some hot water and start the journey to Betty's
Hope, not too far away from Sandersons, the distance maybe just three
miles. They reach there in quick time, but nobody know anybody by the
name of Minty. Frustration was just about to creep in when they see her.
Well, them let loose, for God help them find Minty. That was the freedom;
only when they find Minty they really believe that slavery was all over for
sure. Minty had a brand on she hand. My mother said it was number
104. And that's the number massa know she as. Governor Patrick Ross
end the branding of slaves in Antigua in 1828.

Rachael and her daughters, in love and joy, settle in at Betty's Hope.
Them wipe foot [they left Old Road Plantation] from Old Road. They hate
the old plantation where they used to live. They hate the people that sold
them loved one. Old Road with all its plenty food could not behold them
again. Even if they did not find Minty, they would not go back to Old
Road. They lived at Betty's Hope until Rachael die. . . .

The family was filled with women. They never told me of any man that
was in the family; most of the children didn't know the father. (You see,
in them days, a nega man could not count himself as father. The picknee
the man make belong to massa.)

It was just a few years a-back that nega man get to take on the responsibility of father, so back then nega picknee carry the name of the estate
owner. That practice live on a long time after slavery end. People seriously had the feeling that the child belong to the bakkra and the mother
would usually take the child to the massa. In most cases, it would be
massa that name the baby. The man that was the rightful father couldn't
have nothing to do with the child. Many times he would not even know
that a particular woman was making a child for him.   (25–33)

• • •

I wanted a house for myself. I was big enough and I didn't want to live any longer with my mother, but she didn't want me to go and live by myself. One day I decide to use a hand of box-money [money pooled together every week by a group of people] to start building my own house.

One of the reasons why I wanted to move from under the roof of my mother was that she never would want any of my girlfriends to come home to me. She had a terrible dislike for any woman that would get too close to her sons, but me more so than the rest. I think it was because I was working more regularly than the rest and I treat her good. . . .

When the house was building, there was a rumour that I was building a house to get married. Now that rumour didn't come from the people in my village because at that time nobody in the village was married. It always seem to me the rumour come from the Goodwins [estate owners]. My mother was disturbed. I try and comfort her, but she rind hell and I couldn't convince her that I have no intention at that time to get married. She would just say that wherever smoke there, fire there. A lot of girls was around me, but I wan't ready yet and I didn't want to upset my mother.

In 1906 I had six children within that same year, so people start to call me "Sam the Ram." The house was finish building around the same time and the Goodwins, mostly Massa Affie and family, start to encourage me to get married. I just couldn't take them on. Affie Goodwin use to goon about how I was not in Africa where one man could have many wives and the wives feed them children. He would go on about how I was in Antigua and if I don't work, the workhouse will pick me up.

During the same time a girl by the name of Isabel had just had a child for me. . . .

Soon after, Isabel, her picknee and her mother left the land for St. Kitts. I told the Goodwins—even though it was far from what the truth was—that the woman I was going to marry went away. That keep them from talking about married for awhile, but they never give up the fight.

Of the many girl friends I had back then, there was two of them—Clara and Lou—that was very close to me. Clara was from the village of Liberta and Lou was from All Saints. In 1907 Clara had a boy-child for me and Lou was pregnant. . . .

Clara was gone, but I was not a man to lose out. I got Lou . . . to come and meet me. She had our first child, Ann, on the last day in February in 1908. Ann was the first child for Lou and the fifteenth for me. I was thirty-one at the time.

The Goodwins—them hardly every give up on anything—finally convince me to get married. I decide to marry Lou. When the news broke, naturally Clara get angry with me. I went to look for her at Liberta, but she close the door in my face and drove me out of the yard. She parted from me and parted for good. I haven't behold her and child up to this day. I hear she and the child went to St. Kitts.

I was under pressure, for my mother was also mad with me. I asked Massa Affie to call her and talk to her. He did and that quieted her for a while. You see, in them days, man and woman married when them old, so nega man wedding was far and few between. In fact, I doubt that the people of All Saints ever saw a nega man wedding before I get married. . . .

Affie Goodwin give me a big cake and two bottles of wine for the wedding and told me after that I would go down in history as the youngest black man in the island to get married. (When black people start to get married at an early age, it was just about the time of World War I and they start to do so because of the religion coming from the churches around that time.)

After the wedding my family start to get big. Lou had our first boy-child in 1909 and the second in 1913. But I couldn't resist temptation, so I had other children outside.   (116–120)

• • •

Within the same year [1921], my wife had her fifth and last child for me. By then I had thirty-five children alive. That number isn't too much because I start to make children in 1894, when I was seventeen, and to have two a year would be normal.   (134)

Scarborough, Ontario, Canada: Edan's Publishers, 1986, 25–33, 116–120, 134.

THE IMPACT OF FAMILY LAW ON FAMILY RELATIONSHIPS IN ANTIGUA

The following document describes the history of family law and its influence on family relationships in Antigua up to the present day. It also explains the significance of the new law, recently passed in Antigua, that prohibits discrimination against illegitimate children. This article helps to clarify Annie John's family situation and social status.

FROM MINDIE LAZARUS-BLACK, "BASTARDY, GENDER HIERARCHY, AND THE STATE: THE POLITICS OF FAMILY LAW REFORM IN ANTIGUA AND BARBUDA" (1992)

In a landmark act at the end of 1986, the Parliament of recently independent Antigua and Barbuda legally banished bastardy and made "illegitimacy" legitimate. The Status of Children Act, and two companion measures, the Births Act and the Intestate Act, redefine centuries-old kinship relationships and restructure the duties, obligations, and property rights of kin. Three important changes resulted. For the first time, discrimination against a person on the basis of birth status is now illegal; men can acknowledge their illegitimate children by complying with a simple procedure; and all children so recognized inherit from their fathers' estates. Since over 80% of children in these islands are born out of wedlock, these bills bear on the lives of a great many people.

I explain here why these statutes and the events that contextualize their passage mark a critical turning point in the history of Antiguan family organization and in the use of family law as an instrument of class, kinship, and gender relations. I begin with Antigua's earliest kinship statutes, documenting critical changes in their content in conjunction with evolving social and economic organization, and then examine the events surrounding the recent and radical reform. . . .

I present my argument in three parts. First, I examine the role of kinship law as part of the foundation for domination in early colonial Antigua. This will shed light on the force of law historically and on the symbolic and pragmatic significance of the latest family laws. . . .

In part II, I review what measures lawmakers took after slavery to reinforce earlier class, kin, and gender hierarchies. . . .

In the final section, I argue that the recent effort to banish bastardy

belongs to the long struggle in Antigua for a more equitable division
of labor and resources, representative government, and political autonomy. . . .

I. Class, Kinship, and Gender Law in Early Antiguan Society,
1632–1834

. . . Contrary to local assumptions nowadays, a great many Antiguan
laws never duplicated those of Great Britain. Among the indigenously
written codes were kinship rules that bore clearly the marks of the unusual situation in which the colony's lawmakers found themselves. One
historian estimates that 60,820 slaves were imported to Antigua between
1671 and 1763. Slaves accounted for 41.6% of the population in 1672;
80.5% in 1711; and 93.5% in 1774. The white population peaked at 5,200
persons in 1724.

One striking similarity between the early family laws of Great Britain
and Antigua is that both assigned power over persons and things to legitimate males. A striking difference between the two is that the West
Indian laws were intentionally designed to create and maintain a social
hierarchy that the ruling elite believed to be necessary to maintain order
and the division of labor. One of the earliest statutes, for example, pro-
scribed "Carnall Coppulation between Christian and Heathen." The latter
category included both Amerindians and Africans. . . .

By the end of the 18th century, the island possessed three separate
marriage laws corresponding to its three social ranks of persons: free
individuals, indentured servants, and slaves.

The first marriage law, Act No. 2 of 1672, regulated marriages in the
free white population. . . .

A separate Antiguan marriage code, however, governed the marriages
of free persons and indentured servants. A free person who wanted to
marry a servant either had to serve that master for two years or pay 20
[pounds] to secure the servant's freedom. . . .

What was the consequence of the legal restriction on free servant marriage? In 1720, almost one out of five whites in Antigua (19.1%) was a
servant. A large portion of the colonists, therefore, could not marry unless
they could obtain permission from their employers, buy out their contracts, or pay heavy fines. Perhaps both servants and free persons were
discouraged from marrying by the statute that only recognized marriages
performed by Anglican ministers. Legal separations and divorce were impossible to obtain locally. Given this combination of statutes, and the
well-known fact that West Indian plantation owners preferred employing
unmarried men because married men with families cost the estate more
for support, it is little wonder that concubinage and prostitution were
common among free whites and servants and that some of these persons

failed "to keep harmless the parish." In Antigua, as in Jamaica, there evolved a kinship system for these men which enjoined "marriage with status equals and non-legal unions with women of lower status." In contrast, "respectable" free women married and refrained from extramarital affairs. . . .

Law contributed to the establishment of an informal family structure, but illicit unions inspired still more legislation. An act of 1786, for example, compelled "reputed Fathers of illegitimate White Children to make a competent Provision for them." Parish funds maintained them, "altho' their reputed Fathers have been in circumstances sufficiently competent to provide for such Children." Although precedent for caring for illegitimate children came from the English poor relief acts, the Antiguan law clearly reflects local reproductive practices because both an individual's place in the division of labor and his or her color were issues when Antiguan lawmakers legislated relationships between parents and children. The 1786 bill is important on another account: Precedent was first set for women to utilize the courts to establish paternity, win child support, and act as advocates for their families in the courts.

As these examples show, some of the earliest Antiguan laws regulating reproduction, marriage, and illegitimacy were devoted to controlling the behavior of free settlers and indentured servants. Legislators were anxious that sexual relationships, love, and/or marriage not threaten the boundaries between workers in different legal categories. By 1818, visitor Dames Walker wrote about what he perceived to be an unusual correlation between upper-class status and marriage in Antigua. He reported that "rank and privilege, which are strongly marked in everything, seem to turn marriage into a distinction somewhat of the nature of nobility, and to reserve it in general for the proprietors and leading men of the colony." The island's elite intermarried among themselves.

For all of the 17th century and most of the 18th, lawmakers mostly ignored conjugal and reproductive practices among slaves. After all, slaves were not persons but freehold property. The earliest slave codes were designed to promote labor and prevent resistance. . . .

As the growing value of slaves and the profitability of the sugar crop became apparent, however, local legislators passed measures to increase the number of persons who could be counted as slaves and to further discourage relationships between free persons, indentured servants, and bondsmen. In 1644, a mulatto child produced by a racially mixed union was enslaved until ages 18 or 21. After 1672, such a child was enslaved for life. In 1697 the Assembly decreed that no minister was "to presume to marry a slave to any free person." For the crime of marrying a slave, a free person was fined 20 [pounds]—or subjected to four years of servitude to his spouse's master. The provisions were incorporated into the

1702 Act for the Better Government of Slaves and Free Negroes and the fines and penalties were increased. . . .

The Leeward Islands Amelioration Act, adopted in Antigua in 1798, set minimum food, housing, and clothing allotments for slaves, condemned "excessive punishments," and established marriage rules specifically for slaves. Masters were advised to induce their slaves to choose one mate. Such encouragement of "monogamy" did not spring from Christian piety since the law also held slave marriages by religious rites "unnecessary and even improper." More likely, it came from greed because the planters believed licentious behavior inhibited reproduction. In any case, this slave marriage system only partially resembled the lawmakers' own. The planters insisted that the Africans were still too uncivilized to comply with a contract. Their plan for slave marriages, therefore, preserved the idea of a faithful union but without the element of contract.

By law, slave marriages were monogamous, but not contractual, since the parties won none of the privileges implied in marriages of free persons. A child of a slave marriage, for example, was not allowed to take the surname of the father or inherit whatever property he might have accumulated. The law did include provision for a public declaration of a couple's intention to live together, monetary awards from their masters for marrying, and a brief ceremony in which the marriage was officially recorded in the estate records. Reading these codes, one cannot help but be struck by the irony of the symbolic gesture of recording slave marriages in plantation account books. Instead of preserving these marriages in the church registers, the planters noted them in the double-entry ledgers in which transactions involving the estate's capital were recorded.

At the time of the Amelioration Act, Antiguan slaves made up 94% of the population of the island. The majority worked under severe conditions on large sugar estates. The few historical records which speak to their conjugal and reproductive practices suggest that here, as elsewhere in the Caribbean, there was never a single type of slave family. There were long-lasting as well as short-term unions between men and women. Single and multiple unions coexisted in different proportions in different places and at different times since the social, economic, and ideological contexts in which slaves labored influenced both the number and types of their conjugal relationships and patterns of reproduction. . . . The record suggests a pattern in which slaves experimented initially with a number of partners and later settled into more permanent and long-term unions with single partners.

Historians have also traced some differences in the conjugal practices of field workers, domestics, and skilled artisans. Men who were recognized as leaders within the slave community, for example, were able to maintain multiple unions which were accepted as "legitimate" relationships within the community. Slave women who lived on very large estates were also more likely to become involved in miscegenistic [mixed-race] relationships. Sexual unions and blood ties with whites in different ranks of society obviously influenced the family lives of slaves and the course of their future relationships. A white overseer or craftsman, for example, might free his child by a slave woman to work at his side. Plantation elites rarely permitted such an arrangement, but they sometimes manumitted their lovers and children.

Slaves who labored in towns where demographics and daily life were decidedly different manifested a different conjugal pattern. A large percentage of town slaves were domestics and laundresses, tasks assigned to women. Although slave men worked as messengers, on public works, on docks and in a variety of other pursuits, their masters were unlikely to allow them to establish independent households. Subjected to constant supervision, domestics were also much more likely to live in mother-children households than were field laborers.

Finally, in the late 18th century, town slaves and free persons of color in Antigua, most of whom lived in urban areas where they could find employment, were more likely to come under the influence of Anglican, Moravian, and Methodist missionaries who introduced to their converts the notion that marriage was a critical component of one's religious salvation. . . .

At the end of the 18th century, then, the Amelioration Act and Christian marriage offered to the majority of the island's population, the slaves, opportunities to acknowledge formally familial ties. The assembling of slaves on the large estates, the announcing of marriages, pressure from masters and ministers to end relationships with more than one person, and the psychological effect of having one's union recorded for posterity in the great book of the estate influenced slaves' courting and conjugal practices—even if many refused the gifts, to give up mates, or to participate in the rites, and even if some masters ignored the law. . . . By the end of the slave era in 1834, a legal church wedding had assumed a special meaning across the ranks of this society. Socially, it was a mark of civility, education, financial stability, enduring love, and religious salvation. Pragmatically, it assured certain legal protections for men, women, and their children.

When slavery ended, Antigua's kinship organization was marked firmly by directives from the state. . . .

When slavery ended, the complexity and variability that characterized familial relationships among slaves, particularly men's proclivity for retaining multiple conjugal partners, became less tolerable to the planter/lawmaker. Multiple unions gave men enlarged networks of kin and friends, some of whom might provide them with alternatives to working full time on the sugar estates, while leaving a great number of children without fathers legally responsible for supporting them. Exactly what behaviors lawmakers regulated and what they left untouched by the rule of law colored the events that unfolded after emancipation and until independence. The specific dynamics of legal intervention in matters of class, kinship, and gender would change, but the centrality of its role would not.

II. The Post-Emancipation Era: Free Laborers and Belabored Families

Much remained the same in Antigua immediately after emancipation in 1834: the economy still depended on sugar and the working people labored under profoundly difficult conditions. Nevertheless, the abolishment of slavery altered class relations and the organization of power; it generated significant changes in laws related to labor and the management of families. Because people were no longer commodities, and the earlier marriage laws governing slaves, servants, and free persons expired, the local elite was forced to rethink the rights of individuals, the conditions of labor, and the functions of kinship. Once slavery was abolished, lawmakers placed increasing emphasis on individuals' rights to enter into contracts and, concomitantly, developed a new relationship between individuals, families, and the state.

Slaves' new freedom to accept or decline labor was quickly converted into a new form of bondage by means of statutory contracts between owners and freed slaves who "chose" to remain on the plantations. In fact, lack of suitable land ensured that most remained on the estates under the terms of the Contract Act. The contract provided a job, minimum wages, shelter, medical attention, and gardening rights. Wages were set at 6d sterling per day for able-bodied men; women and children received a percentage of that pay. The Contract Act fostered continuity between slavery and freedom by binding laborers to the lands and houses they had occupied during slavery and, in most cases, to similar work patterns. Nevertheless, the change involved granting former slaves the legal status necessary to enter a contract—a status that conferred the legal competence enjoyed by free persons. . . . The Contract Act was modified slightly over time but not fully abolished until 1937.

A second development, however, tempered the ideology of individualism that underlay the freedom of the former slaves to bind themselves to their former masters. . . .

Like England, Antigua would also eventually build a poor house. Beginning in the 1850s, however, the island's poor laws were rewritten so that the maintenance of applicants for relief became the legal responsibility of every relative. The responsibility for children, the elderly, and other nonworking persons was shifted in law to an "extended" family that specifically included grandparents. For example, in 1864, one could not refuse to work to maintain one's family. Any person accused of abandoning his or her family could be tried before a magistrate. Any such person was also prevented from migrating. By the mid-19th century, the state "policed" as much as it "governed" families.

Antiguan lawmakers may have extended kinship obligations to prevent a potential fiscal nightmare: They were avoiding the possibility that an impoverished working class with an extremely low marriage rate might leave the sugar estates or apply for parish relief for illegitimate children. The legislators accomplished much more than this, however. Relationships between men, women, and children suddenly had new implications because law now infiltrated what had previously been conceived of as "personal" matters. If it had become illegal to enslave a worker, it was now legal to bind a laborer to virtual slavery by means of a contract. If it had seemed immoral to abandon one's kin, it was now also illegal. Civil codes redefining kinship duties and obligations recreated the planters' control over their emancipated slaves. Poor "relief" was a response to the "problem" that the earlier and continuing regulation of families created. . . .

Of acts passed by the [new Leeward Islands] Federation [1871], three in particular had long-term ramifications for family life in Antiguan communities and bear on the events surrounding the efforts to reform family law in the 1980s. Each also illustrates the continuing and constitutive ties between political economy, law, and kinship. These laws include an act establishing new procedures for determining paternity and maintenance for illegitimate children, a statute enabling married women to hold and transfer property, and a divorce act. Products of the late 19th century, the paternity law and the married women's property act remain extremely relevant to the making and breaking of family ties in contemporary Antigua. Of more recent vintage, divorce was infrequently resorted to until the 1970s. . . .

As in the past, the magistrate's court continues to serve as a forum for the kinship disputes of unmarried persons—persons who are today, as in the 19th century, also likely to be poor. In sharp contrast, married persons, many of whom are also middle class, can apply to the High Court to resolve their kinship disputes. In the High Court, judges take more time to listen to disputes and rule according to the circumstances of each individual case. They regularly issue orders for child custody and maintenance that take into consideration the financial positions of the parents and the educational needs of the children.

The fact that the magistrates' courts are used regularly for resolving kinship matters, but mainly by one class—poor and unmarried women—

is evidence that law continues to influence family patterns and the economy of households, even as it reproduces the legal disabilities associated with lower-class kinship patterns. The persistence of these two alternative legal channels for married and unmarried persons preserves the earlier hierarchical class structure—a fact that does not go unnoticed in the community. Antiguans I interviewed, including lawyers, magistrates, and ordinary citizens, thought it highly unjust that the law discriminates in this fashion. Nevertheless, and despite the limitations of the present code, the courts are often utilized by unmarried Antiguan women. Speaking out for the legal, social, and moral rights of one's children is important for women in Antigua. As we shall see, those kinship norms, in conjunction with a long tradition of using magistrates' courts to obtain rights, helped fuel the effort to rewrite illegitimacy laws in the 1980s.

The Federation's Married Women's Property Act (1887), which was modeled on the English statute of the same name and gave married women the right to hold and transfer property in their own names, has been adapted for use in Antigua primarily to deal with problems women face because of local kinship practices. . . . According to the lawyers I interviewed, adultery is the most common reason for divorce in Antigua. While Antiguan wives "look the other way" and ignore some of their husbands' affairs, a man's decision to share "his" assets with his "friend" and illegitimate children infuriates his wife. Hence the custom that presupposes a man's control over matrimonial property causes women's lawyers to use an 1887 code when there is trouble in the marriage. Again, the pervasiveness of such marital tensions, coupled with the norm that encourages women to speak on behalf of their children, proved critical to the recent struggle to legitimize illegitimacy.

The other product of the Leeward Federation with long-term effect on the lives of Antiguan families and of influence in the politics of family law reform in the 1980s was the divorce bill. Judging by the late date of its passage—1948—Leeward Island lawmakers were long reluctant to permit divorce, even though divorce had been available in Great Britain since 1857. Interestingly, the Caribbean statute made divorce retroactive to 1913 without explanation. There has been little further innovation in matrimonial law since the 1940s. In fact, the act under which Antiguans were divorcing during my fieldwork replicated almost exactly an English law of 1937. To obtain a divorce one has to prove desertion, adultery, or cruelty. Its general unavailability in Antigua until the relatively recent past helps explain not only the very low divorce rate on the island but also the custom whereby married couples simply live apart when they cannot live together. Indeed, "living in sin" and having children out of wedlock reflected not so much a failed morality as the near impossibility of canceling a marriage contract in the 19th century and for most of the 20th.

Thus although the divorce law did not originate in an attempt to regulate the nonlegal Antiguan family, it contributed to their numbers by making it extremely difficult to change marriage partners. . . .

III. Independence and the Efforts to Banish Bastardy

In sharp contrast to earlier lawmakers, and for the first time in Antigua's history . . . this elite used kinship codes to remove rather than to create new bases for social hierarchy within the society. In this respect, the Status of Children Act, the Births Act, and the Intestate Act mark a critical turning point in the use of family law as a vehicle of class relations. These statutes, which end discrimination against illegitimate children, are critical on another account too; the story behind their passage heralds significant changes in Antiguan women's participation in lawmaking. Women's historical role as advocates for their children encouraged them to exercise power as the legislature considered changing the status of children. . . .

As in the past, Antigua's marriage rate remains low and its illegitimacy rate high. In the early 1980s, for example, the marriage rate per one thousand persons was less than three, while the illegitimacy rate at birth averaged 80%. A variety of reasons account for these continued rates, including the legacy of laws that discouraged marriage and prohibited divorce, individuals' reluctance to marry until they have established a home and some financial security, an unwillingness on the part of men to wed until they feel they have "sown their wild oats," the critical relationship between marriage and individual religious salvation which becomes especially important in one's later years, and individuals' outright resistance to this form of state intervention in their personal lives. Visiting "friends" and long-term, nonlegal relationships are common and prevail alongside formalized unions. Although both men and women say marriage is an ideal to which they aspire "some day," parenting outside of marriage is also highly valued. Within marriage, husbands and wives have segregated roles and nobody ever suggested to me that they were equal in any respect. Both sexes believe firmly that a wife should defer to her husband when the couple faces important decisions. Men usually determine what economic contribution they will make to the household, and they rarely explain their comings and goings. A cultural prescriptive, common throughout the region, holds that men "by nature" love to love more than one woman and ensures that many men will father "outside" children even after they are wed. Since Antiguans typically acknowledge relationships through both blood and law, families become complicated alliances in which individuals strive for love, attention, respect, and social, political, and economic support.

Prior to the recent legislation, however, marriage and legitimate birth continued to convey certain legal, social, and economic advantages. As late as the 1950s, some secondary schools would not admit illegitimate children. Almost all the churches baptized illegitimate children on days set apart from the baptisms of legitimate children. Moreover, even in the 1980s the illegitimate children of a man who died intestate [without a will] had to wait for the approval of the Prime Minister's Cabinet before they could inherit their father's property—and then only in cases where legitimate heirs did not claim the estate. Illegitimate children also faced difficulty obtaining papers enabling them to travel and work overseas.

The legal changes that addressed these disadvantages awaited a shift in the composition and goals of the lawmaking class. When slavery ended, many planters left the island, leaving their posts in the civil service and commerce to be filled gradually by the children of people of color, indentured servants from Portugal, traders from the Middle East, and men and women from the working class who achieved social mobility primarily through teaching, the professions, and the church. These groups had lacked any political voice until the 1950s when Antiguans won universal suffrage enabling the working class to gain representation in government. In contrast to government by white planters or a colonial federation, the contemporary political leadership is Antiguan born, black, and locally educated. They are people who have "come up": the sons and daughters of working people. Moreover, many of them held jobs such as carpenter, artisan, timekeeper, secretary, or clerk before assuming their posts in Parliament. The exemplar is V. C. Bird, Sr., the Prime Minister, who has served continuously as chief executive since 1961 with the exception of 1971–76 when his Antigua Labour Party lost one election. Bird was born out of wedlock in an Antiguan slum, which meant that a secondary school education was out of the question "both because it was expensive and the schools did not permit entry to illegitimate children." He and his associates now in Parliament were active in the labor disputes and strikes of the 1920s and 1930s, led the fight to legalize the unions, helped write Antigua's successive constitutions, and brought the nation to independence. Those lawmakers are familiar not only with the commonsense understanding of family in Antiguan communities but also with the plight of illegitimate children. Moreover, it was common knowledge in the legal community that Jamaica, Trinidad, and Barbados, nations with kinship histories similar to Antigua's, had revised their statutes to end discrimination against illegitimate children. . . .

The Status of Children Act and Births Act of 1984 failed to reach the Senate because of lobbying by a group of married women who believed strongly in the equality of all children but who refused to ignore the practical consequences of family and gender norms in their community. Antiguan men's proclivity to father and provide for children outside of legal unions, together with the custom of holding a couple's marital assets in the man's name even if a wife works outside the home, suggested to them that the Status of Children Act and the Births Act posed possible social embarrassment together with considerable financial threat. A man's decision to legitimize a child born outside of the marriage could jeopardize his wife's own and her children's financial security. Alert to this possibility the women initiated a political struggle over family law reform lasting two years, waged completely in accord with local kinship and gender norms, espousing human rights and the sanctity of marriage, and ultimately gaining for married women the legal protection they sought. . . .

The concrete result of the women's efforts was a new Intestate Act that offered financial protection to wives and legitimate children without seriously disadvantaging illegitimate children whose fathers had legally acknowledged them. If a man dies intestate, the act gives his wife one-third of his property and all of his personal effects, including automobiles, tools, jewelry, and household furnishings. The remaining two-thirds of the property is shared by his children, including those legitimized under the new Births Act. A man can defeat the provisions of the Intestate Act, however, if he makes other arrangements in a legal will.

With new kinship legislation drafted to the women's satisfaction, Antigua's legislators pressed ahead. The Births Act passed the House on 5 June 1986, with little fanfare. The Status of Children Act and the Intestate Act were introduced together six months later. Proponents emphasized again the need to protect the rights of every child regardless of birth status and expressed pride in being part of an effort to end discrimination in society. They associated these kinship laws with the political goal of promoting a more just society. The acts were lauded as indispensable to a democratic nation and protective of the "real" family. One Representative explained it this way:

> Mr. Speaker, we have a state in this country where the attitude of our people must be changed. We are trying to change them from the top but they have to be changed from the bottom too. . . . I am saying even though we are talking about all children as one, we are also saying, Sir, that they must realize although they are one, their attitudes must be of the same nature. Don't let those from the married family feel they are higher up than those of the unmarried families. They all must go down the road together and behave and hug up one another. For instance, my son, a daughter, one in wedlock and one out of wedlock, they should be together, hug up and kiss up and so on. This is what we are trying to do, to bring together the family.

While they acknowledged that a great many Antiguan children were born out of wedlock, the Representatives insisted that protecting the rights of these Antiguan family members had nothing to do with condoning "immorality," condemning Christianity, or advocating African polygamy: "What I am saying, I hope that it is not in the spirit of creating all sorts of families here and there that this bill is brought here today. It is not a situation in Africa where one man can have two, three, four wives and all sort of concubines, although we have them here, and I hope we are not trying our best to encourage such. We do feel a Christian society is really a welcome one."

The "family" the legislators hoped their new kinship system would protect was "Christian" in its ideal union and "Christian" in its tolerance of bastard children. In accord with the still pervasive influence of the churches, their rhetoric privileged marriage as a religious phenomenon, although not as fully determinative of a married man's resources. Members of the House, and later the Senate when it unanimously ratified these bills, understood that the "family" they envisioned was a family whose blood was thicker than water or any contract. The legislature reordered kinship law so that it would more closely resemble "family" in the Antiguan community, a family defined first through socially recognized blood ties. They understood that they were reformulating the kinship order in the image of the classes from which they had come and which they now represented. . . .

IV. Conclusions

Antigua's newest family laws express and reflect relatively recent changes in the backgrounds and interests of political leaders, in the nature and power of the state, and in the role of law in class and gender relations. No reassessment of the legal implications and consequences of legitimacy, illegitimacy, marriage, and inheritance could occur until a local bourgeoisie emerged with strong identification and ties to the working class, an agenda for social and economic change, and the opportunity to put those plans into action. In sharp contrast to the past, these new codes were specifically intended to break the cement of the old social hierarchy and to remove rather than to create bases for discrimination in society. The newest kinship laws are heralded as mainstays of social equality and justice. Most certainly, these codes resonate more closely with the family norms and practices of modern Antiguans and not with those of the former colonial elite.

Outlawing illegitimacy, the lawmakers outlawed condemnation of the kinship organization of the working people. Simultaneously, of course, they legitimated their own postcolonial rule—one which has not been without its critics. While Antigua's latest kinship statutes redefine kinship relationships and restructure the duties, obligations, and property rights of kin, they emphasize individuals as "free agents," part of the legacy of the labor laws of the 19th century. The state, however, now enters into the lives of families in a radically new way in that law protects the illegitimate child from discrimination and allows that child to inherit. Today the state recognizes and supports a different definition of kinship—one which affects families in every social class.

Law and Society Review (Winter 1992): 863–899.

political independence from Great Britain (beginning in 1962) and Great Britain ended migration by passing the 1962 British immigration law, migration shifted to the United States, which was undergoing an economic boom.

In 1965, the Immigration and Nationality Act in the United States imposed a ceiling of 20,000 immigrants in any year from a particular country in the Western Hemisphere, but this figure excluded close relatives, so the actual numbers could be more than 20,000 per year, per country. Between 1925 and 1989, 2.25 million people migrated from the Caribbean to the United States, with 91 percent of this migration occurring after 1961. The largest percentage of immigrants (35 percent) came from Cuba, largely for political reasons; the largest numbers of economic immigrants have come from the Dominican Republic, Jamaica, Haiti, and Guyana. Since 1961, one-third of all Caribbean immigrants to the United States have come from the four major English-speaking Caribbean countries—Jamaica, Trinidad, Barbados, and Guyana—these migrants account for 18 percent of the current population for Barbados, 17 percent for Jamaica, 14 percent for Guyana, and 10 percent for Trinidad. These figures show the large scale of this migration out of the Caribbean (Palmer, 12–13).

This large flow of migrants out of the Caribbean has had both positive and negative effects on the Caribbean. On the positive side, the money that immigrants send back home helps to bolster the local economies; on the negative side, such massive migration causes familial dislocation and a "brain drain" (or loss of skilled workers) to the local economies (Lowenthal, 213–232). The first document in this chapter discusses these effects in more detail.

The vast majority of West Indians in the United States live in New York, particularly in Brooklyn, although they can be found in many other cities, such as Chicago, Philadelphia, Detroit, Baltimore, Washington, D.C., and Hartford, Connecticut. In Brooklyn, the West Indians maintain a separate ethnic identity from both white and black Americans (although they do support civil rights issues regarding the black population), through close family ties, civic associations and self-help organizations, public events, and carnivals. They are noted for their drive for education and economic success, particularly their passion for home ownership. This hunger for land can also be seen in the interview with Antiguan

Samuel Smith and is perhaps an effect of slavery, overpopulation, and lack of money and land in the Caribbean.

Besides Brooklyn, two other areas of particular interest are Washington, D.C., with its large numbers of West Indian professionals, and Hartford, Connecticut, which has a close-knit community of West Indians with its origins in farmwork. They began picking apples and tobacco in Connecticut in the 1940s and grew into a vibrant community of 25,000 by the 1980s. They are well organized, with two West Indian community groups that own their own buildings and have achieved great economic success (Palmer, 20–23).

Jamaica Kincaid's migration to the United States is also a success story. She came as a teenager after high school and eventually secured employment as a writer in New York, later marrying an American and putting down roots in Vermont with her family. Although perhaps less connected to her island of origin and to West Indian communities in the United States than the typical immigrant, she is an example of an artist who had to leave her small island in order to find her own artistic voice, much as Annie John feels she has to do in order to find herself and achieve independence from her family. In this novel, Annie John goes to Great Britain, but in her next novel, Kincaid has the main character, Lucy, migrate to New York, as did the author herself. The documents that follow should provide some perspective on this migratory movement from the West Indies to larger communities outside.

SOCIAL FORCES OF EMIGRATION

This document provides a useful overview of the social forces that cause emigration from the West Indies and the consequences for West Indian societies and for the emigrants. It was written in 1972 and reflects conditions around the time that Annie John left Antigua, in the mid-1960s.

FROM DAVID LOWENTHAL, *WEST INDIAN SOCIETIES* (1972)

The West Indies have been emigrant societies ever since European settlement. Emigration was a corollary of the absentee spirit. The yearning for Europe pervaded Creole life; for even those who lacked personal connections there regarded it as home. Not only whites went "home"; thousands of their coloured descendants were assimilated into eighteenth- and nineteenth-century European society, never to return to the Caribbean.

Europe continues to attract those who are ambitious, energetic, and impatient with, or fearful of, local conditions. Elite and middle-class West Indians regularly travel abroad for business or pleasure. To many, a first-class education still means a European education. The University of the West Indies, too elite to cater for most local needs, is not elite enough to suit some; more than half of all Commonwealth Caribbean college students attend British and North American institutions. For French West Indians, university and professional training still more frequently entails Paris.

But many emigrants are less pulled toward "home" than pushed out of the Caribbean by economic need. Since the seventeenth century hundreds of thousands, perhaps millions, of West Indians have been forced out by agricultural unemployment. And emigration will remain all but inevitable as long as population growth outstrips economic development. Most Caribbean birthrates hover between 3 and 4 per cent a year—twice those of developed nations; public-health programmes have reduced infant and adult mortality to low levels. Government sponsorship of birth control in Barbados, Trinidad, Jamaica, and the French Antilles cannot soon overcome West Indian pride in procreation, suspicions of racist motives, and local apathy and ignorance—not to forget the real advantages of large families in parental eyes. Without any further increase the

West Indies would still be over-populated; there are too many people now for the jobs available.

Moreover, job opportunities are contracting. Both industrial and agricultural development require more skilled and fewer unskilled labourers. Sugar mechanization is the prime example: using less than half the man-hours of work today, the Caribbean produces five times as much sugar as fifty years ago. Large-scale agriculture is increasingly labour intensive, and since agriculture employs four-fifths of the labour force, technological advance throws many out of work. One West Indian worker in four is now unemployed; seasonal imbalances in estate labour needs, fragmentation of peasant holdings, and fluctuations of demand and supply leave many more chronically underemployed than jobless. Technology not only displaces labour; it increases its seasonality. A century ago it required 250 days in the year to cope with the sugar crop; today no more than 150 days are needed. The toll of agricultural under-employment is probably most severe in Martinique, where out of 39,000 farm employees only 800 have permanent jobs; in other words 97 per cent work only seasonally.

Scale further constrains West Indian opportunities. Production, processing, and marketing are more costly for small territories than for large, and the disadvantage widens with technological progress. Montserrat grows quality bananas but cannot sell them profitably because it produces too few to pay for good harbour facilities or to attract shippers geared to regular interisland schedules. The smaller the island, the greater the relative cost of marketing any product.

Small-island goods and public services are likewise costly. West Indian societies of 10,000 cannot afford a hospital, nor islands of 100,000 a university, because they cannot use so wide a range of services continuously or economically. Students and patients instead must leave home, which is expensive and socially disruptive. Smallness puts many ordinary amenities out of question. Paved roads, electricity, telephones, and movies may all require equipment, capital outlay, and levels of consumption beyond small-island capacities.

Small size handicaps public services too. In larger lands, bigger schools replace one-room schoolhouses, suppliers of books and furniture are geared to bulk distribution and consumption, and everything is concentrated in ever larger centres. In an island of 50,000 what seemed adequate a generation ago is today outmoded by advances that are not locally realizable. Yet Caribbean islanders want the things they learn about from radio, television, magazines, and returned migrants. Thus even if the population remains stable, each passing year leaves a small territory less viable.

Stable populations are a rarity. Small islanders regularly leave home

for larger places to find better pay and a wider range of goods and services. At the same time, social and cultural impoverishment magnifies the
difficulties of rejuvenating their homelands. It is the rare school teacher
or mechanic who elects to live in a place too small to afford the rudiments
of modern comfort. . . .

West Indians abroad resist appeals to come back home not only because salaries are low but because aside from work there is so little to
do. . . .

All Caribbean territories suffer a steady attrition of young people who
find local rewards meagre and local society stultifying. The bonding of
scholarship students only briefly detains West Indian teachers, doctors,
and other professionals; between 1955 and 1959, eighty-five Trinidad
government scholarship winners defaulted on their five-year service obligations. . . .

The local prospects of West Indian writers are no less discouraging.
No Caribbean market is large enough to support much cultural creativity;
authors who stay or return home must combine writing with teaching,
journalism, broadcasting, or public relations. Lionized by small local fol-
lowings, they often cease to be artistically productive and become merely
local celebrities who write.

To escape creative paralysis or impoverishment West Indian authors
generally go to New York, London, or Paris, in search of a publisher and
a public. Even as emigres, they find a psychological and spiritual refuge
in the metropolitan milieu of words and ideas, philosophy and world
affairs. The liveliest minds of West Indian society and many of its potential
chroniclers thus absent themselves; what they might contribute to West
Indian life is never born or is soon lost to local view.

West Indians learn early that success, psychological as well as economic
and social, requires emigration. . . .

Built-in pressures keep pushing West Indians, especially the educated,
out of the Caribbean. Were all economic and social problems resolved
the process would still continue. No West Indian university could cater
for all needs, let alone every new specialty. Breadth of experience and
intimacy with science and scholarship moreover require study, travel, and
contacts in a larger society. From such sojourns many never return, many
more but briefly.

Scope and Destination

Emigrant numbers, destinations, and purposes vary with time and
place of departure. From some islands the outward stream is small but
steady, from others substantial or episodic. Jamaican emigrants probably
outnumber any other. Owing to a net outflow of 200,000 during the
1950s and 1960s, one Jamaican in ten now lives abroad. But emigrant

proportions are higher in the eastern Caribbean. The years 1959–61 saw almost 6,000 people depart from St. Kitts-Nevis, 10 per cent of the inhabitants; Montserrat lost 5 to 10 per cent of its people *each year* over the same period. On small islands where migration is endemic, still larger proportions may be away. One Carriacouan in four is normally off the island, and Anguilla, with only 6,000 residents, keeps close ties with nearly 8,000 Anguillans living elsewhere.

Many West Indian migrants, perhaps most, stay within the Caribbean. . . . But the greatest employment opportunities lie farther afield. At least 100,000 West Indians helped to build the Panama Canal during the early 1900s, and many subsequently found work on United Fruit Company plantations in Central America; two generations later scores of West Indian communities along the coast remain in touch with their island homelands. Between the First World War and the Depression another 100,000 settled in the United States, notably New York and Boston, where their families retain a definite West Indian identity. In the 1950s the tide of emigration turned toward Europe, and by 1968, 320,000 West Indians were in Britain, 150,000 in France, and 20,000 in the Netherlands. The late 1960s witnessed a renewed flow into the United States and Canada.

Many migrants intend to return when they make good. Some do come home as successes, others as failures; but most remain abroad, except for brief visits. Another type of migrant leaves home for specified periods. . . . No sharp line separates permanent from temporary migrants, however. An intended absence of a few months may stretch to a lifetime, whereas someone who means to pull out for good may shortly come back disillusioned. But each type of migrant plays a distinctive role, from which different consequences ensue. . . .

Effects of Migration: The Home Community

Migrant departure and return have profound impacts on West Indian societies. The typical emigrant is a young man or woman who can find no work at home. From some territories men traditionally leave for several years, returning to buy or build a house and settle down. The smaller islands are habitually depleted of young adults, especially males. Off-island agricultural work or sponge fishing at times claims one-third the married men of South Andros in the Bahamas; British Virgin Islanders habitually take work in St. Thomas. In 1960 Cayman Island females outnumbered resident males by four to three; in Anguilla the ratio was five to four, and the 15–44 age group had three women to every two men. Such imbalances are enduring features of small-island life: in Carriacou, where women outnumber men by almost three to one, the ratio has been at least two to one throughout the past century.

The paucity of men is not limited to minuscule islands where emigration is a constant way of life. The entire British Caribbean in 1946 had only 932 males per 1,000 females, and in Barbados and in Grenada the ratio was only four to five. Among those of working age the discrepancy was still greater: fewer than two men to three women in Grenada, three to four in St. Vincent.

The social consequences depend on how institutionalized the sexual imbalance is. Where out-migration is habitual and socially obligatory, family and household organization adjust to the skewed sex ratio. Extra-residential mating involving single women is sanctioned in Carriacou, the Cayman Islands, and South Andros. Barbadian family structure adjusts to sexual imbalance by idealizing the nuclear household and reasserting emigrants' obligations to dependents.

Large-scale, permanent migration has altogether different effects. Young men leave first, typically followed by young women and later by some of their children. The early stages, when wage earners alone are away, can be most burdensome. One inhabitant in three of St. George parish, Monserrat, went to Britain between 1948 and 1962, and three-fifths of these emigrants were aged 15 to 25; estate agriculture was abandoned in 1962 because only 191 folk of working age remained in the parish. Of Jamaica's 162,000 net emigrants to the United Kingdom during 1953–62, 52 per cent were men, 40 per cent women, and only 8 per cent children. Adults who left the island between 1955 and 1960 took 6,500 of their offspring with them but left 90,000 behind.

From the whole British Caribbean during the 1950s only one emigrant in twenty was a child; and by 1960, 250,000 children had one or both parents in Britain. At home the proportion of able-bodied to dependents declined steeply. In Jamaica the working-age segment dropped from 47 per cent in 1943 to 40 per cent in 1960; in Martinique in 1968 it was 41 per cent. In many West Indian rural districts less than one-third of the remaining population is able-bodied. The burden of dependency is great: in Martinique for every 100 working age adults there are 125 children and 189 persons over 60, compared with 64 and 35 respectively in mainland France.

Acute distress often ensues. Some emigrating parents make little or no provision for their offspring. . . . Complaints that emigrant fathers neglected their families were heard from every territory. Difficulties arise even when parents remit regular sums. Foster agencies frequently neglect or ill-treat their charges. At one Jamaican "baby-farm" an eye-witness observed "about twenty little children queuing up for food" in Dickensian fashion.

Conditions were not usually this bad, to be sure. Most children were—and are—left in the care of grandparents or other relatives, often in remote districts. Grandparental upbringing is a common feature of West Indian family life, but mass emigration magnifies its incidence and effects. Growing up in these confining circumstances deprives many children of adequate schooling, supervision, and contact with the modern world.

For elderly adults left at home, child care is not the only problem. The scarcity of the able-bodied makes it hard, if not impossible, to cultivate family farms, to cope with marketing and transport, and to keep up community organization. Moreover, migrants often sell their land, livestock or standing crops to buy passage, leaving those behind propertyless. With little income except what is remitted, some are so bereft that they try to prevent children from joining their parents abroad. Accounts from Montserrat describe children forcibly being taken from grandparents loath to lose their best claim for support.

Once emigrants establish themselves abroad, they regularly bring over their children. The British immigration act of 1962, limiting entry except for dependents, accelerated this trend. . . .

Money sent home helped to offset the absence of the able-bodied. Indeed, remittances are a *raison d'etre* of emigration, and the sums involved are substantial. . . .

Small-island remittances may play a still greater role. Montserratians abroad sent back nearly one-fourth of the island's 1960 income. Remittances are the principal resources of Barbuda and Anguilla. Goods flow in with money; parcels of clothing are frequent gifts, especially at Christmas. Although few depend entirely on emigrant aid, remittances enable many to eschew ill-paid or distasteful labour, making do with occasional jobs such as road mending. Governments frankly schedule public works to help people anxious to "meet the food bill until they receive their next remittance from overseas."

Large-scale emigration may simultaneously raise living standards while undermining the local economy. As the labour force dwindles, field crops give way to cattle and coconuts, pasture succeeds tillage, and wilderness encroaches on pasture; in Montserrat well over half the arable acreage now lies idle, and production steadily diminishes. But remittances have noticeably improved health, nutrition, housing, and education.

The net economic impact of emigration is far from certain. Some maintain that the debits—the price of passage, the expense of raising children to become wage earners abroad, the cost of training and then replacing skilled workers—outweigh remittance benefits. Trinidad and Tobago, for example, trained 696 nurses between 1965 and 1969, but in the same period 586 nurses resigned and emigrated. But others cite population relief and income gains; emigration was a prime factor in Jamaica's phenomenal 6.8 per cent annual rise in per capita gross domestic product over the decade 1953–62.

The social consequences of large-scale emigration are more obviously negative. Emigration, even of the unskilled, deprives communities of the most progressive and ambitious inhabitants. In the absence of vigorous adults, community guidance, like child rearing, rests with the elderly or the weak. Mass emigration aggravates the normal attrition of the educated; almost nine-tenths of Montserrat's secondary-school graduates since 1950 have gone away. Everywhere, the coloured middle class leave in disproportionate numbers, because they are better educated and more knowledgeable about opportunities, can more easily raise passage money, and are more apt to gain acceptance abroad than the rest. Thus the coloured population of Montserrat declined from 2,503 in 1921 to 287 in 1960; that of Nevis from 2,288 in 1881 to 616 in 1960. Their departure opens up opportunities for the working class, but education and talent remain in short supply. High turnover in government, education, and commerce causes administrative chaos; with skilled persons unavailable, the untrained get "temporary" appointments, and the unqualified are seconded to senior positions.

Large-scale emigration also undermines village and rural community relationships. Communal work groups and reciprocal labour services fade away, remittance receipts magnify real or imaged differences in wealth and arouse jealousy, people do not get along together as well as they did before emigration. Loneliness is pervasive; people complain that all their best friends have gone away, leaving behind only idlers and vagabonds. When too many people leave, the remainder lose both social nexus and self-respect, and life becomes altogether less rewarding.

Effect of Migration: The Emigrant

Some West Indian societies adjust to migration as the norm, others endure it as a trauma. The effects on emigrants themselves are also manifold: often atypical from the start, experience abroad makes them yet more unlike those at home. But insights acquired overseas ultimately affect the homeland, too. Many migrants return only briefly or late in life, if ever. But others come home to play significant roles in Caribbean society. Their energy and self-awareness equip them at least to articulate if not to solve problems that defy traditional West Indian approaches. Virtually every major Caribbean leader, in fact, has spent several years abroad.

London: Oxford University Press, 1972, 213–223.

WEST INDIANS IN THE UNITED STATES

Although Annie John leaves Antigua for Great Britain, Jamaica Kincaid actually immigrated to the United States, ultimately to New York and then Vermont. The following article describes the life of West Indians in the United States in 1966, around the time that Annie John and Jamaica Kincaid emigrated from Antigua.

FROM GENE GROVE, "AMERICAN SCENE: THE WEST INDIANS"
(1966)

Small island mon, go back where you come from,
Small island mon, go back where you come from.
You come from Trinidad in a fishing boat
And now you're working in a great big overcoat.
Small island mon, go back where you really come from.

—A calypso

Great big overcoats are the fashion for Brooklyn winters, a bleak, cold, gray time of year when the warmth and blue skies and bracing air of Trinidad seem as distant from the borough's Bedford-Stuyvesant section as does the wealth of Park Avenue, across the East River in Manhattan. It is a time when more than one immigrant from the West Indies wishes to go back to the small island where he really came from.

Even in summer the very name of Bedford-Stuyvesant evokes a vision of slums, and indeed, New York's Mayor John Lindsay last month said that all the city's urban renewal funds must be poured into what he called "the three hard-core ghetto areas that are the shame of the city," Harlem, the South Bronx and, of course, Bedford-Stuyvesant. Yet Bedford-Stuyvesant is not an unbroken panorama of peeling plaster, leaking pipes and dark, dank hallways: there are many pleasant sections and not the least of them are blocks along Hancock Street and Chauncey Street and others, blocks of neat three- and four-story brownstone homes, most with high stone stoops and black-iron grillwork fences draped with ivy, some with bay windows, some with Gothic stonework, some with Victorian turrets, all neatly kept.

In these blocks and in the middle-class and predominantly Jewish section of Crown Heights nearby live dwindling numbers of first-generation immigrants from the British West Indies and increasing numbers of their second- and third-generation offspring, an immigrant group as unique as—in some ways more unique than—any which have ever come to the United States.

Behind those brownstone fronts still stand women in spotless kitchens slowly pouring yellow cornmeal into simmering pots of okra and water, flopping it when the cornmeal is done into butter-lined bowls, pouring a thin gravy of flaked salt codfish over the yellow mass speckled with red and green okra—making cuckoo in Brooklyn just as it always has been made in the islands, in Nevis and Jamaica, in Grenada and Trinidad, in Barbados, Antigua, St. Kitts, St. Lucia, and St. Vincent.

The West Indian enclave in Bedford-Stuyvesant is not the only one in the United States—there are more than a quarter-million West Indians now in the country—but it may be the largest. There are others, in the Sugar Hill section of Harlem, in Miami, in Philadelphia, in Los Angeles, in Charleston, S.C., even on one of South Carolina's sea islands, a tiny speck called St. Helena where the descendants of slaves brought from Barbados to work in lumber camps survive as a group known as the Gullah.

Wherever they live, West Indians—or, at the least, first-generation West Indians—have clung fiercely to their own identity and, in turn, have sometimes felt alienated from both races in the United States. They are set apart by many things, tangible and intangible, by the rich Anglicized cadences of their English, by their stubborn loyalty to their British past, by a drive for property, by their religion, by their resentment of a racial discrimination they were not accustomed to in their islands, even by their names.

Cyril Anderson lives now in a big home in Queens with a coat of arms on the door but he remembers snubs by both races after he came to the U.S. from Trinidad in 1923 and became the Duke of Iron, perhaps the most famous singer of the islands' unique music, the calypso.

"We came here and lived in Harlem," he says, "American Negroes thought that all West Indians came from Jamaica. In the old days we caught hell from the American Negroes but it's different today. The young people don't care much about that.

"It wasn't until 1941 that calypso came downtown to the white people and that year we played for 10 months at the Village Vanguard in Greenwich Village.

"I never went South until 1948 and on opening night in Miami I tore the house down, leading all the people in the show around the stage in a carnival atmosphere. The newspapers raved about the show but I was the only Negro in the act and the next day the deputy mayor came and said I couldn't sing and dance on stage with all those people. After that I had to stand offstage in a corner and only sing. Man, if I didn't have a contract I would have left that damned Miami. Do you know that I spent Christmas in my dressing room alone, while the rest of the cast partied?''

The isolation from native Americans of both races which the West Indian felt especially in the period between the two world wars has largely disappeared, partly because of assimilation, partly because of improved race relations, partly because of the restrictive McCarran-Walter immigration act which has severely limited immigration from the islands since 1952. It was there, though, in the early part of the century when the native Negro greeted the West Indian as every other native group has greeted the prospect of new competition for jobs: with resentment. He called the West Indian ''monkey chaser,'' ''ringtail'' and ''King mon.''

The native white who saw only the color of the West Indians' skins was equally distrustful because the islanders, unused to racial discrimination at home, frequently reacted with anger when he encountered it in the United States. The Pullman Company once refused to hire West Indians as sleeping car porters because they were too likely to strike back when passengers threw racial slurs at them.

West Indians are not new to the United States. If the Gullah were among the first West Indians here when they arrived on slave ships, there were other scattered early immigrations: Alexander Hamilton, for example, was born on Nevis and Alexander Dallas, Secretary of the Treasury under James Madison, was from Jamaica. Dr. Lucas Santomee, the first Negro physician in North America, was brought by the Dutch to New York in 1650 from Curacao and John Russwurm, the first Negro college graduate in the United States and the founder of *Freedom's Journal*, the first Negro newspaper in the country, was a West Indian. So was Denmark Vesey, leader of the famous slave insurrection. The Negro speaker of South Carolina's House of Representatives during Reconstruction was Robert Brown Eliot, a second-generation Jamaican.

But the great flood of immigrants, driven by poverty, by hurricanes, by the pressure of population, came later. Many Jamaicans, for instance, went to Panama in the 1880s to work on the canal and, when it was completed in 1914, moved on to the United States. There was a rush of immigration from all the islands at the turn of the century until it was slowed by restrictive legislation in 1924. Until the McCarran-Walter Act, though, West Indians were allotted half of the unused portion of the British yearly immigration quota of 60,000 but the act cut the West Indian quota to 1,000 per year, 600 of whom must be professional people, 200 of whom must already have parents here and 200 of whom must have relatives here. (It was the restrictions of the McCarran-Walter Act, as a matter of fact, which redirected the tide of West Indian emigration toward the British Isles where one of the results has been the growth of racial tensions.) The vast majority of West Indians in the United States come from the British, rather than the Dutch or French islands of the West Indies, first because they have many times the population of the other islands, but also because of the absence of a language barrier and because of the relative ease before 1952 of immigration under the generous British quota.

Among the immigrants of this century and their children were historian J. A. Rogers, poet Claude McKay, performers Bert Williams, Dean Dixon, Canada Lee, Pearl Primus, Cicely Tyson, Sidney Poitier and Harry Belafonte, musicians Sonny Rollins and Wynton Kelly, Federal Judge Constance Baker Motley, political figures J. Raymond Jones and Hulan Jack, civil rights leaders Stokely Carmichael, Lincoln Lynch, Roy Innis, Ivanhoe Donaldson and Cortland Cox, track stars Herb McKinley, George Kerr, George Rhoden, Wendell Mottley and Mike Agostini.

If the immigrants from the West Indies felt at first that they were being set apart by natives of both races, however, they themselves clung sturdily to their own tradition. They brought with them an intense loyalty to the British flag which seemed, even after they became naturalized, to make them citizens with reservations. There are large West Indian colonies now in Toronto and Ottawa, in fact, because many islanders continued their migration to Canada in order to return to British soil. Their religion was Anglican rather than Baptist and Methodist and their names often had a British ring: Carlton, Basil, Austin, Sedgwick. When they encountered racial discrimination here they often took their complaints to the British consulates.

And they clung together when they came to the United States, an accepted practice of the immigrant groups which preceded them here, the Irish, Jews, Italians, and Poles, but a practice considered by both whites and blacks to be presumptuous for a Negro group. They organized their own association, the Jamaican Association, The Antiguan Progressive Association, the Grenadan Mutual Association, the Sons and Daughters of Barbados.

The American Aid Society to the West Indies still survives, run by founder Hilbert Wilkinson out of his Bedford-Stuyvesant printing shop. It sends help to the islands and recently, for instance, collected money and used clothes to send back after the recent Hurricane Inez. One of the society's dance programs is a casebook of West Indians in Brooklyn. Its advertisers include the Sons and Daughters of Barbados Benevolent Society of America, the West Indies Freight Service, the Association for the Advancement of Caribbean Education, the Paragon Progressive Federal Credit Union and St. Cyprian's Episcopal Church. It is studded with such names as Cadogan, Pierrepont, Weekes, and McVey.

Even the recreations of the West Indians separated them from the natives. Soccer and cricket were their sports and cricket is the sole universal sport of the islands. Scholar David Lowenthal has noted that although teams may have been formed along color and class lines everyone played the game in the islands and it still is played in the West Indian communities in the United States: New York's Van Cortlandt Park is a frequent setting for matches. The music was imported from the islands, too, and calypso and its great practitioners like the Duke of Iron, the Mighty Sparrow and Lord Nelson may in fact be the islands' best-known exports.

The music can be heard any day drifting from those neat brownstones in Bedford-Stuyvesant, those houses which themselves are a part of the West Indian character. They are neat primarily because they are owned by West Indians and the landlord still lives in the home: the West Indians moved to Bedford-Stuyvesant when it still was a white middle-class neighborhood, rented rooms in the tenements that constitute 75 percent of the area's housing, saved pennies until they could buy one of the brownstone homes, and now that the tenements of the absentee landlords are slums, the West Indians' owner-occupied brownstones are a stark contrast to the remainder of the neighborhood.

The ownership of a home is important to West Indians, perhaps more important than it is to their neighbors. During the period of slavery in the West Indies slaves were permitted to grow their own produce, keep the profit, and buy their freedom and after slavery, even, it was only property-holders who were permitted to vote. Too, the islands are small and the ownership of a piece of land in Barbados, for instance, which is only 166 square miles in size, takes on a special significance.

As a result, if there is one pervasive stereotype of the West Indians within the Negro community it is the image of the West Indian as an acquisitive person, a person obsessed with property. In their book, *Beyond the Melting Pot*, Daniel Moynihan and Nathan Glazer insist that the most striking difference between the West Indian and the native Negro is the West Indian's greater application to business education, to buying homes, to advancing himself economically. And it is true that many West Indians have been notably successful in business. . . .

If West Indians are proud of their business success, proud of their thrift, proud of ownership of their homes, some of them occasionally translate their pride into disdain for those who don't hold to the same virtues. . . .

Paule Marshall wrote of the West Indian feeling of thrift in her novel, *Brown Girl, Brownstones*, and at one point talked about the West Indian women working as maids in Brooklyn:

"Each morning they took the train to Flatbush and Sheepshead Bay to scrub floors. The lucky ones had their steady madams while the others wandered those neat blocks or waited on corners—each with her apron and working shoes in a bag under her arm until someone offered her a day's work.

"Their only thought was of the 'few rawmout' pennies at the end of the day which would eventually 'buy house.' "

The pennies did "buy house," of course, and those ivy-draped homes along the side streets of Bedford-Stuyvesant stand now as monuments to the single-minded insistence of the West Indians upon the virtues they brought from the islands.

Tuesday Magazine, November 1966, 12–15.

STUDY QUESTIONS

1. What are the major reasons why West Indians decide to leave home? What are the main consequences for those who are left behind? Does Annie John seem to fit the norm, or are her circumstances different in some ways? How?

2. What problems do you think Annie John will face in another country?

3. Describe the typical life and attitudes of West Indians in the United States in the 1960s. From what you know of Jamaica Kincaid's life, is she typical of other West Indian immigrants? How?

TOPICS FOR WRITTEN OR ORAL EXPLORATION

1. Imagine Annie John's life in either England or the United States after she leaves Antigua; write a short sequel to the novel.

2. Look up books and articles on West Indians in the United States today. Have conditions changed since the 1960s? How?

3. Imagine that you are immigrating to Antigua. Using your knowledge of the islands, describe your new life. What problems would you encounter in adjusting to your new life?

4. Imagine that you are an Antiguan who has just moved to the United States. What kinds of American attitudes and customs are different for you? How do you adjust to your new environment?

WORKS CITED

Lowenthal, David. *West Indian Societies*. London: Oxford University Press, 1972.

Palmer, Ransford W. *Pilgrims from the Sun: West Indian Migration to America*. New York: Twayne Publishers, 1995.

SUGGESTED READINGS

See the full text of the Lowenthal book excerpted in this chapter.

Bryce-Laport, Roy, and Delores Mortimer, eds. *Caribbean Immigration to the United States*. Washington, D.C.: Research Institute on Immigration and Ethnic Studies, Smithsonian Institution, 1976.

Klevan, Miriam. *The West Indian Americans*. New York: Chelsea House Publishers, 1990.

Levine, Barry B. *The Caribbean Exodus*. New York: Praeger, 1990.

Palmer, Ransford W., ed. *In Search of a Better Life: Perspectives on Migration from the Caribbean*. New York: Praeger, 1990.

———. *Pilgrims from the Sun: West Indian Migration to America*. New York: Twayne Publishers, 1995.

Pastor, Robert A., ed. *Migration and Development in the Caribbean: The Unexplored Connection*. Boulder, Colo.: Westview Press, 1985.

Smith, T. E. *Commonwealth Migration: Flows and Policies*. London: Macmillan, 1981.

Stinner, William F., Klaus de Albuquerque, and Roy S. Bryce-Laporte, eds. *Migration and Remittances: Developing a Caribbean Perspective*. Washington, D.C.: Research Institute on Immigration and Ethnic Studies, Smithsonian Institution, 1982.

Sutton, Constance R., and Elsa M. Chaney, eds. *Caribbean Life in New York City: Sociological Dimensions*. New York: Center for Migration Studies, 1987.

Index

ABOUT THE AUTHOR

DEBORAH MISTRON is Professor of Spanish and Literature at Bradford College in Bradford, Massachusetts. She is the author of many papers on Latin American popular culture, with a special interest in the cinema. She teaches Latin American literature and area studies in Latin America.